EOAN GROUP
WE LIVE TO SERVE

EOAN

Our Story

Eoan History Project

On my programme, as I sat planning, I wrote 'Eos',
the beautiful Greek word meaning 'dawn'.
Eos ... Eoan ... pertaining to the dawn. And so
I named the new group Eoan ...
  – Helen Southern-Holt, founder of the Eoan Group

The publication of this book is made possible through generous funds provided by Stellenbosch University, The Nussbaum Foundation and the LW Hiemstra Trust, established by Riekie Hiemstra in remembrance of Ludwig Wybren (Louis) Hiemstra.

ISBN 978-0-9870429-1-0
© 2013 Fourthwall Books, Johannesburg and DOMUS, Stellenbosch
© of texts: the authors

AUTHOR
Eoan History Project
BOOK COMMITTEE
Santie de Jongh, Ruth Fourie, Christine Lucia, Stephanus Muller, Wayne Muller (editor), Hilde Roos (editor), Ronnie Samaai, Phillip Swales
TRANSLATION
Edwin Hees
BOOK DESIGN
Oliver Barstow

Published and distributed by Fourthwall Books
Unit S14a
44 Stanley Avenue
Milpark
2122 Johannesburg
South Africa
T +27 (0)11 482 2899
F +27 (0)86 645 2022
info@fourthwallbooks.com
www.fourthwallbooks.com

Contents

—

Introduction

Weaving the rich and manifold strands of memory of the Eoan Group –
South Africa's first grassroots opera, dance and theatre company – into
a tapestry of history felt more like the task of a curator rather than that
of an editor. Curators have to bring together divergent artworks into one
exhibition so that each work tells a story in its own distinct voice. At the
same time, these diverse and multiple voices must contribute to the unity
and coherence of the exhibition. In a similar fashion, the varied voices of
Eoan members relating their own memories are what make up this book.

In creating *EOAN – Our Story*, we immersed ourselves in the words of
those who lived their artistic lives through the Eoan Group and told us
their stories. We found photographs that said more than words could, and
we handled countless fragile archival documents that carried the traces
in ink of this extraordinary organisation. Curating these memories into a
narrative oral history proved to be a daunting task. What has resulted from
our efforts is a history filled with impressions, emotions, opinions and facts,
distorted by the effects of time on human memory but also informed by
the sensibility that hindsight brings. This book is not written by authors or
editors, but by those who generously shared their experiences.

As the transcribed interviews were shaped into a narrative, the singular
voices of Eoan members emerged. But the real challenge lay in reading and
rereading all forty-five interviews that were conducted for this project, to find
the essence of each and allow the reader to hear each interviewee's voice.
In order to do this, we decided to maintain, as far as possible, the spoken-
language register of the interviews, with little editorial intervention. This
seemed important to us, because language editing was potentially another
way in which the stories told by interviewees could be over-written and
misrepresented by institutional concerns.

Then there was the extensive Eoan Group Archive, housed at the
Documentation Centre for Music (DOMUS) at Stellenbosch University,
which contains hundreds of documents and photographs that corroborate,
enhance and interpret what the interviewees tell us. The photographs
become windows to the past, while the many documents reveal the zeitgeist
of a moment in our collective history. They paint a picture of elation and
success but also reveal pain, frustration and thwarted expectations and
hopes. Selecting those photographs and documents that would serve this
narrative was indeed a difficult endeavour.

This book makes no claim to a comprehensive representation of
everyone who was at one time or another connected to Eoan. Although we
tried to speak to the central figures as well as to some who experienced the
group from the periphery, it is possible that important perspectives and
memories exist that are not documented here. Indeed, one of the positive
outcomes of this book may be that more people are prompted to come

forward with as-yet undocumented stories and material. We are honoured
and fortunate to have captured the stories of a few Eoan members. Some
of those we interviewed, however, passed on before they could see their
forgotten history captured here.

Also, this book is not a chronological history of Eoan, but a fabric
of memories structured around a number of themes that emerged from
the interviews. These introduce readers to vivid characters, nostalgic
reminiscences, political turmoil and musical exuberance. Our hope is
that the book will resonate with a great variety of readers and echo in
historiographical spaces yet to be research and narrated.

Hilde Roos and Wayne Muller
Stellenbosch, September 2012

The Making of
This Book

The story of this book starts with a telephone call on 14 November 2006 to Santie de Jongh, the archivist of the Documentation Centre for Music (DOMUS) at Stellenbosch University. The enquiry about Eoan documents by Mr Charles de Long, a former Eoan member, and De Jongh's diligent pursuit of information to help him, set in motion, over the course of the next twelve months, a series of visits and meetings between the University's department of music and the Eoan board. Eventually, aided by generous funding from the University, the Eoan archive was transferred to DOMUS in the department of music on 23 February 2008. This happened after a permanent-loan agreement had been reached between the current Eoan board (based at the Joseph Stone Theatre) and DOMUS, subsequent to which a contract was signed on 28 January 2008.[1]

The pre-sorting of the collection took place from the middle of March until June 2008. During these months, De Jongh listed and stored 105 document holders and more than 750 folders. By the end of April, Dr Hilde Roos (then still a doctoral student in opera history in the department of music), began a chronological reconstruction of Eoan's history in order to ascertain how a book project about this celebrated group could be attempted. Dr Jerome Slamat, who heads the division of community interaction at Stellenbosch University, Mr Hilton Biscome (coordinator of the book *In Ons Bloed*), Mr Ronnie Samaai and Prof Albert Grundlingh (head of the department of history, Stellenbosch University), gave valuable advice on how this project could be realised. It was of primary importance to find the names of people who had been involved with Eoan over the years, in order for ideas to be developed about the possible content and themes of the planned publication.

On 1 October 2008 a meeting was held with the Eoan board and important role players in the Eoan community in the Joseph Stone Theatre in Athlone. This was followed by a meeting with a larger group of former Eoan soloists, choir members, dancers and administrators in the District Six Museum in Cape Town. Subsequent to this meeting, Hilde Roos was appointed as the coordinator of what became known as the 'Eoan book project'. Hilde's academic research interests (opera production in the Western Cape) and specifically her interest in the Eoan archive meant that she was ideally placed to hold together a process that we knew was going to make substantial demands on time. After advertising the fact widely in provincial and local newspapers and on radio, a public meeting was held on 9 November 2008. It was attended by about twenty-five people, and had the

---

1   Most of the material presented here was taken from agendas and minutes of book committee meetings that had been compiled by Hilde Roos and Christine Lucia. My heartfelt thanks to these colleagues for this work. Some of the information was taken from a talk presented by Hilde Roos at a departmental colloquium on 14 September 2009.

primary purpose of finding volunteers to participate in the book project.
Four attendees volunteered: Bishop John Ulster (brother of the conductor
Dan Ulster), Mr Ronnie Samaai (brother of the tenor Gerald Samaai), Mrs
Ruth Fourie (widow of the baritone Lionel Fourie) and Mr Wayne Muller
(then still a journalist at *Die Burger*). Together with the DOMUS team,
they formed the Eoan Group book committee. The committee's first
meeting was held on 10 February 2009, chaired by Prof Christine Lucia
(Extraordinary Professor in the department of music), followed by a bigger
meeting on 26 February in which themes and ideas for the book were
explored. Mr Phillip Swales, chairman of the Eoan Group Trust, joined
the book committee and Bishop John Ulster resigned owing to his already
overextended commitments.

Early on in the project, we realised that the process of making a book
about Eoan would bring to light the ways in which the South African past
is negotiated, claimed, used, contested and eventually written by South
Africans. We thus commissioned Aryan Kaganof to make a documentary
film about the process and he was present at our meetings from an early
stage. Our idea was not only to compile an ethnography of memory as an
historical celebration of Eoan, but also to document engagements between
role players as a way of understanding how a painful past is mediated in
the present.

During a meeting on 5 March 2009, the committee decided to structure
questions for interviewees on the basis of the seven themes that inform the
chapters in this book:

Origins beginnings (group, tours, opera, branches); social welfare
(cultural upliftment, 'we serve', religious conviction); the role of Southern-
Holt/Manca (originators).

The body 'the dancer'; racial categorisation; inclusion/exclusion; the
voice; separate amenities; 'coloured' construct.

Structure leadership; finances; administration (Trust, Board); hierarchy.

Work livelihood; in-work/out of work; rehearsals/performances; teaching
others; training self; backstage (sets, costumes); skills.

Play/on stage productions (drama, operatic disasters, successes,
musicals, oratoria, opera, operetta); stardom; voice coaching and vocal
roles; orchestra; dance; chorus; directing.

Place venues (performances, rehearsals, admin spaces); homes; tour
destinations/accommodation; overseas (aspiration, diaspora).

Support family; community (white, Jewish, coloured, black); government
(municipal, provincial, national, international); funding; individuals.

On the basis of these themes the committee formulated questions for the interviews. This was important not only because it would facilitate a focused collection of data, but also because the interviews were being conducted by a team of people whose backgrounds, interests and personal involvement with the interviewees and Eoan's history were vastly different.[2]

xviAs these preparations for the interviews progressed, a ceremony was held in the Fismer Hall in the department of music, Stellenbosch University, to celebrate formally the transfer of the Eoan Group Archive to DOMUS. The evening of 23 April 2009 marked a shift in focus from the acquisition and ordering of the archive to the creation of the book. At this occasion, Prof Russell Botman, Rector of Stellenbosch University, quoted three questions from the book *There Was This Goat* by Antjie Krog, Nosisi Mpolweni and Kopano Ratele about the testimony of Notrose Nobomvu Konile before the Truth and Reconciliation Commission:

> How do we 'hear' one another in a country where the past is still so present among us? How much of what we hear can we translate into finding ways of living together? How do we overcome a divided past in such a way that 'The Other' becomes us?[3]

Botman's reflections tell us much about why the history of the Eoan Group is an important one:

> The first question in particular – 'How do we hear each other?' – resonates meaningfully with the events this evening … The history of Eoan is an important history because it does not only echo the liberation narratives of apartheid. It concerns the stories of individuals who, as artists and music lovers, tried to do their best in extremely difficult circumstances. These stories are not primarily stories of political activism, but stories of love for music, of caring for one another and of shared dreams. This is the history of people rather than of activism and perhaps because of this it is a moving, precious heritage of how humaneness survives through music in inhuman circumstances. Somewhere in our past, we know, thanks to these

---

2 A consent form was prepared stating clearly that the purpose of the interviews was to 'document the history and legacy of this group as a book, film documentary and web-based media hub' and making it clear that 'the entire interview will become part of the Eoan archive at DOMUS and will be made available in an interactive Eoan book project and web-based media hub.'

3 Antjie Krog, Nosisi Mpolweni, Kopano Ratele, 2009. *There Was This Goat: Investigating the Truth Commission Testimony of Notrose Nobomvu Konile*, University of KwaZulu-Natal Press, pp. 42–43.

people and their perseverance, there existed voices that sang and did
not stop singing. Somewhere in our past, in the darkest hours, there
was music that was not drowned out by bulldozers or the sound of
gunfire. We want to hear that, I think, as the sounds of hope that never
lost courage.[4]

Early in May 2009, the committee embarked on a series of interviews with
former singers, dancers, administrators, journalists and, in some cases,
their own family members.[5] These interviews, forty-seven in total, were
filmed and recorded and now constitute a part of the Eoan Group Archive
at Stellenbosch University. During this time, the committee met regularly
to discuss progress and problems, to reflect on the challenges and make
adjustments. At a meeting on 28 May 2009 at the home of Ruth Fourie
in Grassy Park (memorable for its offerings of homemade chicken pie,
smoorsnoek, bread, fruit cake and coffee), the importance of releasing a
CD with recorded material by Eoan was discussed. This was prompted by
donations of four reel-to-reel tapes from Ruth Grevler (Dr Manca's daughter)
and thirty-five reel-to-reel tapes from Jocylyn Liedeman (daughter of
soprano Josephine Liedeman). Eventually fifty-five tapes of Eoan recordings
were delivered to Milestone Studios in Cape Town for digitisation.
Simultaneously, as they progressed throughout 2009, the interviews were
digitally copied and given to students who began the laborious process
of transcribing them. Eventually more than seventy-five hours of audio
material were transcribed.

At a meeting on 25 February 2010, it was decided that enough interviews
had taken place for the book project to go ahead. Although new names of
potential interviewees continued to crop up, the committee decided that
further interviews were more properly a future responsibility of the archive
and that priority now had to be given to shaping the book from the material
that had been collected.[6]

On 6 October 2010 the committee met at the Nook Eatery in Stellenbosch.
After much discussion it was decided that Hilde Roos and Wayne Muller
would be given the task of selecting and arranging a pilot chapter for
the book from material that had emerged from the process. This was a

---

4   Translated from the Afrikaans by the author.
5   A full list of who was interviewed when, and by whom, is included at the back of this book.
6   At the same meeting it was decided that Ruth Fourie would start listening to the newly
digitised reel-to-reel tapes in order to identify the singers and the works for future research, but
also for possible use on a CD that would accompany the book. The transcripts of the interviews
were divided between the members of the committee with the instruction methodically to
flag passages as they pertained to the themes according to which the interviews had been
structured. Hilde Roos was asked to organise all selected material by theme.

seminal meeting, characterised by robust debate. We were concerned that the 'heartbeat' of the project (as Ronnie Samaai put it) would be lost if the construction of the narrative were to pass from the committee to an outside auctorial agency at this point. At a subsequent meeting the pilot chapter was discussed and adjudged a resounding success by the committee, and Hilde and Wayne were asked to follow the same modus operandi for the other chapters. By the end of April 2011, the book chapters, timeline and appendices had been compiled by Hilde and Wayne and read, commented on and approved by the committee. By the next year, the book had been accepted for publication by Fourthwall Books and funding obtained from the Nussbaum Foundation and the Hiemstra Trust to proceed to the final stages of the project.

This is how the story unfolded from that telephone call made by Charles de Long to Santie de Jongh on 14 November 2006. What has resulted in the five ensuing years is a book by committee, something I would not have believed possible at the outset.

By the time the editorial duties passed to Hilde and Wayne in October 2010, collective input into the material and relationships of trust in the committee were such that this 'editorial' function happened seamlessly within the dynamic of group consensus. This was in no small measure attributable to the group loyalty and seriousness of intent displayed by Hilde and Wayne, who worked hard to allow the material full expression and listened carefully to the committee's concerns and advice in reworking submitted chapters.

As an academic who works and publishes mostly on my own, I don't mind admitting that I was filled with apprehension on how successful making a book 'by committee' could be. I couldn't imagine in 2006, and find it difficult to believe now, that not only can it work, but that it has worked better, considering the task at hand, than the conventional academic enterprise of the single-author monograph. But perhaps we were just extraordinarily fortunate in the kind of people who ended up making this book, and without whom it might very well have been a risk too great, an experiment too daring. It is difficult to imagine, for instance, what would have happened to us in our more delicate discussions if Ruth Fourie, whose directness and honesty in combination with her disarming, ready smile, had not pushed us beyond our self-involved hang-ups and differences. Or how we would have kept the momentum of the process going without Hilde Roos's countless telephone calls, e-mails, circular letters, agendas and memoranda. What would have become of us had not Ronnie Samaai urged caution and reflection (and practiced it) in some of the more difficult moments we had to negotiate, or if Santie de Jongh had not kept us on the straight and narrow with our 'interview packs'. I have little doubt that we

would be stuck somewhere between 'perhaps' and 'not quite' without Wayne
Muller's journalistic sense-of-deadline work ethic and pragmatism about
how interviews became text. And we would not have pushed as hard as we
did to address difficult political and social questions in our interviews and
discussions without Phillip Swales. How all of this stayed together had a
lot to do with Christine Lucia's wise chairmanship of many meetings and
her measured and quiet critical astuteness and scholarly integrity. And
then there was the presence behind the camera: filming, moving, filming,
winking, filming, laughing soundlessly. How much of what transpired was
directed by Aryan Kaganof? I suspect more than we think.

Stellenbosch University, through its Strategic Fund, the former Vice-
Rector (Research), Prof Arnold van Zyl and Vice-Rector (Community
Interaction), Prof Julian Smith gave generously for this project. The Dean of
the faculty of humanities, Prof Hennie Kotze and Ellen Tise, director of the
JS Gericke Library, have continually supported this and other projects by
DOMUS. This book is therefore in no small part made possible because of
the University's firm commitment to our society, informed by our particular
historically framed responsibilities. It is a sensibility I articulated in my
speech on 23 April 2009 when the transfer of the Eoan Group Archive was
formally celebrated in the department of music, and with which I should like
to conclude:

> To all of those who have been involved with Eoan over the years, my
> express wish would be that what happened to the Eoan archive that
> now rests in Stellenbosch is not seen as a 'transfer' of the material
> from your community to Stellenbosch University. Rather, I should
> like to suggest that like the archive, you are here individually and as
> a community because we are now part of you, as you became part of
> us when this process started more than two years ago. Although I no
> doubt welcome many of you here tonight for the first time, I anticipate
> a time in the future when I will encounter you or your children or
> grandchildren or great-grandchildren in these corridors visiting this
> archive, studying at this institution or attending our concerts, a time
> when we will greet each other not as strangers meeting for the first
> time, but as a community united by our love for music and our interest
> in a shared past.

Stephanus Muller
Stellenbosch, July 2012

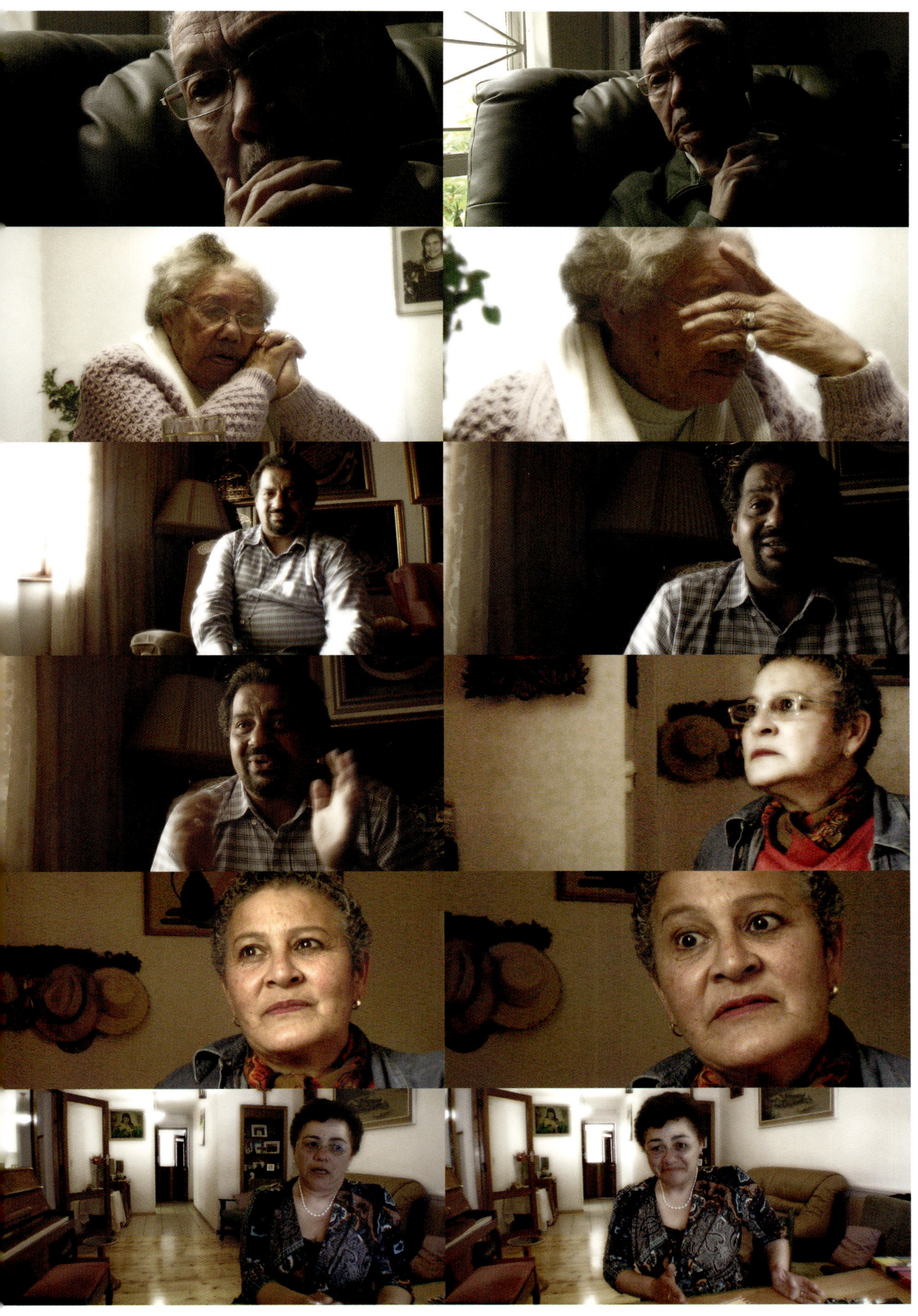

1

Beginnings

*On my programme, as I sat planning, I wrote 'Eos', the beautiful Greek word
meaning 'dawn' – Eos … Eoan … pertaining to the dawn. And so I named
the new group Eoan, in the consciousness that through its illumination the
coloured people could realise the dawning of a new cultural expansion in
themselves, and a new understanding of well-being, physical and mental,
for their race.*

With these words, Helen Southern-Holt, a British immigrant living in Cape
Town, described the beginnings of a small cultural and welfare organisation
for the coloured[1] community in District Six in Cape Town. Situated within
the city centre, District Six was a multi-cultural neighbourhood until 1968,
when coloured and black people were forcibly moved to other settlements
outside the city centre, as apartheid laws regarding racial segregation
stipulated. The Eoan Group, founded in 1933 by Southern-Holt, was South
Africa's first grassroots opera, dance and theatre company.

The community in District Six itself was very mixed. Not many African
families, do I remember, but there were some Jewish families and there
were some English-speaking families and, of course, predominantly
coloured families.
Bishop John Ulster

I started at the [Eoan] Group when I was nine, going on for ten, in 1938.
At that time, the group had their headquarters and classes at St Paul's
church in Bryant Street [in the Bo-Kaap] in Cape Town. You see, this
organisation was the first of its kind for us people, coloured people, as
it were.
Tillie Ulster

Southern-Holt had a clear vision for the Eoan Group:

*My first desire in giving help to the coloured community was to start classes
for clear, articulate speech. Having had to engage coloured workers as well as
European, I knew from experience that the mass of coloured boys and girls
entering the labour market were ill-equipped, and had not the power of the
spoken word to aid them.*

---

1   In South Africa, the term 'coloured' refers specifically to a person of mixed racial origins
rather than, as is the case in most other parts of the world, to a 'black' person. The ancestors
of coloured people in South Africa include Europeans, black Africans, Khoisan, Malaysians
and Indonesians. Under apartheid law, all South Africans were required to be identified as
belonging in one of four racial categories: white, black, coloured or Indian.

District Six, Cape Town, in the 1950s.

Initially, the group offered speech classes. These expanded into literature classes and soon drama productions were staged. In 1935, a ballet section was set up and in 1940 the brothers John and Dan Ulster started a choir.

4

> I think [Southern-Holt] heard some of the teachers speaking and she listened to them and she said, 'Hey, you're not speaking proper English. I think I'm going to start a class in elocution.' And that's exactly what she did. She started it in a little hall, or a little room, in District Six, got some teachers and she taught them elocution – how to speak proper English.
>   *Ruth Goodwin*

> There was a centre in District Six, it was called the Liberman Institute, and at that time [Southern-Holt] went there because people were using that place as a recreation place. But her main interest at the time was speech, because she recognised that people didn't speak well, from her point of view, as an articulate person. The main thing she started was speech, thinking that good speech is important, because the power of the spoken word goes everywhere. I mean, when people speak to you, they don't look at your dress, they look at you and hear what you say. And then going on from speech, she started physical education classes with little children. And she saw quite a lot of potential for doing other kinds of activities with these growing children.
>   *Alethea Jansen*

During the first fifteen years of its existence, the Eoan Group set up branches of the organisation throughout the Cape Peninsula.

> They had Athlone, Newlands, Maitland, Brooklyn, Goodwood, Salt River, Parow, St Paul's, Retreat, Simon's Town, Walmer Estate, Strand, Somerset West, Paarl, Stellenbosch, Wynberg, Port Elizabeth, Grassy Park, Van der Stel and Chiappini Street. At each centre there was a family that one could depend on. The Paarl group, the family that we dealt with, was the Carolissen family, in Stellenbosch it was the Weaver [family], in Port Elizabeth it was the Bruwer [family], in Maitland it was the Kronenburg [family], in Newlands it was the Wicks, in Athlone it was the Bucktons, at St Paul's it was the Adams's. Every centre had a family behind them.
>   *Tillie Ulster*

> When I came to know the Eoan Group, that was more or less from 1943 on, Mrs Southern-Holt *was* the Eoan Group for me. She was a very dynamic, a very good leader in that aspect. She opened many doors for us, went wherever she could find some support for the Eoan Group. I

Helen Southern-Holt in the 1930s.
PHOTO Eoan Group Archive

think her vision was good. But one cannot neglect to say, there were some people, even in the choir, who thought she was too enthusiastic and leaving out the participation of others who were in the committee. But I think that's just a matter of interpretation.
Bishop John Ulster

6

From its inception, the group's constitution placed 'service to the group' above 'self-glorification'.

My professional job was to serve mankind. To bring education to the children, okay. And my whole life was geared in that direction. It didn't worry me a thing, even when I was a teenage girl, at high school and that sort of thing. If people asked me to go to the shop for them or, 'you're coming on a bus, you're coming through Plein Street, bring us that'. That sort of person I always was. And please God, until I close my eyes I'm that type of person. So, but to me it's the group that matters. It's the good of the group. And such service seeks no special thanks. Serve for the pure joy of serving. That was one of the group's aims.
Alethea Jansen

We were supposed to be going out there, getting all these kids off the street and getting them into some form of recreation. Mrs Southern-Holt never set it up to be a high and mighty cultural institution, she just wanted the coloured people to realise their full potential in all directions. In the beginning stages there was weight lifting. There was, you know, a whole host of things that people could just occupy their lives with and also develop and grow as people. You know, it wasn't this high and mighty cultural thing.
Merle Falken

Helen Southern-Holt actually started with ballet and drama. It wasn't the opera. She had the vision to bring people like Joseph Manca, Alessandro [Rota] into the Eoan Group to create the reputation of the Eoan Group to have performed *La Traviata*. But Helen did start with ballet, with dance first of all, before even the opera came into play. [It was for] the people who didn't have it, and that was our people, our people in the community. Normal basic people: artisans, people working in the building industry, people working in the street. She took people and actually made them artists. And that was, I think it was for me, amazing.
Abeedah Medell

"We Live to Serve."

BROTHERHOOD.

To live a life which will be free from all bias, and free from all prejudice of creed, race and colour.

UNITY.

To live and work always for the good of the whole Group, forgetting the personal self, knowing that Unity is born out of the unselfish life.

PURITY.

To keep the body pure and clean, knowing that it is a temple of the living spirit. To control the thoughts, to keep the actions pure at all times. Fully to understand EOAN "dedication".

JOYOUS SERVICE.

To give service to the Group joyously; such service seeks no special thanks or self glorification but serves for the pure joy of serving.

THE GROUP.

To believe in the symbol of service as defined by EOAN and to take EOAN teaching only, for the purpose of becoming efficient so as to be ready to give to others those cultural arts embodied in EOAN. In order to keep up and advance the standard of EOAN not to re-teach, show class work or perform publicly without the Group's permission.

"My Word is My Bond."

Typex

The Eoan Group poster, outlining the group's values.

Although the group was not affiliated to any religious grouping, Southern-Holt's Christian religious convictions shaped the principles on which the group was founded and had a lasting effect on the functioning of the group.

The man that kept her always where the Lord was concerned was the Bishop of Cape Town, Bishop Sydney W Lavis. He was the man, from a religious point of view, that kept that woman going. He was a brilliant man. He used to come from time to time, just to come and bless the children and make them, make us, realise how fortunate we are in having this gift and giving it over to the people.

We're not keeping the talent to ourselves. You know he kept that part of us going. Not that we didn't go to church. But she loved having him around.

I remember once, I don't know what happened one day, but we were in the office at her place in Glengariff Road [in Sea Point, Cape Town] and something triggered off, and all of a sudden she says: 'You know, I honestly feel like Jesus today.' And innocently, I said to her: 'Why, Ms Southern?' She says: 'I'm being crucified!' And you daren't laugh if there wasn't a joke, because she didn't miss a thing.

Tillie Ulster

It was a wonderful way in which the group and its branches, under the steermanship of Mrs Southern-Holt, got on and grew. And it grew very well because she always kept us very close to the aims. And you know one which I will never forget: not for the self, but for the whole. Always!

You know, if a child left [his/her] ballet shoes at the bar and all the kids were gone, dressing and all that, and one would just come in, she'd forgotten something, [Southern-Holt would] say: 'Are those your ballet shoes?' 'No Miss,' the child would say. 'Whose are they?' 'I don't know.' 'Pick them up, they're ballet shoes.

Pick them up and go and find out in the room where you're dressing, whose ballet shoes they are.' You see? And then she'd call them all together and say to them: 'Remember, you live not for the self, but for the whole. Be mindful even if another girlie leaves her shoes there.' What a world it would be if we could practice that philosophy, hey?

Alethea Jansen

Eoan's dance section started in 1935. Southern-Holt's daughter, Maisy, was the driving force behind the ballet during those early years. In later years, ballet classes were taught with the assistance of professional dancers in Cape Town.

The Eoan Group offered ballet classes at several branches across the Cape Peninsula.
PHOTO Cloete Breytenbach, 1965

At the time [the 1940s], the late Dulcie Howes was in charge of the dance-teacher training at the University of Cape Town, and quite a number of the University of Cape Town's dance students under Dulcie Howes came and gave assistance in teaching these children. And at the same time, this became part of their practical work. You see? So the children were getting good sound training at that time. And that is how the group grew, branches sprang up.

Alethea Jansen

I was born in 1947, so Stella, my sister, was already in the Eoan Group and I would go sitting around there, but I was still very young. And then, of course, going with her every week and seeing what is happening. But I didn't really know what was dance about, although I was a busybody sitting there and seeing everything happening. That was still the Ochberg Hall, in Hanover Street [in District Six]. The teacher's salary was low in those years because of the state not subsidising the arts. So the ballet always made the name for the Eoan Group, before the opera came in. We had Greek dancing, we had tap dancing, we had modern, which they call contemporary now, but we were the first to have it all. And as the years went on, the dancing section developed, with Maisy Southern-Holt.

Then they discovered Dr Manca, who was the treasurer of the City Council. He was an Italian, and he then invited everybody who could sing. And Dr Manca went around to all the various Coon carnivals [the Cape Minstrel carnivals] in Cape Town and at the Sea Point Trek, and he was adjudicating every year there. And that is how he discovered Joseph Gabriels. Joseph sang in the Coons and Dr Manca discovered him and so many others. Dr Manca invited them all for training. They came to the Ochberg Hall, but the Ochberg Hall just couldn't keep everything so they went to Upper Bree Street where there was another building and they had the opera training there. Then all the different people, from the street sweepers to the City Council, from domestic workers, from teachers, from clerks, from toilet cleaners, all those people came for Italian training with Dr Manca. Manca, I tell you, really worked his butt off.

Cecil Jacobs

Eoan's activities were many, but the group lacked money and infrastructure.

When I started working for the group, the Eoan Group didn't have a real office. We had a little room in [Cape Town's] old post office, the tail-end of which is now part of the new post office. But at that time it was facing the station. And there we did lots of work from. And we couldn't afford to pay, but Mrs Southern knew somebody from the post office and we

Ada Alethea Jansen, principal of the Eoan Group in the 1950s.
PHOTO Eoan Group Archive

were pushed in there. And at a given time, we were told, we can't stay here anymore, because we can't pay. So we moved to Trafalgar [public swimming pool, in Woodstock], and we acquired a room there, and the next thing, we had to get out there because they needed the room.

We didn't have money to run offices. Now, when we went from Trafalgar, the Adams's offered us their place. They had a garage [filling station]. They had a big place, which they ran, it was their garage. So they could afford to keep us there. I don't remember what happened then but we moved from there after about four, five years and then Mrs Southern said: 'Well, we're not going to hunt for offices anymore.' And then Mrs Southern said: 'No, from now on, the offices will be run from my home in Glengariff Road.'
Tillie Ulster

In 1943, Joseph Salvatore Manca became the conductor of Eoan's choir and over the next thirteen years he developed the choir into an opera company. In 1944, they performed a choral concert in the Cathedral Hall in Queen Victoria Street with approximately thirty-five choristers. After this concert the productions went from strength to strength: the choir expanded in numbers and the works grew in scale, soon including soloists and orchestra.

In 1946, Martin Shaw's *The Redeemer* was performed with organ and 100 singers and in 1947 the children's cantata *Sherwood* by Christopher Edmunds was performed with 500 singers and the Cape Town Municipal Orchestra. From 1949 to 1954, the group staged a string of operettas, preparing the group for its first opera production in 1956. Among these early operetta performances were *A Slave in Araby* by Alfred Silver, *Hong Kong* by Charles Jessop, Harold Fraser-Simson's musical comedy *The Maid of the Mountains, The Gypsy Princess* by Emmerich Kalman, and George Posford's *Magyar Melody.*

The first concert that we had, the big concert that we had, was in the Cathedral Hall in Queen Victoria Street. I remember that concert so well. Now that was the first concert Manca had, because it was held on a Thursday night and they started calling it the Eoan Group Choir. We had finished the last item, it was a waltz by Strauss, I remember so clearly. The concert was over and the people were almost going when this person shouts right from the back of the hall. He applauded and walked down towards us and he says we need to sing that last number again. And it was William Pickerill. He was conductor of the Cape Town Municipal Orchestra.
Tillie Ulster

The Eoan Group Choir in 1946. Seated in the front centre are Helen Southern-Holt and Joseph Manca, with John Ulster (in black suit, left) and Dan Ulster (in black suit, right).
PHOTO Eoan Group Archive

[The choir] became sophisticated. Before that, you know when the Eoan Group came into being, Mrs Southern would never allow names of individuals to appear on the programme. You would perform as Eoan grouper or Eoan chorister or no name. No, that is something Manca brought into it, with photos and the lot which was unknown to us. The group has a set of aims that any member that comes into it, doesn't matter how young you were, you had to learn those aims, and you had to live by it, accordingly.

Mrs Southern was a God-fearing person, as harsh and hard she was sometimes. She was a hard taskmaster, but she got things done. If you have a talent, you don't hide it under the bushel, you use it. And if you're too scared to use it, she brings it out of you.

We had drama people, we had Donald Inskip, Billy Jones, Rosalie van der Gucht, Rose Erlich, Leonard Schach, Basil Warner and his wife Minna Milston, Erwin Plought, John Packham and Jack Cardieu. And Jack Cardieu, we remember so well, because the first time he came to South Africa, he produced something for the Camps Bay operatic choir. No, no [Southern Holt] had a massive circle of friends.

Tillie Ulster

Tillie Ulster, secretary of the Eoan Group in the 1940s.
PHOTO Eoan Group Archive

Maar as jy daaroor dink eintlik, regtig realisties daaroor dink, die Eoan Groep was die eerste operagroep in Suid-Afrika.
~ *But if you actually think about it, really realistically think about it, the Eoan Group was the first opera company in South Africa.*
   Mimi Coertse

Their first encounter with the group and its opera productions left a deep impression on many Eoan members, inspiring some to become artists themselves. Access to the world of opera and vocal training, however, was not necessarily self-evident.

I used to stand on the bed and lock myself in the room with my mother's beautiful satin gown on and I used to sing at the top of my voice, looking in the mirror, and used to pretend I'm a grown opera singer. From quite a little girl, I loved singing. Anyway, my father took me to a concert in the City Hall once. I was so impressed and I said to my father, Dad, you know, I'd really like to go and sing with that choir or to sing on stage, because May Abrahamse sang a solo that night with this beautiful white dress, and I said, 'I'd love to do that one day.' So my dad said, 'Well, you can go join, you can go audition.' So he asked Mrs Kellerman to take me because she accompanied the singers in the Eoan Group and she said, 'Come along, I'll take you.' And so I went. And then Dr Manca auditioned me and sort of said, 'Sing a few notes' and said, 'Oh that's fine, go and stand with the first sopranos.' That's how I joined.
   Patricia van Graan

My first contact with the Eoan Group was when I was working. I started working in a clothing factory in 1955 when I was fourteen, I think. And when I was there about two years there was what we call a 'welfare officer human resources person' and she managed to get tickets from the Eoan Group to see certain productions. The tickets she managed to get were for the factory workers, gratis. So the very first opera I saw was *Rigoletto* and I was very impressed by that. Then followed *Cavalleria Rusticana*, I don't know who sang the lead but that was also beautiful.
   Trevor Pretorius

I studied accounting, shorthand, and I was at a commercial school. So that was my job, I worked for the trade unions. I did all their documents, their bookwork. There was a conservatoire of music, which was run by two English women, that was in Strand Street. But I always wanted to go and study singing, and I had asked whether one could go to the conservatoire in Stellenbosch. But we were not allowed to go there because of the colour of our skin. So a friend of mine, who was studying

at the conservatoire in Strand Street, told me: 'Ruth, you always sing, why don't you go and study music?' And that is where I went. I was there for three years on a part-time basis.
  Ruth Goodwin

16 En hierdie Woensdag sing ek onder die *shower* [by die koshuis van die Eurafrica Training Kollege in Coronationville, Johannesburg], en ek hoor iemand klop daar aan die deur en hy sê: 'Wie ben de jong man met de pragtige stem?' En ek meen, 'n jong man, en hier kom iemand en sê jy het 'n mooi stem en jy het Elvis Presley gesing. En in my gewaad: 'Meneer dit was ek gewees, meneer!' En toe is dit Henk Grysenhoud ['n Nederlandse sangonderwyser wat aan die Hoërskool Coronationville in Johannesburg verbonde was], en hy sê: 'Ons begint vanaand met sanglesse.' Vir my was dit 'n grap! Eerlikwaar, vir my was dit 'n grap, want nog niemand het vir my gesê ek het 'n stem wat kan sing nie. Daardie aand, net ná sewe, laat roep hy my. Ons is op die tweede verdieping, nou vir elke *scale* wat hy met my doen – na,na,na,na – [staan] al die studente daaronder en sing hulle dit na. So daardie eerste aand was 'n lag aand vir my. En hy is so verskriklik kwaad, hy sê vir my: 'Jy weet nie watter talent jy het nie. Kom wees ernstig, wees ernstig.' Volgende aand is hy maar alweer daar. Kom haal hy my uit die kamer uit. Ek dink dit het my 'n week geneem, toe besef ek dat as die man so aanhou dan is daar seker iets. Ses maande daarna toe sing ek met die SAUK Orkes. Kan amper nie glo nie! So het ek gekom tot sang.
~ And on that Wednesday I was singing in the shower [at the hostel of the Eurafrica Training College in Coronationville, Johannesburg] and I heard someone knocking on the door and asking [in Dutch]: 'Who is the young man with the beautiful voice?' And I thought, a young man, and here someone arrives and says you have a beautiful voice and you were singing Elvis Presley. And then me all dressed up: 'Me sir, it was me, sir!' And then I saw it was Henk Grysenhoud [a Dutch voice teacher who taught at the Coronationville High School in Johannesburg], and he says: 'We start with singing lessons tonight.' This was just a joke for me! Honestly, this was just a joke, because no one had ever said to me that I have a voice that can sing. That night, just after seven, he called for me. We were on the second floor, and with every scale he does with me – na, na, na, na – all the students downstairs imitated the sounds. So that first evening was a fun evening for me. And he became terribly angry, says to me: 'You have no idea what talent you have. Come now, be serious, be serious.' The next night he comes again. Hauls me out of my room. I think it took me about a week before I realised that if this man is carrying on like this, then there must be something to it. Six months later I was singing with the SABC Orchestra. Could hardly believe it! That's how I started my singing.
  Gerald Samaai

Patricia van Graan and cast rehearsing in the Cape Town City Hall.
PHOTO Cloete Breytenbach, 1965

2

The Colour of Music

In the 1950s and 1960s, when the Eoan Group performed their regular opera seasons, it was against the oppressive backdrop of a racially segregated society living under apartheid laws. In 1948, the National Party government under DF Malan had come into power. This signalled the beginning of formal apartheid with laws such as the Group Areas Act and the Separate Amenities Act, fragmenting society into 'white', 'coloured', 'Indian' and 'black'.

When I sang in Johannesburg, [radio personality] Esmé Euvrard and her husband, Gilberto – they were very fond of me – came to me, and she had some friends with her. They entertained me at their home. And this woman said to me: 'Excuse me, but are you, are you also coloured? In all the papers it's coloured people, are you coloured? Because I'm not sure, aren't you white?' You see that time they didn't know [if you] are white or are you coloured. If you're just a little bit fair, you have to test with the pencil [to check whether a person's hair was straight or curly, thereby determining their race]. That sort of thing.

The orchestra members were, I would say, mostly foreigners, people who didn't know much about apartheid. There were quite a few who said, 'Ruth, can I take you out for tea?' I said, 'No, you can't because I'm black.' They would say, 'But you're not black.' I said, 'But I'm not white.'

Once, I was walking to the butcher and a woman came to me. She's German, and she stopped me, she said to me, 'Are you the opera singer who sang Madama Butterfly?' And I said, 'Ja.' So she says to me, 'Come, come, I will take you for tea.' There was a little restaurant opposite this butcher. I said, 'Sorry, I'm not allowed to go in there.' 'Why not?' I said, 'because I'm not a white.' She said, 'You're not a white? You will go with me, I'm going to buy for you a cup of tea.'

Ruth Goodwin

One day – now my middle sister is quite dark and I'm olive skinned; my eldest sister was fair – so we're standing on the steps and these little white kids were standing there, and the one said to us: 'Is julle susters?' [Are you sisters?] So my middle sister, the dark one, she said yes. And he looked at us and he looked at her and he said, 'Nou lieg jy? Jy's dan 'n kaffir' [Now are you lying? You're a kaffir then.][1] Oh, and she was … she never forgot that. She *never* forgot that, because she was the dark one. But hey, you know, they used to call us corks – if I press you down here, you'll pop back up over there. Ja, they used to call us corks. It's amazing. I believe our sense of humour really just carried us through.

Benny Arendse

---

1   'Kaffir' is a derogotary term for a black person.

Ruth Goodwin.
PHOTO *The Star*, 14 September 1960

Benny Arendse in 1960.

In order to study at white institutions such as the University of Cape Town, coloured people had to apply for a permit from the government.

> But now came the nonsense: being the only coloured [student], I had to get a permit and Ms [Dulcie] Howes [ballet teacher at UCT] said to me, 'Oh Cecil, you had better go to Coloured Affairs, and you'll have to fill in a form and that form must go to Pretoria and the permit will come and then you'll be accepted into ballet school,' she says. 'But bugger the thing, you just come and don't tell anyone, you just come to the classes and bugger the bloody permit because I'm sure this thing will only be coming in June/July.' And she was right. The permit only came in June/July. But I started with her. The classes went on well.
>
> *Cecil Jacobs*

By accepting funding from the Coloured Affairs Department of the then government, the group had to comply with apartheid legislation, which forced them to perform to racially segregated audiences only. From 1965 onwards, Eoan had to apply for permits from the Cape Town municipality to allow coloured people to enter 'white' buildings and for coloured singers to perform in these venues. Coloureds had to use a separate entrance and the audience was seated in separate blocks in the hall. The white audience sat in the centre block, while coloured people were placed either at the back or the sides of the hall.

> Look, you should know, there was also the apartheid thingy going on. So certain places we couldn't go to and certain places we could. Let me tell you my personal view. I was never interested in politics. I couldn't care what went on, it was just music, music, music. And then mostly the teachers, and not only them, but they were very politically minded. This is why quite a lot of them left [South Africa] when the apartheid laws [came into being] and we then of course had to get out of Cape Town. And you know, then we went to Athlone, ja. And then a lot of guys, especially, left. You know, teachers. They were, you know, they were politically minded and so on. But you know, I was never interested in politics ... up till today. Up till today I never ... Yes, it was just music all the time, you know? Ja, I don't know. I suppose in the world not of the world ...
>
> *May Abrahamse*

> Politically, I was never ... I never really worried about that. You know, only if it ... only if it affected me then I would open my mouth, but I was easy-

G.P.-S.
Ref. No. 19/3/5

KB-E 135

DEPARTMENT OF COLOURED, REHOBOTH AND NAMA RELATIONS

APPLICATION FOR PERMISSION TO ATTEND CERTAIN UNIVERSITIES

Name and address:

P. VOGES
15 ORPHAN STREET
CAPE TOWN
8001

Write your initials, surname, address and postal code in the space opposite in BLOCKLETTERS. Mention Mr, Miss.

1. General instructions:

   (a) Please complete this form in duplicate.

   (b) This form must be completed by Coloured students who wish to attend universities other than the University of the Western Cape. Students who wish to attend the University of the Western Cape or the University of Durban-Westville must not complete this form but should apply direct to the university.

   (c) Separate forms must be completed if the applicant wishes to apply for more than one course or for admission to more than one university.

   (d) Students who are unable to attend the University of the Western Cape as a result of financial, medical or domestic circumstances, must make a sworn statement in support of their application in paragraph 6 of this form, otherwise the application will not be considered.

   (e) Before submitting this application, students are advised to consult the university of their choice about the course they wish to follow and the admission requirements pertaining thereto.

   (f) Application forms must be addressed to:

   The Secretary for Coloured,
   Rehoboth and Nama Relations
   Private Bag 9058
   Cape Town
   8000

2. (a) Christian names...... PETER

   (b) Date of birth...... 11. 10. 56

   (c) How long have you been residing at your present address?...... 3 years

   (d) Tel. No...... 93 14 39

   (e) Population group...... COLOURED

   (f) Highest educational qualifications (Std 10, B.A., etc.)...... STD 10
   obtained at (name of school or institution)...... TRAFALGAR HIGH ...... Year...... 1954

   (g) Are you at present registered at a university? Yes/No...... NO. If so, mention the name of the university......
   ...... Year of first registration...... and course......
   ...... Number of permit issued......

3. Parents' name and address......
   ......
   ......
   ......

4. (a) University the applicant wishes to attend...... CAPE TOWN

   (b) Year of first enrolment at the above University for the course mentioned in paragraph 4 (c)...... 1981

   (c) Course for which applicant wishes to enter (B.A., B.Sc. etc.). See paragraph 1 (e).
   HIGHER EDUCATION DIPLOMA (SPEECH & DRAMA)

   (d) Is the course offered at the University of the Western Cape?...... NO

3

Coloured people needed a permit such as this, dated 6 November 1980, to study at institutions for white people.

5. Subjects to be taken in each year of study:

1st Year	2nd Year	3rd Year
ENGLISH I		
EDUC. PSYCHO		
SPEAR } PERFORMANCE		
SPEECH} TEACHING		
EDUC DANCE		

4th Year	5th Year	6th Year

6. Should the course be offered by the University of the Western Cape furnish reasons for not being able to attend the University of the Western Cape [please read paragraph 1 (d)]...

I am aware of the fact that if permission is granted to me it may be cancelled if any information furnished by me in this application is found to be false in any material respect and I do hereby solemnly declare that to the best of my knowledge and belief the information given above is correct.

S. Voges 29. 9. 80.
Signature of applicant   Date

The deponent has acknowledged that he/she knows and understands the contents of this affidavit. Sworn to me at ....CAPE TOWN... this .....29TH..... day of ....SEPTEMBER.... 19 80.

NAMENS SEKRETARIS VAN KLEURLINGSAKE
FOR SECRETARY FOR COLOURED AFFAIRS.
Commissioner of oaths' stamp

.... Commissioner of oaths

FOR OFFICE USE

1. Permission granted/~~Not granted~~
2. Permit No. 158/81

Permission granted to study at the University of ....Cape Town........
for the course ........H.E.D. Speech/ Drama........
including the major subject/s. .... as from 19 81.

CONDITION OF PERMIT:
(i) This permit applies only to the above-mentioned University and the course indicated.
(ii) Deviation from this course without the prior approval of the Minister is not permissible.

Secretary for Coloured, Rehoboth and Nama Relations

DEPARTEMENT VAN KLEURLINGBETREKKINGE
KAAPSTAD
6 -11- 1980
CAPE TOWN
DEPARTMENT OF COLOURED RELATIONS

going at the time. Though it was heart-breaking to see my own people
having to sit out at the back. Even my own family having to sit right at the
back, or just on one side. They couldn't sit where they wanted to sit in the
City Hall.
   Winifred du Plessis

That is something; politics kan jy nie uithou nie ~ *you cannot get away
from it.* Look you didn't obey, it's politics! But I must say, out there, there
were many of our people who ostracised me because I sang for the group.
Because the fact remains that [Eoan] sang for separate audiences. But that
was the only time when I did it, and that was in Johannesburg, because
I had no alternative. I couldn't let the show not go on because of this,
because it was for separate audiences. All of us, it was not only me. There
was Lionel [Fourie] and Joseph [Gabriels], they felt the same way. [The
community was] very much against it, very much so. Many of them didn't
speak to me and, I mean I couldn't explain. It's a wonder my husband
didn't divorce me, because he was very much against it too.
   Ruth Goodwin

I remember that we were going to have the production of *Carmen Jones*,
the musical. So when we performed at the Joseph Stone [theatre in
Athlone, Cape Town], it would be so-called coloureds only and non-whites
only. Then we'd perform at the Alhambra Theatre in Cape Town, and it
would be whites only. Then there was a slight wind of change after two
or three years, of getting used to 'tonight is coloured audiences only',
Tuesday night and Wednesday night is white audiences only. Then I
remember the concerts in the early 1970s, which the Eoan Group staged
at the Cape Town City Hall. If there was eight rows of chairs and each has
got about 200 up, two of the rows then became for non-whites only to sit
on. And the other four was for whites only. But you see, one audience, non-
whites there, and the whites there, and the people who was in the political
sphere of South Africa was against that. They wanted us to boycott
performing for white people. Yet, the bulk of the audiences that carried
the shows, the financial parts of it, was white people.
   Fuad Sawyer

Whenever Eoan performed to racially segregated audiences, community
support was put in jeopardy. As apartheid legislation intensified and Eoan
became increasingly entangled in political compromise, the boycott from
the coloured community resulted in the group performing to empty concert
halls by the 1980s.

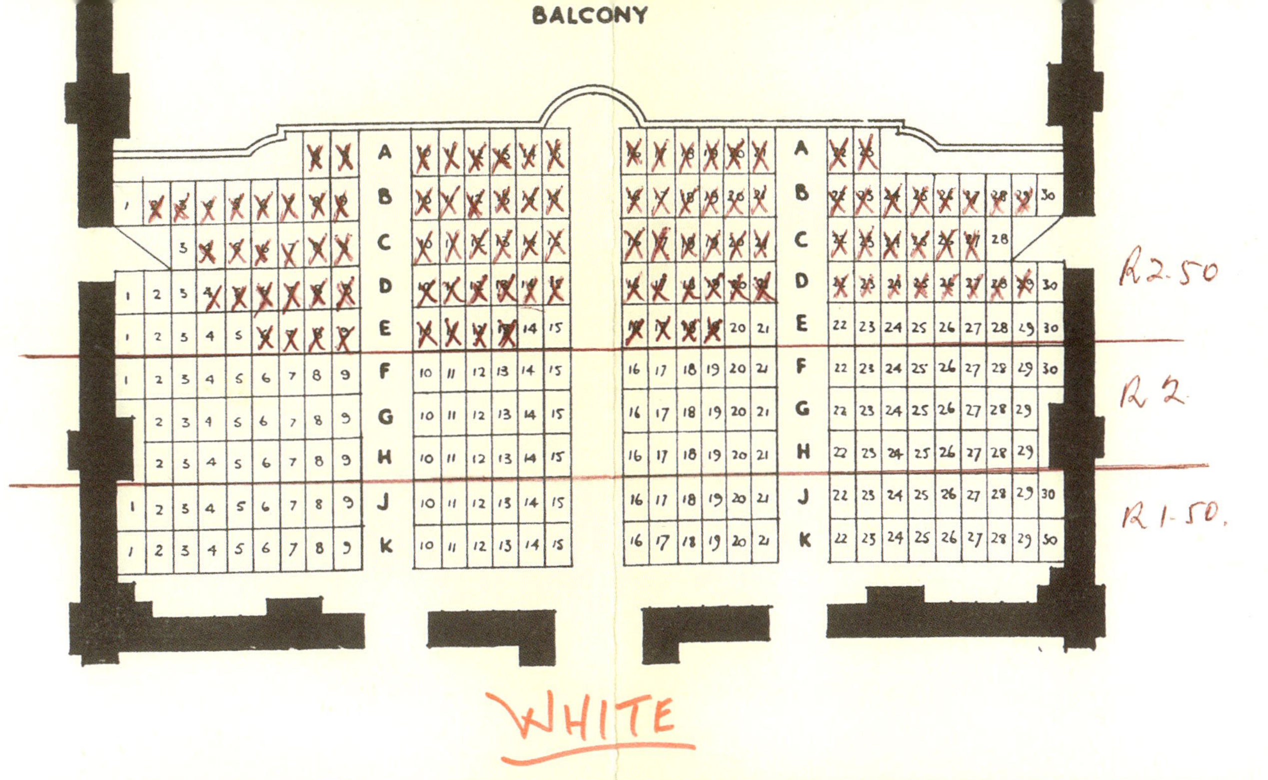

The seating plan for a 1972 operatic concert held in the Cape Town City Hall.
The white audience was seated in the centre block, with the coloured audience
at the back and sides of the hall.
SOURCE Eoan Group Archive

After the Eoan Group performed at a concert in Stellenbosch to a racially segregated audience, this cartoon was published in the now-defunct publication, *The Torch*. *The Torch* was a news publication of the Teacher's League of South Africa, a liberation organisation, similar to today's teachers' unions, to which coloured teachers belonged. The cartoon was critical of Eoan's performances to segregated audiences, saying: 'Stellenbosch bosses come look at coloured culture,' and 'Whites here; Non-whites this side'.
SOURCE *The Torch*, 24 November 1947

Ons het baie swaar gely gedurende daardie tydperk. Ek onthou daar was 'n tydstip wat mense gesê het: 'You are accepting the grant from Coloured Affairs, so we don't support you any more.' My vraag was altyd aan die onderwysers: 'Where do you get your cheque from?' Toe sê hulle: 'Yes, but we are forced to.' Toe sê ek: 'So what? We are also forced to.' Ek het altyd vir myself gesê: 'Manca says you must be ready when the time comes.' En ek het geglo dit gaan kom. Maar daardie tyd toe is hulle net besig om die kunsterade te stig [wat deur die destydse regering begin is en wat professionele wit kunstenaars in diens geneem het]. Ons het gevoel daar was 'n rede hoekom hulle die kunsteraad gestig het. Ons het mos al ons uitvoerings gehad in die Stadsaal, en toe wat doen hulle? Die regering revamp die City Hall, neem die gordyne weg, toe het ons nie meer 'n venue nie. Toe gaan ons af na die Alhambra-teater. Dit was een van die mooiste geboue aan die binnekant. Maar ná 'n tyd toe gooi hulle daardie gebou ook af. Gooi hulle die Alhambra af, toe het ons weer nie meer 'n venue nie. En toe soos dit later gekom het, toe het ons na Athlone toe gekom. In Athlone, Joseph Stone.

Want kyk hiersa, toe begin die studente mos opstaan by die universiteite. Hulle het jou beskou as 'n traitor: 'You are singing for the whites.' Toe gaan ons na Manca toe en sê vir hom: 'We've got a problem ...'

Ja, 1976 begin alles tot 'n punt te kom. Opdrag gekom vanaf Coloured Affairs, 31st of May: 'We would like the Eoan Group to give a performance. Doesn't matter which opera, we will fund it.' Toe sê Manca: 'You either do the opera, or we will take back the funds.' Toe besluit ons ons gaan nie die fonds neem nie, van Coloured Affairs nie. Hulle doen toe 'n beroep dwarsdeur die hele land: 'If everybody can contribute R1 or R2, we can survive.' Hulle het nog nie R100 ingekry nie, dwarsdeur die hele land. Dit het eintlik gelei tot die tyd dat die Eoan Groep partykeer gesluit was. Want jy het begin twyfel of jy veilig is. Jy het nie geweet wat gaan aan nie. En die probleem was eintlik: dis nou jou eie mense wat opstaan en jy weet nie wat om aan die saak te doen nie. Jy beweeg daagliks tussen hulle, nou hoor jy die mense praat ook daarvan: 'Yes, but the Eoan Group is still accepting the grant.' Hulle het geen keuse gehad nie.

~ We really struggled during that period. I remember that at the time people were saying: 'You are accepting the grant from Coloured Affairs, so we don't support you any more.' My question to the teachers was always: 'Where do you get your cheque from?' And they say: 'Yes, but we are forced to.' And I say: 'So what? We are also forced to.' I always said to myself: 'Manca says you must be ready when the time comes.' And I believed it was going to come. But they were just busy establishing the arts councils at the time [which the then government established and which employed professional white artists]. We felt there was a reason why they established the arts council. We were

giving all our performances in the City Hall, and so what do they do? The government revamps the City Hall, removes the curtains, so we no longer have a venue. Then we went down to the Alhambra Theatre. It was one of the most beautiful buildings on the inside. But after a while they knocked that down as well. Knocked down the Alhambra, so again we had no venue. But after a while we came to Athlone. To Athlone, Joseph Stone.

Because you see, that's when the students started their uprising at the universities. They regarded you as a traitor: 'You are singing for the whites.' So we went to Manca and said to him: 'We've got a problem …'

Yes, in 1976 everything came to a head. Instruction from Coloured Affairs, 31st of May: 'We would like the Eoan Group to give a performance. Doesn't matter which opera, we will fund it.' Then Manca said: 'You either do the opera, or we will take back the funds.' So we decided we were not going to take the funds, not from Coloured Affairs. They then made an appeal throughout the country: 'If everybody can contribute R1 or R2, we can survive.' They did not get even R100, from the whole country. This actually led to the time when the Eoan Group was closed down sometimes. Because you began to doubt whether you were safe. You did not know what was going on. And the problem was actually: it's now your own people who are rising up and you don't know what to do about it. You are moving around among them every day, and then you hear people talking about it: 'Yes, but the Eoan Group is still accepting the grant.' They did not have a choice.

Gerald Samaai

Well, for instance when they went on tour in 1960, they went on their first national tour. They were not allowed to perform in certain places, for mixed audiences. It was always, I think there was one or two performances where they had to perform for whites only. But there was times when certain of the groupers, like Lionel [Fourie] was one of them, who refused to sing, because it was for whites only. And there Ruth [Goodwin]'s husband refused to allow her to sing, where there was, it was, a mixed audience.

Ruth Fourie

In 1965 toe was ons byvoorbeeld op baie goeie plekke. Ons was byvoorbeeld in Durban by die Admiral Hotel, en orals waar ons gesing het, het die mense ons baie goed ontvang. Ons was maar altyd met daardie agter in ons kop in: 'This is not really what your people want.' Een aand het [Manca] lekker met ons gesit en gesels. Hy sê toe vir ons: 'I'm aware of what is going on. I know exactly how you feel, because you have been ostracised by your people. So am I. You're at least thirty-five, forty people together, you can talk. I'm standing here alone. But I'm prepared to fight till the death.'

30

[Oorsee is ons] baie goed ontvang. Ek het so gelag. Mister Sydow het so lekker gesê, om sy woorde te gebruik: 'My son, for the first time the word "coloured" is going to mean something good for us.' Maar orals waar ons gekom het, toe ons in Skotland kom, toe weet ons eintlik nie: 'They are the people who are denied access to all the theatres and look what we can produce.' Toe gebruik ons nou eintlik die apartheid-situasie tot ons voordeel. Ons het 'n wonderlike tyd gehad in Skotland. Ek dink die resensies en almal daardie goed wat uitgekom het, hulle het ons [genoem] 'on a par with England's best'.

~ In 1965, for example, we were in many good places. In Durban, for example, we stayed at the Admiral Hotel, and everywhere we sang the people received us very well. But always at the back of minds: 'This is not really what your people want.' One evening [Manca] was sitting and chatting with us. He said to us: 'I'm aware of what is going on. I know exactly how you feel, because you have been ostracised by your people. So am I. You're at least thirty-five, forty people together, you can talk. I'm standing here alone. But I'm prepared to fight till the death.'

[Overseas] we were received very well. I just had to laugh. Mister Sydow put it so well, to use his words: 'My son, for the first time the word "coloured" is going to mean something good for us.' But everywhere we went, when we arrived in Scotland, we did not actually know: 'They are the people who are denied access to all the theatres and look what we can produce.' So we then actually used the apartheid situation to our benefit. We had a wonderful time in Scotland. I think the reviews and all that stuff that came out, they said we were 'on a par with England's best'.
    Gerald Samaai

There was one stage that I remember whilst in the Eoan Group: Dr Manca had opened the doors to what we would say black people, Xhosa, Bantu – whichever way we're gonna put it over – and he felt that they, that there was a need to get some black singers into the group. I remember two or three of the rehearsals we had a few black people. It was not long, a week or two after that, where Dr Manca had to ask the very same people to leave, because it had reached the ears of the government so quick, and they had tramped on his toes for that.
    Fuad Sawyer

A tall African man came to audition, beautiful bass voice, and so Dr Manca said to this man: 'I'm sorry my friend, I cannot accept you in the Eoan Group because of you know, the laws.' An African man and he had a beautiful voice. And he said, so sorry but I cannot accept you. And he had to leave. And I had a friend [Fred Martin] at the time, this friend was very

Fred Martin and Patricia van Graan singing at a concert in 1971 to raise funds for Martin to study singing in Italy. Due to Martin's political outspokenness, Joseph Manca did not want him as a member of the Eoan Group.
 Supplied by Patricia van Graan

much involved in politics and we used to sing together in concerts. He won a bursary too.

We used to sing lots of duets together. He never belonged to the group because he was very political, and Dr Manca didn't like him because he was very, very political. But we were sort of going out at the time to sing and he tried to stop me from singing with him. No, Manca didn't like him 'cause he was too political.

Patricia van Graan

Well, I don't think they saw themselves as musicians. I mean Lionel [Fourie] was, I don't think he ever had any tuition in playing the piano and he could play the piano from tonic solfa. You know, he'd have a bit of score there and play the piano from there.

I didn't think [the audiences were patronising], I didn't get that impression. You know, I think people just came there to hear the music. It was people who loved music, you know. Musicians is a culture on its own, music is a culture on its own and people go because they love music and they listen to it and they appreciate it as it's given to them. You know, I didn't get any idea that they were patronising, but they came. People came over and over and over.

Ruth Fourie

En daarvandaan toe begin ek al hoe meer ernstig raak. Toe sê ek, ek wil bladlees, ek wil al daardie goed doen. Ons twee het begin baie intieme [vriende] raak, ek en [my sang onderwyser] Henk Grysenhoud. Maar met die beleid van die land, vind hulle uit dat ek studeer onder hom, en toe soek hulle hom orals. Want ek mag studeer, maar ek mag nie uitvoerings gee nie, onder sy naam nie. En met die apartheidsbeleid, toe ek weer van hom hoor, toe het hy selfmoord gepleeg. Want hy het nie toegelaat dat hulle vir hom aansê wat om te doen nie. Toe sit ek nou; hierso het ek net begin met sang, waantoe gaan ek nou?

~ And from then on I became more and more serious. I said I want to be able to read music, I want to do all that stuff. The two of us became very close friends, me and Henk Grysenhoud [my singing teacher]. But with the policy of the country, they found out that I was studying under him, and they looked for him everywhere. Because I could study, but I could not give performances under his name. And with the apartheid policy, when I heard about him again, he had committed suicide. Because he was not going to allow them to order him around. So there I was; I had just started with my singing, what must I do now?

Gerald Samaai

Joseph Gabriels.
PHOTO *Sunday Tribune*, 17 August 1960

Die politiek het my so geaffekteer dat ek altyd ge-push het om baie harder te werk as my medesangers wat blank was. Ek moes altyd tien of twintig maal sterker oorkom om gesien te wees.
~ *The way that politics affected me was that I always had to push myself to work harder if my co-singers were white. I always had to come across as ten or twenty times stronger to be noticed.*
   John van der Ross

In 1962, Mimi Coertse, a well-known South African soprano singing in Vienna, Austria at the time, was prevented from awarding Joseph Gabriels the bursary she had launched to support upcoming young singers.

Nou ja, toe't ek nou gesê hy [Joseph Gabriels] moet dit kry, want hy het ongelooflik pragtig gesing, hoor. Heerlikheid, hy't mooi gesing! En nou ja, toe was daar destyds vir my gesê, ek meen, dit was toe nou seker maar die bewind daai tyd van die [Universiteit van Pretoria]: hulle kan nie dit vir 'n anderskleurige gee nie. Toe't ek gesê, wel, dan word my beurs die jaar nie toegeken nie. Dit was die einde van die storie. En net 'n paar [jaar] daarna toe sing hy in die Metropolitan. Jy weet ... Nou ja ...
~ *Well, I then said he must get it, because I'm telling you he sang unbeliev-ably beautifully. My goodness, he sang beautifully! Anyway, I was told at the time, I suppose it was the policy of the [University of Pretoria] at that time: they could not give it to a non-white. So I said, well, in that case my bursary will not be awarded that year. That was the end of the story. And just a few [years] afterwards he was singing in the Metropolitan. You know ... What can one say ...*
   Mimi Coertse

Both Gordon [Jephtas] and I had to apply for a permit to study at UCT [University of Cape Town]. You've got to swallow your pride to become a great singer, violinist, pianist. So you apply and somebody else says, 'Yes you can and these are the conditions.' Then you can go to UCT. So that is what I mean by being kept in a harness. Thank goodness that is over, we never thought we are going to live long enough to see that coming to an end. And that is why it is so important for young people now today, to recognise what people did that time with very little resources, few oppor-tunities and that they could do what they did, and today it is, everything is open, supposed to be open. You can live your dream, if you are willing to work hard enough.
   Ronnie Samaai

The people never ever thought that the so-called coloureds can do things
like that. And I have, how can I say, I don't hate the person, I just hate
what they did. And that is the way I was brought up. My father used to say:
'It is not your colour, it is what is in you, your spirit, that is important.' It's
not the colour, we are all God's children, you understand, hey? And that is
the way you must live, and that is what I tried. And that is why in my daily
life I never gave in, I never gave in because of my colour. I showed them
what this colour can do and behave.
   Benny Arendse

**By day the performers of the Eoan Group lived a 'coloured' life, but when the
stage lights went on, they were in a 'white world'.**

We were a coloured company when we performed in the Alhambra. It
was a time when we coloured performers who performed in white areas
went in as a Portuguese, change the names, and that was the only way
you could do it, is to become Portuguese. It was a strange world that I was
living in. Look I was a teacher during the day teaching coloured children,
totally coloured, in a coloured area as defined by the Group Areas Act.
And when I come home, at quarter to four – I had to leave, four o'clock
honest to God – and I arrive in Cape Town by the back door. You come
through the station and you come through the non-white exit and you
head into a white theatre which is in a white area. And the audience is
white, but you can't see them, because when you look into the lights you
don't see an audience. There is no contact between you and the people
because the theatre [the Alhambra] is not built that way, for backstage
visitors. Strange situation of coming in, all the workers, like the doorman
and the costume people are all whites. The stage hands and the stage
manager is white. But somehow in your time, the time that you are there
in your dressing rooms, wonderful dressing rooms with lights and things
like that, you lose it. You get transported away. After the performance
little mini vans line up and has a number on it, and if it is your number
it is going to Wynberg. You get in and go back to the coloured area and
you go home. The next day it is all the same again, this is Mondays to
Saturdays, in the season for six weeks.
   Most of them did it [crossing between the two worlds] quite
successfully, there was not much of a struggle among coloured people.
We came to accept things. It was sort of, 'Ag, nou ja, wees nou die minste.'
['Ah well, just give in].'
   And in 1979–80 with the [State of Emergency and school riots],
because the Eoan Group was getting money from Coloured Affairs it

Peter Voges on stage in 1980.

did not sit well with the students and the teachers. So they very kindly, because I was well thought of, came to me and spoke their minds. 'And this is what we would like you to think about: you cannot be here and there, we don't want to force the issue, but if you go there you are not here.' And this is the way I was earning my bread and butter, teaching. So that is what I had to do. Gordon [Jephtas] had, it was the second time he put me in as the artistic coordinator, so at the end of 1980 I had to resign from there. So then the two worlds somehow did not match anymore, I had to become aware of the facts. I could not take more of it, this was not going to be an easy ride. This was 1976 onwards to 1985 – my whole world changed and my whole consciousness changed. So I then knew there was something different.

> *Peter Voges*

Living in these two worlds became difficult for some, standing in the way of their artistic endeavours. Some, like David Poole, had themselves reclassified as white. Poole was a ballet dancer and choreographer who, in later years, held influential positions at both the UCT Ballet School and the Ballet Department at CAPAB.

David Poole was a coloured South African. And one of them remembered that, talking about him, one of his friends from the Eoan Group, and said, 'Oh, David Poole, you know, he went to London coloured and came back white!' So, he just forgot his roots. Well, you know, I suppose, he actually came back a ballet person. And that's international.

   Emma Renzi

How can I put it, [David Poole] is very distantly related to me, from my granny's side, you know, her cousin or somebody was his mommy's sister or whatever. But they were fair, they were very white-looking. Even his sister also, he had a sister by the name of Gail and they lived in Woodstock. Now Basil Poole, his brother, was also a dancer, he made no bones about it that he was coloured. He always referred to his backside, he said: 'You know, this is my heritage'. You know, he was really jovial about it, he would always joke, Basil, and he was always with the coloured students.

But now David Poole, he's a born coloured. Just when he came back [from London], you know, he became, he was white. If you had the right connections and knew the correct people in the right places, then it was just accepted and he had Dulcie Howes behind him, you know, those people. Look, David Poole wasn't even qualified as a dance teacher or somebody to take over UCT's ballet school, he had to go back to London and he had to do crash courses in administration and qualifications to become a qualified dance teacher and all the others. But through Dulcie Howes also, he got all these things right in London. She sent him to the correct places, channels and whatever.

   Lydia Johnson

They all knew because [David Poole] taught at a coloured school, and his mother lived in Duke Street [in Woodstock]. And the wonderful thing about these performances in the City Hall – on Commemoration Day there was a performance there to which invited people came. And Mrs Poole came right round me, at the side through the back and right through the men's dressing room to a bay and she left the same way. She was a cunning woman. We all knew, this is not a thing that you can hide to coloured people. They know.

   Peter Voges

The government of the day used various ways to check which race group a person belonged to. One method – the 'pencil test' – was to slide a pencil through the hair. If it slid out, the hair was straight enough for the person to be classified as 'white'. If the pencil stuck, the person was classified 'coloured'. Coloured people would often joke amongst each other about their

David Poole in 1965.
PHOTO Eoan Group Archive

'touch of the tarbrush', in reference to the roots of the hair, which always
gave away their race, no matter how much they tried to straighten their hair.

> If you turn sideways, you can see the tar mark ['touch of the tarbrush']
> ... on the waist. That is where the tarbrush sits. The tarbrush here in the
> neck and on the sides, that is where the tarbrush sits, we knew it. But
> David would sue anyone who called him other than white. We knew his
> mother lived on Duke Street, Woodstock. His brothers were all different-
> looking, say no more. And David poured a lot of energy into the Eoan
> Group. He just over-rode and overcame, one hell of a person to work with,
> but he demanded absolute perfection.
>
> *Peter Voges*

> Nobody really had associated [David Poole] with dancing for the Eoan
> Group. The public didn't know that he had danced, only the groupers,
> and part of the public. Because you see, he danced on the stage, nobody
> knew his name, as I say, names were not on the programmes. No, nobody
> [queried his race]. Nobody did. No, no, no, he had the talent, you see? This
> is the thing.
>
> *Tillie Ulster*

In 1963, the provincial arts councils were established by the government
for each of South Africa's former four provinces – the Cape Performing
Arts Board (CAPAB) in the Cape Province, the Performing Arts Council of
the Transvaal (PACT), the Natal Performing Arts Council (NAPAC), and the
Performing Arts Council of the Orange Free State (PACOFS). For the first
time in South Africa's history, the state sponsored the performing arts in
full. The arts councils were, however, for white performers, and it was only
after 1980 that legislation allowed singers of colour to perform for them.

> Ja, sommige van my persoonlike vriende het gedink, 'Nee, julle gaan na
> die wittes toe,' jy weet. Toe sê ek, waar gaan ek die geleentheid kry? Ek kry
> dit tog nie hier [by Eoan] nie. Hulle is vandag trots, en daar's een of twee
> wat nog altyd nie hier [Kunstekaap] kom nie, maar baie van hulle is trots
> [oor] wat ek bereik het, jy weet. Maar daar was moeilike, moeilike jare
> daai tyd as 'n lid van KRUIK. Toe lateraan toe kom [ander bruin sangers
> soos] Keith Timms en Sidwell [Hartman] en Jennifer Hartman en Virginia
> Davids – sy was in die koor saam met my. Ek het gedog hulle gaat nooit
> vir my die geleentheid gee nie, en ek wil sing! Ja. En daar was baie van
> onse mense [wat gesê het]: 'Oh no, you're singing for the whites now.' Ek
> sê: 'But where else must I sing then?' Ek het vir die Coons [Kaapse Klopse]
> gesing ook al.

Nou kom ons hier [by Kunstekaap] – ons mag mos nie hier gekom
het nie, bygewoon het enige van die operas hier nie. Dan gaat ons na [die
tenoor] Gé Korsten se kleedkamer, dan sê [my vriend] vir Gé: 'Ou Gé, hoe
sing jy daai noot dan so laf, jong? Ronnie gee vir hom 'n top C daar!' Daai
was darem nou terrible! Dan sê ek: 'Nee man!' Dan gee ek 'n top C. Dan sê
Gé: 'Ja, julle's goed, julle's goed, julle's goed!' Maar ons kom nie daar nie,
jy weet. Wys maar net hoe die tye gewees het, nè. Jy het die talent, en hier
kan jy dit nie gebruik nie, maar hulle erken dat jy goed is.

*~ Yes, some of my personal friends were thinking, 'No, now they are going
to the whites,' you know. So I said, where I am I going to get such an
opportunity? I'm not getting it here [at Eoan]. Today they are proud, and
there are still one or two who still do not come here [Artscape], but many of
them are proud of what I have achieved, you know. But there were difficult,
difficult times during those years as a member of CAPAB. Then later on
we were joined by [other coloured singers like] Keith Timms and Sidwell
[Hartman] and Jennifer Hartman and Virginia Davids, she was in the chorus
with me. And I thought they were never going to give me the opportunity,
and I want to sing! Yes. And there were many of our people [who said]: 'Oh
no, you're singing for the whites now.' I said: 'But where else must I sing
then?' I had also sung for the Coons [Cape minstrels] already.*

*Now we arrive here [at Artscape] – we were not supposed to come there,
you know, not attend any of the operas here. So we go to [tenor] Gé Korsten's
change room, and [my friend] says to Gé: 'Listen Gé, why do you sing that
note so flat, man? Ronnie, give the man a top C!' And that was really terrible!
Then I say: 'No, man!' Then I sing a top C. Then Gé says: 'Yes, you guys are
good, you guys are good, you guys are good!' But it goes no further, you
know. Just shows you what the times were like, not so? You have the talent,
and you can't use it here, but they admit that you are good.*

Ronald Theys

Eoan's voice trainer and producer, Alessandro Rota, tried to persuade
CAPAB to give Eoan's singers opportunities to sing in their company in
the Nico Malan Centre (now Artscape) in Cape Town. CAPAB required that
singers have a formal qualification in music in order to perform in their
productions.

[Rota says], 'I read the article that people must be able to produce the
paper [qualification]. Now professor, I have brought some paper. I'm
putting down the paper, you tell the paper to sing. I can wait the whole
day! In my country where I come from, Italy, and incidentally I was born
almost on the border where Guiseppe Verdi was born, they don't ask for
the paper, they ask for the voice. That is what opera is about.'

Alessandro Rota in 1956.

Hy sê: 'I've got a chap there, by the name of ...,' en hy noem die persoon se naam, en hy weet toe na wie hy verwys. 'In the day he polishes the floors of the City Hall. Night time he sings the leading role.' En dit was die waarheid, want ek het vir Jimmy [Momberg] persoonlik geken. In die dag werk hy vir die City Council, en vanaand sing hy die hoofrol. En ons het altyd gespot onder ons en sê: 'Jimmy, daardie voorste gedeelte polish jy beter, nè, want jy staan mos daar vanaand!'
~ He says: 'I've got a chap there, by the name of ...,' and he gives the person's name, and he knows who he was referring to. 'In the day he polishes the floors of the City Hall. Night time he sings the leading role.' And that was the truth, because I knew Jimmy [Momberg] personally. During the day he works for the city council, and tonight he sings the lead role. And we always used to joke among ourselves and say to him: 'Jimmy, you really polish up that front part nicely, not so, because you're standing there tonight!'
Gerald Samaai

Other white people also tried to intervene for the coloured community at CAPAB.

Ek was ook aan KRUIK verbonde ... en ek wil so graag gehad het dat die jonger mense van die Eoan Groep moes insit in die aand van die repetisies. Hulle mog nie na die Nico [Malan] kom om te hoor nie. Maar dat hulle miskien by die repetisies, by die kleedrepetisies, kan insit, maar dit was net taboe. Dit was my grootste teleurstelling dat ek daarin gefaal het. Maar toe in 1981 toe verskuif dinge, want die politiek het toe stadigaan beginne verskuif en een van die wetgewings was toe verval en die Nico word toe oopgestel vir alle rasse en toe dadelik het ek daarvan werk gemaak, maar onmiddellik, om te vra dat mense van die Eoan Groep moet kom, hulle moet oorweeg word vir vaste plekke in die koor en, o man, dit was ook 'n stryd om dit gedoen te kry, want dit was nie, jy weet, dis okay as hulle in die gehoor nou sit, maar dit was nou 'n ander saak weer om hulle op die verhoog te hê. Dit was vir my baie erg gewees.

Wel jy weet ... hier is mense wat vyftien, twintig jaar opera agter hulle blad het wat ons kan gebruik in kleiner rolle en hoekom nie? So dit was toe, gelukkig, goddank, kom daar toe 'n Hollander genoem Tom Veldhuys by KRUIK, wat toe deel word van die operabestuur en hy was toe meer vatbaar vir die gedagte, toe kry ek dit so deurgedruk. Maar moet glad nie glo dit was maklik nie, hoor. Soortvan allerhande assosiasies toe van, jy weet, daardie tyd was dit maklik gese jy's sommer 'n dit en 'n dat. Jy't altyd 'n negatiewe konnotasie daaraan gehad.

En toe, dit was so 'n stryd gewees, dat ek toe bedank het uit Kruik, want ek kon dit nie meer vat nie, want dit was net te onsmaaklik hoe

OPLAAS SAAMSING AS GELYKES

VIR die bruin verhoogkunstenaar wat professioneel sy kuns in Suid-Afrika wil beoefen en gelykwaardig naas sy blanke kollega meeding, het die son uiteindelik opgekom.

'n Deurbraak van groot belang is vandeesweek gemaak met die aanstelling by KRUIK van bruin sangers op volwaardig gelyke vlak met blanke sangers.

Dit dui daarop dat dit geen ,,toegewing'' vir individue is nie, maar 'n blink kans vir ons talentvolste mense om in die land van ons geboorte ook met ons kuns ons brood te verdien.

VASTE KOOR

Die aanstelling van die twee Eoan- Groep-sangers, Ronald Theys en Keith Timms, vandeesweek in KRUIK-Opera se vaste koor, beteken nie net erkenning vir die gehalte werk wat onder ons kunstenaars gelewer kan word nie, maar ook die implementering van die Theronkommissie se aanbeveling oor dié saak wat reeds in Junie 1976 voor die Regering gedien het.

Hoewel dit betekenisvol is dat Ronald Theys en Keith Timms in die operakoor aanstelling het — hulle is immers gekies uit sowat veertig kandi-

* Lees verder op bladsy 2.

STIL-STIL het hierdie groepie sangers vandeesweek geskiedenis gemaak toe hulle vaste aanstellings as lede van KRUIK se operakoor ontvang het.

Van belang is die deurbraak wat Ronald Theys en Keith Timms — bekende Eoan Group-sangers — gemaak het. Hulle kan nou die verhoog van die Nico Malan-Operahuis as volwaardige kunstenaars betree.

Van links is Ronald Theys, Brian Windell, Marichen Meyer, Christine Reynolds (koorleidster), Stuart Fifield, Miranda Kark, Constance Dreyer en Keith Timms. (Foto: Jack Lestrade.)

This article about the first coloured singers to join CAPAB's opera company appeared in the Afrikaans Sunday newspaper, *Rapport*.

SOURCE *Rapport Ekstra*, 10 February 1980

dit nou afgeloop het. En toe reël hulle toe 'n perskonferensie om, vir die eerste keer ooit, dan nou kastig die drie nuwelinge wat in die opera, in die koor sing, aan die pers voor te stel. Maar ek het mos nou geweet waaroor dit gaan. Toe gaan ek daarna toe, maar hulle sê nou glad nie dit is drie bruin mense nie. Ek het jare hier gewerk self, ons het nooit 'n perskonferensie aangebied as hier nuwe mense gekom het nie, net vir oorsese kunstenaars. So dit is seker omdat dit julle eerste drie bruin sangers is.

~ I was also attached to CAPAB … and I was really keen for the younger people from the Eoan Group to sit in on the night of the rehearsals. They were not permitted to attend anything at the Nico [Malan]. But perhaps they could sit in on the rehearsals, at the dress rehearsal, but that was just taboo. It was my greatest disappointment that I failed in this. But in 1981 things began to change, because politics began to change gradually and one of the laws was abolished and the Nico was opened to all races and I immediately set to work, but straightaway, to ask that people from the Eoan Group must come, must be considered for fixed places in the chorus but, oh my goodness, this was also a struggle, because it was not, you know, it's okay to have them sitting in the audiences now, but it was a completely different matter to have them up on the stage. This was extremely exasperating for me.

Well, you know … there were people with fifteen, twenty years of opera experience who we could use in the smaller roles, and why not? And then fortunately, thank God, a man from the Netherlands called Tom Veldhuys became part of opera management at CAPAB, who was more open to the idea and so I managed to push it through. But don't for one moment think it was easy. There were all kinds of associations, you know, at that time you could easily be called this and that. There was always a negative connotation to doing this.

And then, it was such a struggle, that I resigned from CAPAB, because I could no longer take it, because the way things went then was just too distasteful. And so they arranged a press conference, for the first time ever, supposedly to introduce to the press three newcomers who were going to sing in the opera, in the chorus. But I obviously knew what was really going on. So I went to it, but no one mentioned that these were three coloured people. I worked here for years myself, and we never had a press conference when new people joined us, just for overseas artists. So this one was held probably because they were the first three coloured singers.
Amanda Botha

Looking back, the impact of apartheid still lives in the memories of these performers. Despite the change of management and name – the Nico Malan was renamed Artscape – the building still holds painful memories.

You know, I went for the first time [to Artscape] ... seeing black people
on stage. Do you know what? I sat there and I actually cried, because I
thought these people never allowed us to come to sing here. And tonight,
look at these coloured people and the black people, and they sang so
beautifully. You know my heart just went out to think: 'Gee, why couldn't
we not also have done this all the years? You know, we weren't allowed to
go there. And here are these people singing so beautifully. It really, really
broke my heart. And when I go and I listen to them today and I think,
listen to these voices, you know, these voices are natural, just a natural
gift from God that they can sing like that.

I don't feel any bitterness towards anybody or anything. I'm not that
type of person who feels bitter. I cannot, I can't be like that. It's happened.
At the time it happened, I was sad to think, here people have talent and
you cannot, you know, use your talent to make people happy. Because I
think that is what we did to people.

Ruth Goodwin

3

Taking the Lead

In the early years, the Eoan Group operated with Helen Southern-Holt at its helm. But even then, before the formal establishment of apartheid in the late forties, government funding for group activities was frowned upon as it potentially linked the organisation to a policy of racial segregation.

> [In the 1940s] the people were very much against applying for a government grant. The group and its activity warranted it, but the committee didn't feel [Southern-Holt] should [apply for it]. She would discuss with the members and as long as they felt a grant hadn't to be applied for, she didn't apply for a grant. But every time we met, she made the people aware that this organisation and its activities are entitled to government support. So eventually, when they saw money was getting scarce, we applied for a grant. We didn't really have a venue, we're moving from place to place. [At that time] there was no Ochberg Hall, so they decided okay, she can apply. At that time R3 000 was a lot of money. When you apply, you apply annually, and that was a lot of money. So the members were happy about that.
> *Alethea Jansen*

Joseph Manca joined the organisation in 1943 as conductor of Eoan's choir, which had been led by Dan Ulster up until that time. Ismail Sydow, who was to play a major administrative role in later years, had joined the group in 1941. During the First Arts Festival in 1956, their special performance for government dignitaries caused a major fall-out between Southern-Holt and other members of the executive. As a result she left the organisation in 1958 and Manca took over the reins with Sydow at his right hand. In the same year, Southern-Holt emigrated with her daughter, Maisy, to Canada, where she passed away in 1972.

> I become sad when I think of how the group just let her go like that. Wow! I'll never forget that day, that executive meeting. It is as vivid in my mind. I was ashamed. That woman, who had done so much to put our people on the map culturally, could be treated like that! It was beyond my understanding. In that meeting Mrs Southern-Holt was blamed for things that she wasn't guilty of. Because, what she did was for the good of the group, like harping on a command performance for the parliamentarians. She had a very logical reason why: those people [the parliamentarians] would never stand in a row to purchase tickets, even if they send their people. They'll never see what has been done, and they'll never see what our people are capable of. That was her point, and she had a very valid point, I think.

Helen Southern-Holt in 1956.
PHOTO Eoan Group Archive

Well, the opposition – you know there's always niggling people with niggling little bits talking in your ear. We made it clear, they are not going to pay for a ticket because if they must pay for a ticket, they won't come. We always had full houses, even the bay seats, people were prepared to pay extra for a bay seat and a seat up in the balcony. So the house could easily be filled with ordinary groupers, people who are interested in the group, you see. And that is also a reason why the people felt, why should the performance be made free of charge for [the parliamentarians]. We come from far and pay our ticket, because we want to support the organisation. But they didn't realise, the government was giving us a grant. So it was government money. And if some of those men disagreed that this organisation should be given money, then it just wouldn't be given. You see, there were other things, other true factors that we had to teach the people, they must understand that.

They held it against Mrs Southern-Holt, because of that performance with the parliamentarians, I don't think she was ever forgiven. You know what they said? 'She's making apartheid'. That's how it was interpreted by the people, she's making apartheid. After all she did.

Alethea Jansen

What [Helen Southern-Holt] did for the people was to be admired, you know. I do know [why she left Eoan], but I don't want to talk about it, because it saddens my heart. Manca didn't give this woman the right deal, in spite of all that she did for him. Mrs Southern had spent her whole life doing this, you know. It was conflict of some kind. The details I can't say, because I wasn't there when it happened, you understand? I don't know. There was conflict and she walked out with Gwen Michaels and [Alethea Jansen], and one or two others, hurt to the core. I don't know what it was all about. I have no idea.

Tillie Ulster

Joseph Manca was born in Cape Town in 1908 of Italian immigrant parents. He worked as an accountant at the Cape Town Municipality and was conductor of the Camps Bay choir before he joined Eoan. Manca had great ambitions for the Eoan Group and, realising that some members' voices were good enough to sing solo parts in opera, musicals and oratorio, he began staging bigger choral productions, followed by operettas and opera. He became the driving force behind South African's first Italian opera company. He not only led the group to unprecedented artistic heights but also played an important role in the private lives of group members. Manca was well loved and admired but also criticised for his leadership during the thirty-three years that he was with the group.

Joseph Salvatore Manca in 1956.
 Eoan Group Archive

He was a very kind man. Today we think that these people were never
paid, that they never got any kind of compensation, or bus fares or any of
those things. But he treated them like his children, you know, and he saw
the talents. And he was an ordinary man, and I would also say that he,
I think he sacrificed his family for Eoan, or for his music, for his love of
music.

Ruth Fourie

Manca was terribly strict, terribly strict. You went to a rehearsal for
probably two hours, and you came to the rehearsal after being at work
and there were no smoke breaks. And you had to be in this rehearsal
room with the man up front. And Manca didn't take lack of discipline
or disrespect. And you had to listen. And he could hear if anybody was
singing the wrong note. Oh, he was very rigid when it came to that. So
we had to be obedient as such, to him. So the discipline was imposed,
yes. And if you did anything wrong, if you spoke, he would silence you
there and then and go into Italian and call you a 'salami' or whatever.
So you had to obey him, else you were out. It wasn't a very democratic
organisation. Manca ran the show, not Sydow. Sydow was the chairman
but Manca ran the show, and if you did anything wrong you were out
and you had no say. There was nothing like, 'now I will appeal against
my expulsion from the Eoan Group'. It did help, it taught us discipline.

Trevor Pretorius

Oh, we were his children. 'You are my children,' he used to say to us. 'I
love you,' he'd say. At the time there were no televisions and things like
that. So this was our life, you know, it was a life line for us, you know.
And we loved it. Everyone who sang in there loved it. That's why you were
dedicated, such dedication. [Manca] used to tell us: 'Don't ever get mixed
up with politics, politics is a dirty word! Don't get mixed up with politics,
I don't want anybody in this room that's involved with politics. If you are,
I don't want you in the group.' But you had to have someone like that on
the top, otherwise you couldn't keep the group together, you know. If it
wasn't for Manca the group would have fizzled out long before that. You
needed a strong person there as a leader, a dedicated person too. He was
really dedicated to the Eoan Group, you know. I mean if it wasn't for him
I would never have been performing opera, I would never have learnt for
instance and be given the chance to perform on stage and sing if it wasn't
for Manca.

Patricia van Graan

If you spoke about the Eoan Group in the context of opera, it was only
Manca. And I think Manca ruled with an iron arm, it's his work. But
we all know when you put a show like that together there are many,
many people, many hands behind the scenes who do the work. Whether
Manca was not prepared to say that, or try to just take all the accolades
for himself, I don't know. But that was part of Gordon's [Jephtas, Eoan's
répétiteur] frustration, for us it was sad then that [Gordon] had left, but
it was the right thing to do.
   Ronnie Samaai

[Manca] was excellent. He was a father figure in the organisation, he really
was. I mean, he was music, like we were music. We wanted music, he was
music. And he was also excellent as a conductor, there's no doubt about
it. He was very good. I mean, he had good guys behind him. I think it was
like Jimmy Adams and Andrew Mackerel and Mike Karelse and the Ulsters
and the Grunenbergs.
   Elizabeth Engelbrecht-April

I got this house from Mr Manca because he was on the council and I was
staying in District Six in a room. I knew he had contacts, so I said to him,
'Mr Manca, I'm living in a little room, is there a possibility that you could
push my papers, because I got a paper for Kensingston's houses and
for Matroosfontein. Could you do so?' He said, 'Matroosfontein is out,
because I belong to the Cape Council and this is the divisional council.'
So I said anything will do. He said to me, 'Is your forms in?' I said yes.
And then he got me this house through Mayor [Gerald] Ferry. He went to
Mayor Ferry and he said, 'I've got a fantastic singer who stays in a room
and I'd like her to have a room of her own.' And Ferry said, 'Has she got
a form for my department in my district?' So he said yes. So Ferry said,
'Okay, I'll push it for her.' In no time – I got such a shock. I got a call from
the office to say I must come look at the house if I like it or not and so on.
And there you are, I am staying in a house [that] Manca arranged for me.
   Sophia Andrews

Manca was a very controlling man. He was very astute. He had a vision
and one must actually commend him for that particular vision. And the
vision was to really develop Italian opera. His heart and soul was in it.
He gave his life to it.
   Phillip Swales

Joseph Manca conducting an opera performed by the Eoan Group in 1960.
PHOTO Eoan Group Archive

Manca was this person who stood there with his magic wand and made it happen.

Peter Voges

Dr Manca was 'n baie eenvoudige mens. Daardie tyd het hy gewerk by die tesourie van die stad en hy het altyd gesê: 'You people must get ready. When the doors open, nobody must be able to match you.' En hy het na ons verwys altyd as 'my musical children'. Ek kan regtig sê ek het hom baie goed geken, want as ons altyd daar oefeninge gehou het, het hy altyd gesê: 'Come for lunch, we will work after that, or come for supper, then we work after that.' Hy het in Ravensgate Mansions – ek sal nooit vergeet nie – in Green Point gebly. Maar 'n fantastiese mens. Ruth, sy dogter, en sy seun … was maar altyd op die agtergrond. Maar ons het vir Ruth geken soos ons ons vriende geken het. Dr Manca het nooit 'n motor bestuur nie, daar moes altyd iemand vir hom gaan haal, met elke repetisie moet iemand hom gaan haal. En iemand moet hom gaan terugneem ook. Mense het gegaan met hul liefdesake, met hul laaste ding. Dr Manca will solve the problem. Dis die persoon wat hy was. Hy het altyd gesê: 'Your joy is my joy, and don't look sad because then I also feel sad.' Hy het dit uitgeleef en sy hele familie het hy grootgemaak daarom. Sy kinders was deel van die Eoan Groep, alhoewel hulle nie mag gesing het nie. Soos iemand dit eendag gestel het: Manca is die Eoan Groep en die Eoan Groep is Manca.

~ Dr Manca was a very simple man. At that time he was working at the city treasury and he always said: 'You people must get ready. When the doors open, nobody must be able to match you.' And he always referred to us as 'my musical children'. I can really say that I knew him very well, because whenever we went to practise there, he always said: 'Come for lunch, we will work after that, or come for supper, then we work after that.' He lived in Ravensgate Mansions – I'll never forget it – in Green Point. But a fantastic man. Ruth, his daughter, and his son … always stayed in the background. But we knew Ruth like we knew our friends. Dr Manca did not drive, so someone always had to fetch him, for every rehearsal someone had to fetch him. And someone had to take him back as well. People went to him with their love problems, with every last thing. Dr Manca will solve the problem. That's the kind of person he was. He always said: 'Your joy is my joy, and don't look sad because then I also feel sad.' He lived his life like this and raised his whole family accordingly. His children were part of the Eoan Group, although they were not allowed to sing. As someone once put it: Manca is the Eoan Group and the Eoan Group is Manca.

Gerald Samaai

We were all scared of Dr Manca. He was like God. He did everything. Mr
Sydow was always sulking, you know. He walked around and they did
have their arguments but never in front of us. But Dr Manca was the Eoan
Group, he was the force behind it and if it wasn't for him, all of the things
would not have happened. I think he was just so passionate about it. I
think it is passion that kept the group going. I can't remember him for
one night not being there. He did the chorusing, you know, he conducted
the orchestras and this one man who had this huge passion that kept us
going and I think when he passed on, where do you find a person with
passion like that? It is a very special passion, that. I think the Eoan Group
was his life. He slept and he woke every day with the Eoan Group, he
planned what was going to be done next. I know he wore these glasses,
these very thick glasses, and he always scared and intimidated me. And
if I look back today, I don't think I would ever be scared of a person like
that again. He was always there, I can't remember anybody else even
taking a chorus rehearsal.
   Virginia Davids

Manca was 'n slim ou. Hy was 'n rekenmeester by die stadsaal, en hy het
sy eie musiek ook geskryf. Hy was 'n harde werker gewees. En jy moet baie
gee van jouself daardie tyd om vir ons opleiding te gee, in daai manier.
~ *Manca was a clever guy. He was an accountant at city hall, and he also
wrote his own music. He was a hard worker. And you had to give a lot of
yourself at that time to give us training, in that way.*
   Ronald Theys

Ja, they were complaining about him, you know – Manca said this or
Manca said that, and what not. He was quite a hard task master, you can
understand that. All those people he had to be in touch with and control.
And sometimes he was quite harsh. But to me it didn't matter, to me
the harsher the better. I said the more learning, I always feel like I'm a
sponge, learn from people all the time, you know.
   May Abrahamse

In 1977, Manca resigned from the Eoan Group because of ill health. As had
been the case with Southern-Holt's resignation some twenty years earlier, it
was clear that management relations were strained, and for many members
the true reason for his resignation was never clear.

I just know that something happened. I wish I knew what it was, I would
really love to know what it was and who it was, but I just know it caused
my father his downfall. It came slowly. You see, CAPAB came into being

Dr. Joseph Manca, with some of the singers in the Eoan group choir.

THE EOAN GROUP
is this the end?

BRUCE HEILBUTH Snr.

In an article, the arts magazine *Scenaria* foretold the end of Eoan as a result of Manca's resignation.
SOURCE *Scenaria*, June/July 1978

and then a lot of money went to them and CAPAB started doing opera
and Eoan had to compete with CAPAB and something happened. Ja,
they didn't have the finances to do the grand opera. That was why they
couldn't get the orchestra, so they had Regina Devereux playing the
piano [as accompanist]. They just didn't have the money for opera, to do
grand opera. I think if they could afford to do it, they would have been
successful at it. But they just didn't have the money.

In 1975, the last tour they went on, that was when they wanted to get
him out. I think after that, when he came back, something happened
and my father had a nervous breakdown and that is the cause of what
happened. Somebody wanted to get him out or something. I didn't know,
he never said.

Ruth Grevler-Manca

Ons moes aanvaar dat hy wil bedank om gesondheidsredes. Want ons
weet ook, voordat ons oorsee was, het hy 'n ope-hartoperasie gehad en
hy het van daai pacers laat insit. Ons weet hy was nie 'n gesonde persoon

nie. Ons weet ook natuurlik sy ouderdom het ook 'n rol gespeel, maar ons het gevoel hy moet net so klein bietjie nog aangaan. Die '75-toer van die jongmense en van die Eoan Groep het grotendeels bygedra dat die Eoan Groep amper tot sy val gekom het, want die ouer garde, wat nie kon saamgaan nie, die't nou amper half en half onttrek, hulself onttrek van die organisasie af. Dis die storie.

~ *We had to accept that he wanted to resign for health reasons. Because we know that, before we went overseas, he had open-heart surgery and had one of those pacers put in. We knew he was not a healthy man. We also knew that obviously his age played a role, but we felt that he had to carry on just a little bit longer. The '75 tour of the young people and of the Eoan Group contributed largely to the fact that the Eoan Group almost collapsed, because the older people who could not go, they sort of half and half withdrew, withdrew themselves from the organisation. That's the story.*
    John van der Ross

Bruce [Heilbuth, reviewer for the arts magazine *Scenaria*] knew all of us. I still have that cutting where he said, 'What is going on at the Eoan Group? I've been trying to get hold of everybody, but nobody can tell me why Dr Manca isn't there anymore.' He just heard that Manca isn't with the group anymore. And that is as far as I can tell you. I heard it first in the paper, in 1977, ja. And nobody knew anything, nobody could tell you anything. Nobody could say anything at all about it. So everybody just said, 'Oh, Manca retired'. And so I said I wasn't falling for that and so on. I used to keep in touch, because then he said, oh, it was through ill health. And I used to phone him regularly, but he never wanted me to meet him. But I used to phone his wife too and she said, 'Oh, you know, he's not so well.'

    [Manca] never wanted visitors. Probably being ill, he felt that, you know, he didn't want to chat. He always said, 'Ag no May, I don't want visitors.' But then I used to phone always regularly his wife and she said, '*That* man is here again,' and that was Sydow. Oh deary me. Ja, so I can only think that they had this altercation. And Manca wasn't well. You know he had a heart thingy, a heart [operation] and he had a pacemaker.
    May Abrahamse

Ismail Sydow joined the Eoan Group in 1941 as an administrator and was the chairman of the Eoan board from 1963 to 1977. His wife, Carmen, was the wardrobe mistress, and was responsible for the costumes for all Eoan's productions. The Sydows adopted two children, Didi and Allie, who both took part in Eoan's productions. Didi was a talented dancer and was sponsored by Eoan to study ballet in England.

Ismail Sydow in 1960.
PHOTO Eoan Group Archive

Well, Mr Sydow was the administrator. He was synonymous with the Eoan Group. Lived, breathed Eoan Group, you know. And within that it shows the control that they had over the people, you know. The man said to whoever it was that challenged him about being paid, he said, 'Sit down!' And that was the end of that.

Jocylyn Liedeman

[Sydow and Manca] kept the Eoan Group together. If there was no money today, then [Sydow] would leave the building and tomorrow he would say there's so much money. You know, he knew the right people, the correct people to get money, funding and that type of thing. And he was strict in his own way also with discipline, the same thing with Dr Manca. But you see, Mr Sydow was a strong person, strong in character and personality. He didn't think two words if he wanted to tell you your fortune, he'd tell you your fortune. As long as he had his facts straight he would put people in their places.

Lydia Johnson

Niks kan gedoen word sonder Sydow se toestemming nie. Hy en Manca het baie vasgesit, hulle het baie argumente gehet. Skoon oorsee wat ons daar gewees het. Oor klein dinge, dan herinner Sydow vir hom dat hy is die voorsitter. Dan sê hy wel maar sonder my kan julle nie voortgaan nie, ensovoorts. Maar hulle was altyd so gewees, maar Moslem en Jood. Dan sit hulle nogal lekker saam met mekaar, dan doen hulle besoek op mekaar en hy gaan baie na Manca se huis toe. En dan is dit weer oraait. Maar hulle't goed aangekom, maar hulle't ook baie gestry. Sydow het baie dinge reg gekry vir die Eoan Groep. Hy het nie sy mond gehou nie, soos hulle sê. Hy was nie bang gewees vir 'n blanke mens nie, hy het vir hulle vertel: 'Kyk dis dié en dié en daai, en ons kleurlinge, ons kry nooit dié nie, maar ons moet dié en daai kry.'
~ Nothing could be done without Sydow's permission. He and Manca had many differences, they had many arguments. Even when we went overseas. Over small things, then Sydow would remind Manca that he [Sydow] is the chairman. Then he says, fine, but without me you can't carry on, etcetera. But they were always like that, just Muslim and Jew. Then they get along well with one another, then they visit one another and he often goes to Manca's house. And everything is alright again. But they got on well, but they also argued a lot. Sydow achieved many things for the Eoan Group. He did not keep his mouth shut, as they say. He was not scared of a white person, and would say to them: 'Look it's like this and like that, and we coloureds never get this, but we must get this and that.'

Ronald Theys

Manca and Sydow worked closely together and enjoyed a lifelong friendship characterised by respect for each other as well as turbulence. It is well known that they often had verbal tussles in front of groupers.

Mr Sydow was nie akademies sterk nie. Maar hy het 'n wonderlike vernuf gehad om mense te lei en vir jou op jou plek te sit. Byvoorbeeld een aand, ons was laat met repetisies en Rota wil aangaan met beweging en Manca wil aangaan met die orkes. En hulle twee skel vir mekaar en ons staan in die middel, hierso op die verhoog. Rota skel met Manca in Italiaans, oormekaar. En wat gebeur toe: Mr Sydow verskyn daar so skuins op die verhoog en hy skree: 'You two shut up! I don't want to hear a thing. I want to see you two after the show.' Ná dit moet hulle altwee gaan na Sydow toe, soos skoolkinders. En Sydow sit hulle altwee op hulle plek: 'You don't do that in front of the singers again.' En dan luister hulle mooi soos kinders. En dan gaat hulle maar weer volgende dag verder.

~ *Mr Sydow was not strong academically. But he had a wonderful talent for leading people and for putting you in your place. For example, one night, we were late with rehearsals and Rota wanted to carry on with movement and Manca wanted to carry on with the orchestra. And the two of them were shouting at each other and the rest of us were standing in the middle, here on the stage. Rota and Manca were hurling abuse at one another in Italian. And what happened then: Mr Sydow appears there in the corner of the stage and he shouts: 'You two shut up! I don't want to hear a thing. I want to see you two after the show.' After that they both had to go to Sydow, like school children. And Sydow puts them in their place: 'You don't do that in front of the singers again.' And they listen nicely like children. And then they just carry on the next day.*

   Gerald Samaai

Manca was more of a person that said, 'This is mine and I want to make it work. This is my Eoan Group, this is my people.' And then you get this man on the other side, Mr Sydow, he's coming in with lots of other things also and he was like the grand old father. Sydow was like the grandfather and Manca was like the father and they were both possessive. And the one will shout, 'I tell you, you do this.' And the other will say, 'No, I tell … I say that.' It was all Italian words coming out, 'basta' and warra warra warra, you know. And I used to think, look at this two old people fighting. But, it wasn't really a fight as a fight in the sense of 'I'm-gonna-get-at-you' attitude.

   Martin Johnson

Ismail Sydow and Joseph Manca during the group's tour to the UK in 1975.
PHOTO Supplied by Anna-Maria Kuipers-Liliefeldt

[Sydow and Manca] were both money people, business people, business men basically. It was a very strange combination. You had an Italian, quite the Italian, he wanted so much to be Giuseppe, but he was Joseph, and he worked for the City Council. And then you had Boeta Maai [Sydow], and you could hear Boeta Maai, and then you are the green grocer ... But he was common, ordinary, both of them were. I mean I went to Mr Manca's house in Green Point and Mrs Manca, Minke, with the eyebrows and the black tinted hair, you could see on the clothing.
Peter Voges

They were always arguing. I remember when we were travelling from London to Aberdeen, we went by train and things like that. And I heard the two of them arguing. And [Sydow] used to give Manca hell. He really used to. And then Manca used to keep quiet. I heard something like this which I never repeated to anybody. But we were in the train and Mr Sydow was arguing with him and this is what Sydow said to him: 'You think because you're a white man, you can tell me what I must do.' Because he didn't even speak nicely, you know. 'Now, I'm chairperson,' you know. And so then already the feeling that Manca was unhappy. And so when I heard that Manca had left and Sydow was in charge, I knew exactly what it was all about, but nobody ever said a word.
May Abrahamse

Before attending the Youth Festival in England in 1975, the group drove by bus from Cape Town to Johannesburg, giving concerts along the way to raise extra funds. In Johannesburg, Manca and Sydow had another memorable fall out.

Toe stuur hulle vir ons 'n bus. Maar dis hier van Soweto af. En hierdie bus het toe deur seker grondpaaie gery. Maar nou's ons nou almal met swart klere aan en manelle en vrouens met spierwit rokke. Niemand kan nou sit in die bus nie, want die bus is nou vuil en dis daai plastiese sitplekke. En die bus is nou vol, vol modder. Niemand van ons kan sit in die bus nie en hier weet ek nie wat sê Mr Sydow vir Manca nie en hier skop Manca vir Sydow teen die maermerrie. Dit was net een van daai snaakse goed. Manca het gesê: 'Nee, die bus moet gaan, ons soek nie daai bus nie.' Maar toe stuur hulle vir ons 'n bus weer, met iemand wat dronk is. Toe ry die man teen die eerste paal vas met die bus, toe's Sydow nou so kwaad toe sê hy: 'Yes, you just want to conduct, you just want to conduct, you even want to conduct on a bus too!' Toe draai Manca net en sê: 'Shut your mouth, Ismail Sydow!' En hy skop hom hier toe onderdeur. Toe sê hy, 'Let me out! Let me out!' Toe wil die ou net uit die bus uit klim. Maar hulle't

baie vasgesit. En dan vanaand dan ry hulle weer, dan ry Sydow weer vir
Manca huis toe.

  John van der Ross

After both of them resigned from the group – Manca in 1977 and Sydow in
1978 – Sydow was the only group member who continued to have a close
relationship with Manca.

When Manca died, you know, passed away [in 1985], Mr Sydow let us know
that Manca didn't want any of us at his funeral. And so I phoned the
family – I used to speak to Manca's brother every now and again. I said
to them, 'I believe that Manca requested that nobody be at his funeral of
the Eoan Group.' And he said, 'Where on earth does he come on that?'
So right up till the end he was, you know, funny. Because the others were
told nobody was going and so only a few of us went. And we sat at the
back there, because he was actually Catholic, you know, and his wife was
Jewish. And you know his wife died a few months after that.

  May Abrahamse

When I heard that Manca had become ill, that he had died and that it was
said he didn't want anybody at his funeral, any of the groupers, I didn't
believe it. But I still felt that Manca had done so much for the people, we
should have given him a grand funeral. But what I heard, which is very
sad, a certain person there had asked him to get out, after this man has
done so much, he was asked to leave.

  But I went to his funeral, whether they said I mustn't come, I went
there. And there were only a few groupers, this man that had done so

much, you know? There was a group, or one or two people, I don't know,
this is what I heard is the reason why he left. Or they asked him to leave.
And that is very sad. The music section went down, because Manca was
the man who kept it up. Who else was there? Who else is there? Do they
know what Manca knew about music? And they weren't even prepared to
get people in to come and teach the people.
   Ruth Goodwin

The group faced enormous financial challenges and so the Eoan Group
Trust was launched in 1964 as a separate entity to the Eoan Group with the
aim of acting as a financial guarantor for the group. The trust consisted
of important and well-to-do citizens who supported the group. Among the
trust members was the lawyer, theatre producer and future mayor of Cape
Town, David Bloomberg, and later also Dr ID du Plessis of the Department
of Coloured Affairs. Although Eoan had been financially self-reliant since
1957 (except for the annual grant of R2 000 received from the Cape Town
Municipality), it became increasingly clear that without substantial financial
support it would be impossible to produce opera and fulfil its mission of
cultural upliftment in the coloured community. Many years later, Professor
Richard van der Ross was the first coloured person to serve on the trust.

   The Eoan Group board and the Eoan Group Trust are, to this day,
separate entities, with the board looking after the day-to-day artistic and
administrative functions of the group, and the trust being the so-called
financial guarantor. When the group moved to Athlone, the Joseph Stone
Cultural Centre became the property of the trust. The relationship between
the board and the trust was seldom a good one.

One of the big problems with the trust was that it was composed of white
businessmen. There was a guy from Standard Bank, he was the chairman
of Standard Bank at the time. The mayor, by virtue of being the mayor,
was a member, Bloomberg. He was actually one of the better trustees,
believe it or not. And as I say, there were white businessmen. Then they
got in Professor [Richard] van der Ross, who was at the University of the
Western Cape at that time. And he said, no look, we cannot operate in
isolation of the Eoan Group, because until he got there the perception was
that the trustees [form the] trust, the Eoan Group was the Eoan Group. We
look after the building; the Eoan Group runs the shows and sees to the
training. And that was it. There was no link there.
   Mike van Schalkwyk

Ons [die trust] het nie die beurs vasgehou vir produksies nie. Ons het net
die gebou in stand gehou, en dit was nogal 'n hele paar pennies elke jaar.

Die instandhouding, die weer en die dak, die heining en die grond daar
rondom. Natuurlik die gebou, die stoele en wat meer, die beligting en al
daai dinge. Nou dit het ons gedoen. Die verhouding was goed tot op 'n
punt. Daardie punt het ook meer na die vore gekom toe ons van die groep
se mense op die trust gebring het. Daar was twee verteenwoordigers van
die groep op die trust om mee te skakel. Nou ek het vas geglo, ek glo nou
nog, die groep se mense was nie opgewasse om die trust te bestuur nie.
Die trust het geld gehad, nie baie nie, ek dink die meeste in my tyd, het
ons gehad 'n kwart miljoen. En dit is niks vir so groot gebou nie, 'n kwart
miljoen of 'n bietjie meer. En dan vreet jy daaraan en neem weg, die
inkomste was min.

67

    Ek wil ook iets sê wat krities is op die trust. Hulle het seker ook
kritiek op my gehad, my groep. Met die verloop van tyd – wat ek nou sê
is heel subjektief – het die geldelike sake van die trust, die algemene
beheer van die groep, sy mense agteruit gegaan. Manca, soos jy self weet,
het ongewild geraak met 'n deel van sy groep, die algehele bevolking,
kleurling, al hoe meer die elite, wat teater toe en so gegaan het omdat hy
die groep laat vertoon het voor verdeelde, op rassegebied gehore.

    Maar dit het so ver gegaan in my tyd by die trust, dit het so ver
gegaan dat lateraan die tweespalt gelei het na 'n verdeling in die groep,
daar was later twee groepe. Jy sê jy is die leier van die Eoan Groep en ek
sê ek is die leier van die Eoan Groep. En elkeen het sy aanhangers en dit
is nie 'n goeie ding nie. Ek sê nie dit is ongewoon in daardie kader van
die samelewing nie, nee, jy kan maar kyk in die koerante elke dag, dis
deel van artistieke mense. Maar dit het daar gewys, want hier was die
een groep en die Eoan Groep was nou twee, letterlik twee groepe. Dit het
so ver gegaan dat as die een groep op 'n Saterdagmiddag sou vergader en
my groep was eerste daar, sluit ek die hek en jy mag nie inkom nie. So ver
het dit gegaan dat eendag, die ander groep wat uitgesluit is, vergadering
gehou het op die sypaadjie.

*~ We [the trust] were not responsible for the budget for productions. We
just maintained the building, and that was quite a bit of money every year.
The maintenance, the weather and the roof, the fence and the grounds.
Naturally the building, the chairs and so on, the lighting and all those
things. That was what we saw to. The relationship was good up to a point.
That point also came to the fore increasingly after we brought some of the
group's people into the trust. There were two representatives from the group
to liaise with the trust. Now I firmly believed, I still believe, the group's
people were not up to the task of managing the trust. The trust had money,
not much, I think the most we had in my time was quarter of a million. And
that's nothing for such a large building, a quarter of a million or a bit more.
And then you eat away at it and take away, the income was low.*

Richard van der Ross when he was chairman of the Eoan Group Trust in 1971.

I also want to say something that is critical of the trust, they probably also had criticism about me, my group. Over the course of time – what I'm saying now is entirely subjective – the financial affairs of the trust, the general management of the group, its people, deteriorated. Manca, as you know yourself, became unpopular among a part of his group, the overall population, coloured, increasingly the elite who went to the theatre and so on, because he allowed the group to perform in front of racially divided audiences.

But it went so far during my time at the trust, it went so far that the dissension led to a split in the group, there were later two groups. You say you are the leader of the Eoan Group and I say I'm the leader of the Eoan Group. And each one has his followers and that is not a good thing. I'm not saying this is unusual in that section of society, no, you can just look at the newspapers every day; it's part of what artistic people are. But it showed there, because here was one group and the Eoan Group was now two, literally two, groups. This went so far that if the one group was meeting on a Saturday afternoon and my group was there first, I lock the gate and you may not come in. This went so far that one day the group that had been locked out held their meeting on the pavement.

Richard van der Ross

When I became the chairperson, at first, I served on the board, and I got to hear about the trust. We always had a member from the trust sitting in the board meetings and we also got to hear that they are people that oversee the building, the interest of the Eoan Group, and they've never really been active. They haven't been around, and then, when I became the chairperson, I realised that these guys are less important. They're not out there and speaking to a lot of people. I've spoken to them also a couple of times and they haven't met, they haven't played their role, they haven't. They pulled back the insurance of the building, so a whole lot of things went wrong. The maintenance, they didn't do anything. The one thing they did do was to send out somebody to come service the curtain every six months. And it was costing me about R200. That is what they did do. So we felt that we need to move on. We've worked extensively without them, we didn't contact them, we didn't worry about them, until one day, I said to them that we cannot progress any further until we've revived the relationship with the trust and the Eoan Group Board. There was a time when they tried to sell off the building, the trust. They tried to sell it off and the people had to come in their masses to try to stop the whole sale. And they did on more than one occasion. So, and they always send the letter saying, 'Now we're going to be violent', from the Eoan Group. So there were a lot of tension between the trust and the Eoan Group.

Shafiek Rajap

I'll probably go down in notoriety as the chairman [of the trust] at the time when we refused government funding [in the 1980s]. Yes, we stopped the funding. People still had these old ideas from the 1970s, and even today there are people who haven't forgiven the Eoan Group for [taking money from the government]. It was one of the things that [popular singer and songwriter] David Kramer – because I managed to talk him into coming on to the committee – one of the things that he insisted on. He probably wouldn't want me to say that. But he wouldn't get involved if we didn't stop the funding. As the chairman it was [my job] to keep the whole thing together because – I don't want to harp on it – but there were always divisions within the group, one group suing another group for doing something. It's amazing but it happened and in the end they ended up with massive legal fees, R20 000 to R30 000, fees which they couldn't pay and then the trust had to fork out that money. Money which could have been put to much better use.

Mike van Schalkwyk

Mike van Schalkwyk in 1989.

4

In Rehearsal

Joseph Manca's vision to perform grand opera with the Eoan Group presented a daunting challenge. Although Eoan members loved classical music, many had received no formal music training and could not read staff notation. Not only did the artists need to learn the technical aspects of singing and dancing, they also needed to be taught the music as well as the Italian language.

> I was always interested in classical music, and I still remember, I used to polish the furniture and sing in my own Italian. My mother used to say, 'For God's sake, your hands can work while you're singing!'
> *Winifred du Plessis*

> To many of us opera was new. We had never seen anything of the sort. And this was wonderful.
> *Trevor Pretorius*

> Opera was in the Italian style, now coloured people in the Italian style … it could not be more bizarre. They produced in the Italian style, which is ornate, old Italian style. But because they were who they were – flower sellers and factory girls and whatever have you – it became charming, because it was so different. They will still hold on to the past glories; it's still there.
> *Peter Voges*

The singers of the Eoan Group were often marketed to the public as a group of untrained people who, against the odds, had achieved professional operatic singing standards.

> I was born to be a singer. I wasn't just scraped off the road. I was born to be a singer. I loved, loved classical [music].
> *Sophia Andrews*

> A lot of people thought, here they've got all these singers and these are people who don't have any training, people who are illiterate. Now of course that was a total fallacy because there were several people in the teaching profession. Several people had clerical jobs or did welfare jobs, social welfare. Many people do not know that Vera Gow has got a diploma and she majored in social science. And so was Tyroni Robertson. He also had that same degree. I also studied in that same direction. So it is wrong to think here are a load of domestic workers or factory workers and people who can't read music. People were trained, lots of people had training.

Alessandro Rota as stage director, Gordon Jephtas as répétiteur and Joseph Manca as conductor coached Eoan singers for their roles on the operatic stage.
PHOTO Cloete Breytenbach, 1965

It was in my opinion a racial thing. You were regarded as being uncultured, uncultured if you couldn't appreciate sculpture or art or the theatre and you didn't have training. Well, these people, what do they know? Because of their race, coloured, black, whatever they may be, had the finesse! And this has always been something that I want to dispel, dispel this fallacy of 'it's a bunch of people from the factories'. A lot of people were highly trained, we had school principals. There was one school principal who was a singer and in fact the guy nowadays is a multi-millionaire, he is in business. And there's a school named after him and that's Ernest Janari. There was Cecil Tobin, another school principal, many teachers, there were people who were musicians.
   Trevor Pretorius

At the beginning, nobody [trained us], just natural talent, yes it was natural talent, you know. And then in between we got a little bit of training with Olga Magnoni.
   Patricia van Graan

Joseph Manca was a music lover who wanted to spread music and teach people music. People often went to his house to learn, including Joseph [Gabriels].

Mabel Kester-Gabriels

76   In order to join the Eoan Group's opera section, singers had to do an audition for Manca. Some singers started out as chorus members, while others immediately got solo roles.

Toe oudisie ek, en [Manca] sê toe okay, ek kan nou in die koor sing. Maar toe is hulle al baie besig en toe moet ek bywoon 'n oefening die Sondagmiddag. Want dis die beste tyd wanneer hulle kon oefen, want almal werk. En toe sing ek, nè, ek het nog ge-oudisie, en ek dink ek moet net soos Mario Lanza sing nou, jy weet. Toe sit hy my in die koor. En toe ek opdaag vir die oefening toe sien ek dis in Italiaans. Ek dink dit was *Il Trovatore* wat hulle geoefen het, en ek het so twee bygewoon toe sê ek nee maar dis nie vir my nie. Dis nou Grieks – dis nou die Italiaans – ek sê dis Grieks vir my en toe bly ek weg. Maar toe 'n jaar later, toe sien ek weer van die oudisies, hulle't weer oudisies vir drie groot operas. Toe sê ek vir myself ek moet weer die kans gaan vat, nè. En hulle is baie beroemd nou, en ek wil ook in die limelight wees. Toe gaan ek vir nog 'n oudisie, maar die keer toe sing ek 'n regte tenoor ding, en toe't hy nou van my gehou. Toe sê hy vir my – maar hy kan ook so spek geskiet het – 'O ja, I know you, I know you.' Hy maak of hy my nog onthou daai tyd, toe sê ek vir hom, 'I auditioned before.' 'Yes I know the voice!' Toe sit hy my in 'n opera, in *La Traviata*, in 'n klein rolletjie wat ek net inkom en so vyf lyne sing. Maar dit wys maar net hy het nou geluister daar is 'n stem.
~ So I went for an audition and [Manca] says okay, I can now sing in the chorus. But they were already very busy and I had to attend a rehearsal the Sunday afternoon. Because that's the best time they could practise, because everyone was working. And then I sang, you see, I was still auditioning, and I thought I must now sing just like Mario Lanza would, you know. He then put me in the chorus. And when I arrived for the rehearsal I saw it was in Italian. I think it was Il Trovatore *that they were practicing, and after I attended about two rehearsals I said no this is not for me. This is all Greek to me – that is the Italian – I said this is all Greek to me and so I stayed away. But then a year later I saw they were auditioning again, they were holding auditions for three big operas. So I said to myself that I must take another chance, you see. And they were now very famous, and I also want to be in the limelight. So I went for another audition, but this time I sang a real tenor thing, and then he liked me. And then he said to me – but he could also have been exaggerating – 'O ja, I know you, I know you.' He pretended*

Olga Magnoni in 1966.
PHOTO Eoan Group Archive

    Ronald Theys

Manca's first words were, 'Where have you been hiding yourself!' I said I
wasn't hiding myself, I have put myself out there and no one took notice
of me. I immediately got into the role of the romantic lead in *Zip Goes a
Million*. And it was not my first time acting, cause I always have been on
and off stage at our community centres.
    Gerald Arendse

Manca co-opted fellow Italians who were living and working in Cape Town
to help in Eoan's opera productions. Alessandro Rota and Olga Magnoni did
vocal training, while Manca himself trained the chorus.

[Olga Magnoni] was brilliant and she certainly taught me a lot. She didn't
believe in forcing the voice, which I think Rota could be guilty of. Rota in
his singing lessons would force, Magnoni wouldn't do this. She'd rather
teach you the technique. And of course, it was mainly Italian school of
singing. A lot of people don't know the difference. There's the Italian
school and there's the German school. And one of her favourites was to
get her students to learn *solfeggios*, these were the vocal exercises. And
yes, I learned some beautiful things.
    Trevor Pretorius

One thing I remember about him [Rota], was when he said, 'You know,
the voice, it's got to be like silk when you sing, it's got to be like silk.
Imagine you're putting on a pair of silk stockings, you know, and it's
got to be so gentle, or else it will rip.' You know, that is the voice, so
everything has got to be like silk. That is just the way the singing is
as well. And then after that, I worked with Olga Magnoni for a good
few years. And it was Olga who said to me at the time, 'Jennifer, just
remember never to use a mic, never use a mic.' You know, so since then
I was scared of using a mic. Really scared.
    Jennifer Wheatley

After I finished at the College of Music [at UCT], I went into private
training. My private training was with Olga Magnoni. With her I stayed
about three years. When that woman heard me sing, she said to me, 'I
want to show you your range. You are the first woman after a long time,

only one person I've heard was overseas that's got a range like you.' She made me sing so many things, ooh, because she was a singer herself.
Sophia Andrews

I [trained with] Alessandro Rota. One thing I always admired about him, he used to say, 'You know, Judita …' – he calls me 'Judita', because that's an Italian name – 'Judita, everytime I work with you, I learn something.' But then in the Eoan Group, it dwindled and there wasn't much of voice training classes there. Then I used to go to his house in Sea Point.
Judith Bailey

Alessandro Rota, toe ek by hom begin sanglesse neem, toe's hy al 'n man seker so van vyf-en-sewentig. Maar vreeslik sterk in die stem, ek kan onthou. Somtyds as hy vir my wil wys hoe dit gedoen moet word, of somtyds dan sing hy bo-oor my en ek het altyd gedink, jô, die man is vyf-en-sewentig en kyk hoe sterk is die stem nog.
~ Alessandro Rota, when I started taking singing lesson with him, he was already a man I suppose of seventy-five or so. But with a very strong voice, I can remember. Sometimes when he wanted to show me how it should be done, or sometimes when he sang over me, I always thought, wow, the man is seventy-five and just look how strong the voice is.
John van der Ross

Manca het jou verstaan gemaak dat God has given everybody a little bit of talent. Try to find out what is your strong point. Because if you have a strong point, surely Mr B does not have that. Exploit it to the best. Alessandro Rota was 'n wonderlike man gewees. Hy het altyd gesê, as ek kom vir sanglesse, hy het vir my gesê, 'My son, when you breathe, you are the only one who can breathe like that.' Nou as jy vir iemand sê jy kan asem haal, dan sê die persoon maar almal haal mos asem! Maar hy het gepraat van asembeheer. En ek dink dit was my sterkpunt in die musiekwêreld. Ek kon byvoorbeeld die 'Il Mio Tesoro', daardie een met die lang frases, dan het ek altyd gelag as ek hoor oor die draadloos hulle sê: 'Tito Schippa breathed only once in this long phrase.' Dan het ek altyd met my vrou gespot en gesê, 'Gerald Samaai does it without breathing in between!' So ons het die talent gehad.
~ Manca made you understand that God has given everybody a little bit of talent. Try to find out what is your strong point. Because if you have a strong point, surely Mr B does not have that. Exploit it to the best. Alessandro Rota was a wonderful man. He always said, when I came for singing lessons, he said to me, 'My son, when you breathe, you are the only one who can breathe like that.' Now if you tell someone they can breathe,

they will say but everybody can breathe! But he was talking about breath control. And I think this was my strong point in the music world. For example, I could sing 'Il Mio Tesoro', that one with the long phrases, then I always laughed when I heard them say over the wireless: 'Tito Schippa breathed only once in this long phrase.' Then I always joked with my wife and said, 'Gerald Samaai does it without breathing in between!' So we did have the talent.

    Gerald Samaai

Jy weet as ek geoefen het met [Alessandro Rota] en ek voel ek smaak nie om nou die hele periode te gaan uitsing, nou sê ek, 'Signore, I got hees.' 'What's wrong?' Dan haal hy 'n lekker uit, 'Here you take for cough.' Nou gaat ek na die deur, ek maak 'n grap, dan sê hy, 'Where you go?' Ek sê toe, 'you say fokoff.' 'No, I mean for cough, for cough!' Okay, nou sê hy nei, ek is net lui, net lui. Nou seg hy, 'Now we are going to a F.' Nou sing ek. 'Now we go for a G, now we go for A.' Nou sing ek hom. 'Do you know what you sang now?' 'An A.' 'Top C, no that was top C.' 'Really?' Nou's ek nie meer siek nie, nou wil ek aanhou sing!

~ You know, when I was practicing with [Alessandro Rota] and I feel I don't really want to carry on singing for the whole period, then I say, 'Signore, I got hoarse.' 'What's wrong?' He takes out a sweet and says, 'Here you take for cough.' So I walk towards the door, as a joke, then he says, 'Where you go?' I say, 'You say fuck off.' 'No, I mean for cough, for cough!' Okay, then he says no I'm just lazy, just lazy. So he says, 'Now we are going to an F.' So I sing. 'Now we go for a G, now we go for A.' So I sing it. 'Do you know what you sang now?' 'An A.' 'Top C, no that was top C.' 'Really?' Now I'm not sick any more, now I want to carry on singing!

    Ronald Theys

Well, I think [Alessandro Rota] was good at producing, because he was bringing in the strong Italian element from operas that he had sung in. So he must have had personal knowledge of these productions. But he did a lot of voice training. I had to go to him for voice training as well. I did not particularly like his style. The technique that I developed was through my lessons with Olga Magnoni. Now, she and her husband, Bruno Magnoni, were involved in the early production of operas in Cape Town.

I did not work with Gregorio Fiasconaro [an Italian opera singer who lived in Cape Town], who did produce some operas for the Eoan Group, but I did not know him. By that time, he and Dr Manca had an almighty fall out. Well, you know, Italians are unusual. When you hear Italians, whether it is Angelo Gobbato, you think that guy is declaring war with the shouting and screaming and storming out of the theatre, the opera house. Italians generally speak very loud as I have experienced in Italy.

    Trevor Pretorius

Alessandro Rota in rehearsal with Gerald Samaai in the Cape Town City Hall.
PHOTO Cloete Breytenbach, 1965

The lady who really helped me was Désirée Talbot. I studied with her at UCT. She quietly just understood the voice. And I think the reason she understood the voice was that she was a pianist and she was very excited about singing and therefore she went on to sing. And she herself didn't have a wonderful voice, but she became a wonderful teacher, you know? And therefore understood singers and worked with singers and was able to just give you the necessary support and choose the right stuff for you to do.
Phillip Swales

Formal tuition in staff notation was never very successful in the Eoan Group.

Toe't ek gevra het vir [Manca] dat in plaas van hy note bashing doen, kan ons nie geleer word om musiek te lees, want geeneen kon musiek lees nie. Toe seg hy, 'Nee, man, that won't work, it won't happen, people won't turn up.' En dit het gebeur, nogal, dat mense nie opgedaag het nie. Soos ek gesê het, daar was omtrent ses tot sewe, want dit was te veel vir hulle om nog van die werk af en nog gaat leer en by die huis gaat leer en miskien moet hulle nog huisdinge doen.
~ So I asked [Manca] that instead of him note bashing, can't he teach us to read music, because no one could read music. So he says, 'No, man, that won't work, it won't happen, people won't turn up.' And it did happen, quite a bit, that people did not pitch up. As I said, there were about six or seven, because it was too much for them to come from work and then still go and study, still go and learn things at home, and maybe they even had to do things around the house.
Ronald Theys

We left the group when we moved to Johannesburg. Joseph wanted to learn to read music with the director Edward Dunn but apartheid on the buses very often left him at the bus stop because only four non-whites could get onto the bus. He therefore missed many lessons and later gave up.
Mabel Kester-Gabriels

Groupers often taught each other notation and singing technique.

I was listening to [Joseph Gabriels] on this recording, the way he sings that, you know. Amazing! And he couldn't read a note of music. Lionel [Fourie] sat with him and taught him to take the top C. On a Sunday night Lionel and I used to go to Dr Manca's house, sit around the table and that's where we taught Joseph. And what an amazing voice.
Ruth Goodwin

Lionel Fourie in 1960.

Lots of the people who had studied music taught the people who didn't know anything about music. For instance, Lionel took months to teach Joseph to take a top C and they even transposed something for him, they changed it so that he could reach there, cause if you listen carefully, some of his notes are strained. But Lionel could do a top C easily. I was there when he taught people that you sing from your stomach, not from your throat. Yes. So he was taught that. Oh, he taught everybody, he was a teacher.

Ruth Fourie

Lionel was very helpful. He used to always refer to me as 'Ou Boet'. You know, 'Boet', and he always encouraged, always used to pump you, tell you things, what you must watch for, what you mustn't do and so forth, you know what I'm saying. In the beginning, I used to have a problem with the high notes as a baritone, because I couldn't get over the bridge, and Lionel used to coach me on how to do it.

Martin Johnson

My mother [Josephine Liedeman] took the part of Anina in *La Traviata*. And so, while we were in the shop and helping people, she'd be singing her part and I'd sing with her. I can't sing to save my life, but I had learnt the words actually, so I would put in my little bit and she'd sing her part. And that's how she practiced her words.

Jocylyn Liedeman

In 1975, the Eoan Group went on tour to the United Kingdom, where they received training in various aspects of opera production.

O, en toe word ons geneem op 'n kort kursus by die Royal Opera House [in Londen]. En daar het hulle spesiale ouens gehet om vir ons te leer om so kort kursus te doen op grimeering, op sang, op beweging. Dit was fantasties. Want daardie sou duisende geld gekos het. Gordon Jephtas het daar aangekom en het baie sessies met ons gehet, en gepraat met ons, want hy't gewoont in Londen gewees. En hoe ons ons moet gedra, ensovoorts. En toe maak hy vir Judith Bailey en myself oudisie met die operahuis se personeel. Toe kry ek en sy nogal 'n beurs om daar te studeer. En daarvandaan wou ek nie meer hier gesit het nie. Toe weier ons dit, want ek was getroud gewees, twee kinders, jy dink nie van die toekoms nie. En dieselde met haar, ons kon dit nie aanvaar nie. Maar toe sê Gordon: 'Dis 'n veer in jou kop, dat jy nou daai kan gekry het.'
~ Oh, and then we were taken on a short course at the Royal Opera House [in London]. And there they had special guys to teach us, to do short courses

Ronald Theys (left), May Abrahamse (middle, back) and members of the Eoan Group during a training session in London in 1975.
PHOTO Eoan Group Archive

*on makeup, on singing, on movement. It was fantastic. Because that would
have cost thousands in money. Gordon Jephtas arrived there and held many
sessions with us, and spoke to us, because he was used to being in London.
And how we had to behave, and so on. And he arranged an audition for
Judith Bailey and me with the opera house staff. And then she and I even got
a bursary to study there. But then I did not want to sit around here anymore.
So we turned it down, because I was married, two children, you don't think
about the future. And the same with her, we could not accept it. But then
Gordon said: 'It's a feather in your cap that you could be offered that.'*
  Ronald Theys

**Eoan's dance teachers predominantly trained at the Ballet School of the
University of Cape Town, where Dulcie Howes and later David Poole taught.**

Mr Sydow sent me to UCT. I was one of the first coloured students to go
there. It was a three-year course. And then I did my intermediate and then
I got my licentiate status. That was the first year, and then the second year
I did my advanced and I got my fellowship status. At that time I was about
eighteen or twenty, and I was one of the youngest coloured teachers in
Cape Town.
  Lydia Johnson

And as time went on, I was doing part-time teaching and Dulcie Howes
came to one of the classes and she observed me. She called me and she
said she will speak to Ms Price. And I just said thank you and I went on
and continued teaching. And Ms Price was the next morning at our house
to say, 'You are getting an afternoon scholarship to the University [of Cape
Town] Ballet School. And my mother said, 'The University Ballet School,
but I don't have enough money!' And she said, 'No, the City Council is
giving you the bursary.' So off I went to the University Ballet School and
when I got there I had to dance in a class with Phyllis Spira and all the
people for an audition. I thought I was going to die but anyhow, the class
was finished and Dulcie Howes called me in and she said every afternoon
I must be at the University Ballet School, I must not be absent. I started
off as a part-time student in 1955, I remember that date very well.
  Cecil Jacobs

Because I came from a family where we were exposed to dance, music and
theatre, we were exposed to all the art forms from the age of ten already.
So I knew it, so I adapted everything I saw on stage and made it my own
thing when I went into these classes. We did do classes with David [Poole],
very strange classes, every muscle ached. But a wonderful story is we had

Cecil Jacobs (back, left) and his group of Eoan dancers pictured in an article in *Rapport Ekstra*.
 Rapport Ekstra, 21 September 1975

a final dress rehearsal with the orchestra. We got through the first act and at half past ten flat the orchestra packed up and left. So we went on for the first night not having rehearsed with the orchestra. Picture it! It was a huge success, but that was the Eoan Group and they had the reputation of producing quality in the City Hall, which was at that time Cape Town's gathering place or theatre, big theatre.
Peter Voges

Although the Eoan Group became best known for opera and dance, drama training was also offered.

I started with the Eoan Group when I was seven years old. In those years all young people were sent to the group by their parents. A community living for culture, I would say. A meeting place to learn something. In my early years it was dance. I then stopped dance because I got very tall. I therefore joined the drama section. Drama classes and rehearsals took place at the Ochberg Hall in Hanover Street. We took turns learning and teaching drama, plus having discussions. Important people here were Eddie Canterbury and his wife Mabel Canterbury.
Mabel Kester-Gabriels

In the early days the Eoan Group also helped members get training elsewhere in skills they could use at the group.

Ms Southern sent me to commercial school to learn bookkeeping and typing because she was adamant that I was going to be in charge in the office, which I ended up being. The group paid for my [training]. Well, I didn't want to go there, my parents didn't want, but she wanted me to go there. So the group paid for it, you know. And I was there for a couple of years when I became secretary. But I tell you, it was hard work, but it was wonderful work; the joy that it gave you to do this work for your community, man. Sometimes during the week when a teacher couldn't go and do a class, I used to go and teach them. I taught at Goodwood some afternoons, Thursday afternoons, and I taught at Retreat, dancing and movement and what have you, but the classes had to go on. And a class that I continued doing and enjoyed for years was going to Simon's Town every Friday evening to go and teach the people there in St Francis school hall, it's on Main Road. That I did for a very long time.
Tillie Ulster

Apart from voice training, much preparation went into staging an opera production. It meant learning the music and rehearsing the stage directions,

Lydia Johnson in 1971.
PHOTO Eoan Group Archive

as well as making costumes and building sets. Manca was instrumental in preparing the singers for their performances, especially during the early years when opera as an art form was new to the group and none of the singers knew Italian.

90

On a Sunday, mainly, [the singers] would come, the whole of Sunday they would come and [my father] taught them at the piano in the lounge. He used to sit at the piano and play a bar of music and they used to have to sing it. And as they got better, they sang together. It took him one whole day to teach Joseph Gabriels eight bars of music.
   Ruth Grevler-Manca

What Dr Manca did is he [translated] the Italian. Every word was [translated] into English, so you knew exactly what you were singing. You sing in Italian, but you know for example 'I love you'. You must know what you are saying. You know what I mean, you can't say, 'I love you', you have to know how to act properly because you're saying, 'I love you'. So that is how I think everybody learned the Italian.
   Ruth Goodwin

We were learning from Manca because he taught us a lot, he didn't only get us to sing. Some people thought we sang parrot fashion but Manca went to great lengths to teach us things. You know, we were taught various things in music. The PPs and the MFs; mezzo forte, pianissimo, and so on. And so we learnt all of this. And so, of course there was the joy of the performances. Because your friends and your family could come along, and it was also a great honour saying, 'I'm a member of Eoan Group'.
   Trevor Pretorius

So you can imagine how little time [Manca] spent with his family, because they rehearsed at least three, four times a week, at Delta House [in Bree Street, Cape Town]. And on a Sunday night we all went to his house, the soloists. And he taught them, word for word, note for note. People like Ruth Goodwin and May [Abrahamse] who had had some tuition, and Lionel [Fourie] of course, Lionel could read some music. But people like Joseph [Gabriels] and Robert Trussell, they knew very little. They couldn't read music, but [Manca] taught them everything.
   Ruth Fourie

[Dr Manca] would give me a set of records that was belonging to him and then he used say to me, 'You listen to your part and then that is how

you are going to learn it.' When we were going through our parts, we all
assembled together. Then he wanted to hear how far you were, if you did
need extra help. But he would work and then he would tell you to get that
word right. Geessh, the way he would tell you! And that was how we learnt.
But he was fortunate to have a band of coloured people that loved singing.

Sophia Andrews

Maar jy moet weet daardie dae dan sing ons by oor nè, dis note bashing.
Dit vat lank, dit neem jou omtrent 'n jaar om iets te leer man, maar jy
moet geduld het, die repetiteurs moet geduld het, jy weet. Sommige ja,
soos Gerald Samaai, hy kon gelees het, ek weet ook nie hoe goed nie, maar
ek het nogal voorgestel dat Manca vir ons iemand kry om ons te leer die
note. 'No my boy, it won't last.' En almal dié. Ek dink hy wou laat weet het
hy is die ou wat vir ons geleer het. Hy het eendag ook gesê by 'n partytjie
ná ons 'n groot konsert gedoen het, 'You know, they can't even read
music.' En dit het vir my gepla. Dat hy vir ons so gebruik het, in 'n manier.
~ *But you must know that in those days we sang by ear, you see, it was note
bashing. It takes ages, it takes you about a year to learn something, man,
but you must have patience, the répétiteurs must have patience, you know.
Some, ja, like Gerald Samaai, he could read, I don't know how well, but I
once proposed that Manca get someone to teach us the notes. 'No my boy,
it won't last.' And all that. I think he wanted to let it be known that he was
the guy who taught us. He once even said at a party after a big concert, 'You
know, they can't even read music.' And this troubled me. That he used us like
that, in a way.*

Ronald Theys

In my geval, ek was gelukkig, ek kon mos toe [note] lees. Ek dink van
die mense wat musiek kon lees, as daar sewe of agt was in die hele Eoan
Groep, was dit baie. Die koor was noot vir noot gespeel. Maar dit kan ek
jou verseker, ek het gesukkel met *L'Elisir d'Amore*, toe ken Jimmy Momberg
dit al dwarsdeur. Want dit wat hy vanaand voorgespeel het, was noot vir
noot, met die woorde dat hy môre nie vergeet nie, hy ken dit al. Waar ek
moes staat gemaak het, hier is die blad, hierso voor my, ek kan dit mos
nou lees. Bitter min mense weet dat Dr Manca nooit die orchestral score
gebruik het nie. Hy het die orkes conduct van die [piano] score. Dan het
hy, byvoorbeeld, geskrywe: 'Enter violins', of 'Enter tuba'. In die geval
van 'n sanger waar hy nou weet hier is 'n moeilike deeltjie, dan het hy 'n
asterisk gemaak. Dan weet hy hy moet die orkes hier bietjie opbring. Hy
het elke singer in detail geken.
~ *In my case, I was lucky, because I could actually read music. I think if
there were seven or eight people in the whole Eoan Group who could read*

Joseph Manca with a singer at the piano in the Ochberg Hall in District Six.
PHOTO Cloete Breytenbach, 1965

*music, it was a lot. The chorus was played note by note. But I can assure
you I struggled with* L'Elisir d'Amore, *when Jimmy Momberg already
knew the whole thing. Because what he was played tonight, was note for
note, with the words so that he does not forget them tomorrow, and then
he knew it. Whereas I depended, here is the sheet music, here in front of
me, I could read it after all. Very few people know that Dr Manca never
used the orchestral score. He conducted the orchestra from the [piano]
score. Then he would write, for example: 'Enter violins', or 'Enter tuba'. In
the case of a singer where he knew it was a slightly more difficult section,
he made an asterisk. Then he knows he must bring up the orchestra a bit.
He knew every singer in detail.*

Gerald Samaai

And every time I went to this rehearsal, I was just hearing all these people
sing. I was just so in awe of the sound that came out there, the sound and
the quality, and I mean Dr Manca worked magic. If I look back, he worked
magic teaching those people all those opera choruses. Half of them
couldn't read a single note. And there were people driving from rehearsals
to as far as Malmesbury every night. That time, Malmesbury was far. Yes,
you drove from Malmesbury and you drove back to Malmesbury, even if
it was a school night. That is the sort of passion people had. You know,
imagine driving from Paarl every night. And going back to Paarl and if
you look back, it was pure magic what came out of there.

Virginia Davids

At seven o'clock rehearsal would start. Then Dr Manca would tell us,
tonight we're going do the slave chorus from *Nabucco*. We each would get
a copy, we'd be sitting in our different voice ranges. He'd first call out –
Dr Manca's favourite thing, he never came in and just started, he would
call out the register. And he would say, and one would just hear: 'present,
present, yes we're all present, yes fine'. Then he would start. And whilst
Dr Manca trained us, he was a very stern person but he also could share
jokes with us, and especially being South African and having to speak in
Afrikaans and listening to some words in Italian, which would make us
laugh. You know we could poke fun. We had all that. So Dr Manca worked
on a schedule. Within two weeks time we must know the full chorus
before we close the books and sing from memory.

The accompanist who took us through the parts while Dr Manca
taught us was the great names like Regina Devereux as well as Gordon
Jephtas and many others. So whilst learning it, Dr Manca would give us
the correct diction on how to pronounce the Italian words. So we'd take
four or five bars, and after listening to Dr Manca we'd pronounce the

Vera Gow rehearsing with Joseph Manca in 1965.
PHOTO Eoan Group Archive

words, we'd speak the words, and then we'd sing the words. And that accumulated up till we knew the whole chorus of that. And Dr Manca would specifically take us through all the parts that we all understood what was going on. He would explain it to us, until it became second nature.
Fuad Sawyer

After rehearsal at Manca's place, for instance, sometimes on Sunday night, we'd go to Ruth [Goodwin's] house where there was a piano. And her husband was the only one who had a motor car. So he would transport us all to Manca's house. And then after a performance you'd go to their house and sing there. It was fabulous. And most of the time we never recorded those things. Those days was the old Grundig machine, reel-to-reel machine. We did do some things, but then Charles would put something else on it. And then Lionel would play the piano, and everybody else would sing. It was really fabulous. Because, he and Ruth sang very well together. They really gelled very well.

Oh, there were lots of fun parts, you know. Like I say, we used to get together and everybody sang, made a noise, and of course the drinks came out. All party animals. Yes, they were all party animals. Yes, well we know that in some cases people had to be. Sometimes they'd worry because Joey Gabriels, for instance, he had to be fetched out of places … He wasn't really a drinker, but he was a lady's man. And Robert Trussel was another one.
Ruth Fourie

Joseph Manca rehearsing with the choir.

Eoan had a rigorous schedule of rehearsals, which performers had to attend strictly. As performance dates came closer, singers were required to attend even more rehearsals.

The rehearsals were twice a week. Once you go into production, of course almost every night and so, yes, you do your homework quickly or you do your homework when you come home from the theatre, still with your false eyelashes on. I did all of those. And of course, weekends, Sundays, Saturdays we rehearse, we go on stage and I still passed matric. I think for me it was just such an excitement just to be on stage, just to be there and to do music.

Virginia Davids

The demands on the soloists were far greater than on the members of the choir. The choir generally got together once a week, may have been twice a week, with Dr Manca for a two-hour session. Although, there were certain of us who twice a week had voice production lessons with either Mr Rota or Mrs Magnoni. The practice sessions and voice production lessons always took place after hours, which meant that it did not interfere with our working lives. Naturally these were stepped up closer to the opera season or concert times. I think that because many of us derived so much pleasure from what we were doing, we never viewed it as an imposition into our lives.

Joan Watson

Ja, die rehearsal schedule het jy lank voor die tyd gekry, so jy weet watter dae jy daar moes wees. En snaaks as jy daar aangekom het die aand vir oefening, en Manca het net een kyk gegee en gesê, 'I didn't see Sam Roth here. I didn't see John here. I didn't see Clive here.' Hy het net een kyk gegee. Hy het mos gesê, 'I know my musical children.' As daar twee of drie op 'n aand afwesig was, was dit baie. Ek dink dit is wat die Eoan Groep gemaak het wat hy is, we lived, we really lived to serve. Dit was die motto van die Eoan Groep.

Toe sit ek met die probleem, ek het nie vervoer nie, hoe gaan ek daar kom? Elke dag in hitchhike. My probleem was ek kry elke oggend tien oor ses die trein in die Paarl in. Nou moet ek kom eers in Bishop Lavis, want ek het onderwys in Bishop Lavis. Tien oor ses begin my dag. Dan klim ek weer op die trein. Dan het ek my onderwys gegee vir die tien periodes. Waarvan somtyds sewe musiek was. Daarna gaan ek na die klasse toe by Olga Magnoni. Van Olga Magnoni af kom ek terug by die groep om te oefen. En vanaand ná alles klaar is, hitchhike ek weer huis toe. Dan kom ek so by die huis weer. Somtyds drie keer [per week]. Maar soos dit nader gekom het na die seisoen, dan is dit elke dag, insluitende Sondag. Ek het net sommer botweg geweier om op 'n Saterdagmiddag te oefen, want Saterdagmiddag speel ek tennis. Ek moet mos maar 'n bietjie tennis ook speel. En so het dit aangegaan en die eerste jaar het goed afgeloop.

~ Yes, you got the rehearsal schedule long in advance, so you know which days you must be there. And it was strange when you got there that night for the rehearsal and Manca just gave one look around and said, 'I didn't see Sam Roth here. I didn't see John here. I didn't see Clive here.' He gave just one look around. He did once say, 'I know my musical children.' If two or three people were absent on an evening, it was a lot. I think this is what made the Eoan Group what it was, we lived, we really lived to serve. This was the motto of the Eoan Group.

So I sat with the problem, I had no transport, how was I going to get there? Hitchhike in every day. My problem was that every morning at ten past six I caught the train in Paarl. But I first needed to get to Bishop Lavis, because I was teaching in Bishop Lavis. Ten past six my day began. Then I get on the train again. Then I went to give class for the ten periods, of which seven were sometimes music. Then I went to the classes with Olga Magnoni. From Olga Magnoni I returned to the group to practice. And tonight once everything is finished, I hitchhike home again. Then I got back home again. Sometimes three times [per week]. But as it got closer to the season, then it was every day, including Sunday. But I just refused point blank to rehearse on a Saturday afternoon, because on a Saturday afternoon I play tennis. I also need to play a little bit of tennis, after all. And so it went on and the first year went well.

Gerald Samaai

Regina Devereux, Eoan's accompanist, 1967.
PHOTO Eoan Group Archive

Sometimes I had to take one train and then the bus. So I said, well, I travel
from Athlone to Elsies River but I get off before, two stops before I should
get off. That's to save one cent, yes, one cent was a lot [at that time]. But
the point is this, I got off two stops before and I walked through the bush
and they warned me about the snakes in the bush. But then I know what I
was doing!
    Dirk Alexander

But it was wonderful being a member of the Eoan Group then. First of all
it required a lot of discipline. You needed to attend all of these rehearsals.
I moved out of the city, so we moved to Bishop Lavis, that was where
I was living then. And I had to get a train into rehearsals on Sundays,
Saturdays. But during the week it was easy because invariably I was in the
city for various reasons like the studies and so on. But it did cost sacrifice.
But this singing brought a great deal of joy. You know, I will never forget
when I first heard some of the Eoan groupers, like Arthur Abrams for
example, singing 'Va Pensiero'. Now you know 'Va Pensiero' from *Nabucco*.
The beautiful Hebrew slave chorus, it's magnificent. To hear a group of
men singing that.
    Trevor Pretorius

**With a rehearsal schedule that took up a lot of Eoan members' time and
energy, their family members also paid a high price.**

[My father] was never at home. In fact, I remember when I went to learn
to play the piano and I came home from my first lesson – Désirée Talbot
was my teacher – and I asked him please to show me how to draw the
treble clef and the bass clef, he didn't have time. He was off to rehearsal.
    Ruth Grevler-Manca

You must remember, this was a group of dedicated people, very dedicated
people. They sacrificed majorly, I mean, lift clubs, getting on buses late
at night, taking trains late at night to go back, because they still had to
get on the train late at night and not have to worry about Jan Bos [the
criminal element] and it was real sacrifice. So these were real dedicated
people.
    Virginia Davids

It is an irony that so much was done for the so-called coloured people
through this group and there were those sacrifices on the other hand.

<u>EOAN GROUP</u>

Opera Rehearsals :   Monday 8th to Sunday 14th March, 1965

Date	Time	Venue	Opera	Details	Music
Mon. 8th	7.30 p.m	City Hall	Elisir	Full Company	Orchestra
Tues. 9th	7.30 pm	City Hall	La Boheme	Principals only	Manca Rota Gordon
Wed. 10th	7.30 pm	City Hall	La Traviata	Full Company and Dancers	Orchestra
Thurs 11th	7.30 pm	Delta House	Il Trovatore	Full Company	Manca Rota Gordon
Fri. 12th	7.30 pm	Delta House	All Operas	Costume call All Principals For Adjustments	Mrs. Sydow Mr. Rota Tailor
Sat. 13th	9.30 am	City Hall	La Boheme	Principals only	Orchestra
Sat. 13th	7.30 pm	City Hall	La Boheme	Full Company	Orchestra
Sun. 14th	2.30 pm	Delta House	All Operas (Costumes)	All Chorus Costume Adjustments	Mrs. Sydow Mr. Rota Tailor

NOTE: During this week it may be necessary to call different types of rehearsals.   You are therefore requested to hold yourself in readiness for all calls.

JOSEPH S. MANCA
Hon. Musical Director

A typical rehearsal schedule for Eoan's opera group.

There were sacrifices of the members of the group themselves and those were really quite serious personal sacrifices. They were financial, they were sacrifices of time, there were relationships that were sacrificed. Mrs Manca for instance became irate sometimes, you know. And I had seen her arguing with [Manca] one night. This was outside the City Hall, out after rehearsal, and we were witness to this. And I'm sure it happened in many other homes. Like Ruth [Goodwin] had children in this period. I had a son in this period. [The singers] were never [at home].
>> *Ruth Fourie*

Well, let's face it, with any artistic community there is always a certain amount of conflict. I mean if we were to say that there was no conflict that would be very naïve. And I think the conflict actually centred around the choice of singers for the roles. The conflicts centred around the people that were, if one could call it, were the favourites of Dr Manca. There were lots of burning issues. But it was also the period in which you didn't really spend much time in deep conversation about these things, because we had jobs that we had to look after, we had families. And a lot of us had problems in our families. You can imagine as artists there was lots of domestic conflict because we spent hours away from home. We were away from eight o'clock in the morning until twelve o'clock at night; five, six days a week sometimes. It was long hours.
>> *Phillip Swales*

Gordon Jephtas was Eoan's répétiteur. He was loved and respected by group members and in the rehearsal schedule for the 1965 opera season, Manca officially refers to him as 'Maestro Gordon'. The group sponsored his formal music education at the College of Music at the University of Cape Town in the early 1960s.

When Gordon was here, we got a lot of tips from him as well. So, of the three [trainers] there is similarities and they have like different attacks of how to do the high [notes] and the breathing exercises and things. Everybody has their own … So you now choose which one, it all depends now on what frame your voice is. If it's tired, if it's warmed-up and things like that. So you just mix with what is best for that.
>> *Judith Bailey*

Trovatore gave me a headache. We had to say our words properly, I had to know the meaning of everything – hey, I need to know what I'm singing – and Gordon used to help me with that.
>> *Sophia Andrews*

Rehearsing for the 1965 opera season.
PHOTO Eoan Group Archive

Thanks to [Olga Magnoni], she could coach me into [my range], work on the bridge of my voice. She did wonders with my voice and I said thank you. And [Alessandro] Rota also. Rota could do the other parts, but Gordon did the polishing. Rota could give me the idea of [a role] because Rota, being a singer himself, but Gordon could do the final edges, pronunciation, you know, he did your pronunciations properly and so forth, that's where Gordon came into play. So I owe it to three people, you know, who really gave me my voice.
  Martin Johnson

Gordon was our répétiteur. He's the one who actually taught me a lot because he used to constantly hammer me at doing things, especially the [difficult] bits at the time, constantly working, every day and night. I had a very good ear and I picked up very quickly, and Gordon used to plonk at all these notes and I used to follow. So I learnt my operas without being able to really, really read music but I could follow the notes. At the time that was our life, we didn't have anything else besides opera and singing. But that dedication is gone out of the window, it will never come back.
  Patricia van Graan

You know, Patricia van Graan, she was always coached by Gordon. Whenever Gordon was available for coaching, Patricia would take it, not the others. You get this thing that says, and I will do it in Afrikaans for you with an accent, 'Wies djy om vir my te kom sê?' [Who are you to tell me?]
  Peter Voges

Gordon Jephtas, you know, it took that guy three weeks for me to learn the whole opera of *Traviata* and I didn't know a thing about opera,

about Italian, and it took him three weeks. He was such a fantastic guy.
Patience. I will never forget him. Man, it was the way he could take his
time to teach you something, and you were like a sponge, you took in and
you held everything that he taught you. He was one fantastic teacher.
   Winifred du Plessis

Gordon was extremely gifted, he was absolutely top-class. And he was like
a sponge, it just went in. Gordon had contacts and he had got engaged at
Zurich as répétiteur. It was, really, he had this absolute instinct for it. He
was a good pianist. But he was a good coach. And that is a very different
thing from being a good pianist, or even a good accompanist. You have
to know the languages, you have to know the style, you have to be able
to give everybody their cues, and that kind of thing. It is a completely
different cup of tea to just playing the piano very well. And he did have
[the passion for it], he was really extremely talented. Then he moved from
Europe to New York, and occasionally, you know, he would contact me.
Lots of singers, well-known ones like Marilyn Horne, did go and coach
with him. You know, if you wanted a role you've sung hundreds of times
but you haven't sung it for a year or so, and you want to sing it in, you
want a pianist who knows it. So you go to the one who is recommended –
he was one of the best ones in New York. He was known for that.
   Emma Renzi

Gordon, hy was 'n absolute begeesterde, entoesiastiese man met 'n
goeie kop, baie musikaal. Natuurlik het hy ook 'n temperament gehad,
maar hy het regtig uit hierdie mense by die Eoan Groep magic getoor uit
hulle stemme uit. Ek het elke aand wat hy met hulle gewerk het, het ek
oorgegaan om daar te gaan sit, want dit was net vir my te wonderlik.
*~ Gordon, he was an absolutely inspired, enthusiastic man with a good head,
very musical. Naturally he also had a temper, but he really conjured magic
out of the voices of these people from the Eoan Group. Every night that he
worked with them I went to sit over there, because it was just too wonderful
for me.*
   Amanda Botha

But the person who did the bulk of the work here was Gordon Jephtas.
Now Gordon was a very accomplished pianist, he was one year ahead of
me at UCT studying music. At that time I said to Gerald [Samaai] that I
don't think there is any music under the sun that he could not sight read,
he had a phenomenal sight-reading ability. Very quiet, very unassuming
but he would teach all the parts. So sopranos, say May Abrahamse or
Ruth Goodwin, would spend three, four hours with him going through

Gordon Jephtas and Joseph Manca at the piano.

PHOTO *The Argus*, 28 February 1959

the recitative and the arias. Then he would go through the tenor, the bass, the baritone. Robert Trussell was a magnificent bass voice, Gordon trained them all. And Gordon at the end, of course, left the country and worked with great voices, voices of real world quality, like Peter Pears. But he had the wonderful ability to bring the voice and the work as an aria or a recitative, to a point that a man could just conduct, but Gordon was the man behind it all.

But that goes to show his ability and I think at one stage Gordon also felt like, 'Yes it is fine to play with these natural voices, but I need to just spread my wings.' Which he did and he went to Italy, he went to America. He could speak Italian and he would understand a text of an opera, so, so well. Apart from just teaching the parts that was to be sung, he could fill them in, exactly what happens when you sing this certain aria, what happens when you do that specific recitative. He was a real teacher, because he would teach those parts. Somebody else would develop the voice, but as far as the actual opera learning was concerned, that was Gordon. And of course Manca put it together.

Ronnie Samaai

Oh, I loved [Gordon] to bits. I mean he's still alive. I have so many recordings of him, you know. He passed away, but to me he's still alive.

May Abrahamse

After leaving South Africa in 1966 to pursue a career overseas, Jephtas visited South Africa often in the 1970s, spending much time training Eoan's soloists. However, his focus shifted away from opera and he introduced a number of singers to German lieder.

We did this [lieder] recital in Durban [in 1971 and] Gordon wanted us to come and do it for the Eoan Group. They wouldn't allow it, they wouldn't allow. No, Mr Sydow said that to me that they don't do concerts with one person only. He said, no, it must be everybody. I don't know, he was a funny man. Anyhow, I came, I chatted to Gordon and Gordon said, speak to [Sydow], you know and things like that. And then I said to him, 'But Mr Sydow it's another art form.' So he said to me, 'Art, what is art?' So, when I came down to stay in 1973 Gordon said we are going to do a recital at the Eoan Group. We are going to do it, he don't care. And then he came down often and we did, you know?

Yes, it happened [in 1979]. We did that at the Nico Malan. I was the first coloured person to sing there, you know. They didn't make a fuss about it, really, but Gordon arranged it. Oh yes, all our people came. You know, but they weren't allowed, because apartheid was still [in place]. I

May Abrahamse and Gordon Jephtas in recital at the Nico Malan in 1979.
PHOTO *Rapport Ekstra*, 18 February 1979

don't know what strings Gordon pulled, but he was very well known and they respected him, because he'd worked with so many, you know, great singers overseas, and he was a very humble guy. He was small and thin and what not, you know, and things like that.

There was this woman, Antoinette, what was her surname? Antoinette, and she gave me such a glowing write-up, you know? Ja, so I have lots of memories. Oh dear, when I sing I still listen to Gordon's records and to me he's still my teacher, you know.

May Abrahamse

I used to go after work up to Bree Street, [the group] had rented the place upstairs and [Gordon] would sit and take me through my part with the Italian words and so on. And you know what he did? He came back [from overseas] and the first thing he said to me, 'I brought a song down for you, because when I heard it, I said, that's Sophia, only Sophia would do that thing properly'. It was out of *Porgy and Bess*, it was 'The Strawberry Song'. And as I say, I got very close to him because I knew he was a lonely person, he didn't have a lot of friends. He was also just somebody that loved music. He also studied at the college. He also got a degree or something. And as I say, he was very strict also. If you don't turn up for his rehearsals and you don't let him know, then he don't want to see you. He don't want to see you until he feels you've been punished enough. He was younger than what I was, I could have klapped [hit] him you know. And the last time he came down was a sad time, because he was dying. Something he did overseas that he ought not to have done, got into drugs. That is the last I saw of him, I wasn't at his funeral or anything, I didn't have the heart.

Sophia Andrews

While Eoan had an enthusiastic leader, répétiteur and singers ready to take on any opera, no opera production is possible without an army of people working backstage to ensure a quality production.

There were always backstage people. Oh that was wonderful, you know, we always had backstage people. Everybody was willing to give a hand, man! And if it was a branch display, the daddies and the big brothers were there, and: 'Who's coming to fetch you? Is your father fetching you?' And we'll have meetings, the branches will have meetings: 'Now we will be requiring so and so backstage and we will be wanting somebody to turn the curtains …', if we're in a hall with a fancy curtain that you turn, you know. That wasn't often, but anyway. Then the parents would say: 'Okay, I'll send my son, or my husband will come, or we must come for Mary …', or whatever. And that's how we covered all that, with no fuss …

Alethea Jansen

Gordon Jephtas coaching Ronnie Theys in 1975.
PHOTO Eoan Group Archive

Die orkes, ja, kyk hulle was professioneel. Ek het nie gehou van hulle manier nie, want hulle is professioneel en Manca was nie 'n professionele dirigent nie, en somtyds het hulle maar net gedoen wat hulle wil. En ons kon sien daai. Hulle het dit nie goed hanteer nie, en hy het dit ook nie goed hanteer nie. Hy wil net dirigeer, en hulle het nooit iemand anders gekry nie. En een musical wat ons gedoen het, toe sit hulle die orkes agter die skerms met 'n opening dat hy kan sien die mense, nou moet hy dirigeer agter, hy het nie van daai gehou nie, want hy wil in die limelight gewees het.

~ The orchestra, yes, look, they were professional people. I did not like their manners, because they were professional and Manca was not a professional conductor, and sometimes they did just what they wanted to. And we could see that. They did not handle it well, and he also did not handle it well. He just wanted to conduct, and they never got anyone else. And one musical that we did, they put the orchestra behind the curtains with an opening so that he could see the people, now he had to conduct from behind, he did not like that, because he wanted to be in the limelight.

   Ronald Theys

After the First Arts Festival in 1956, Carmen Sydow, wife of Ismail Sydow, became Eoan's official wardrobe mistress, making costumes for opera and ballet productions until her retirement in 1978. In the early years many community members assisted with the preparations, but as community support dwindled, so did the sewing ladies. Carmen Sydow also taught young women to sew.

She would sit by the window the whole day with all the sewing and she would sew from the morning till the evening. And Boeta Maai [Ismail Sydow] would come from work and ask, 'Gaya, didn't you make food yet?' Then he would go to the kitchen and he would make the food, you know, so that she could finish whatever she was busy with. She worked very hard. I can truly say that she worked very hard at the Eoan Group. She would sit at my side and we would sew together. Because she was just strict, man. She was very strict, you know, where the Eoan Group was concerned.

   Sheila Beukes

Mr and Mrs Sydow had really dedicated their life to the Eoan Group. They lived in Vrede Street in Woodstock. And I can tell you, Mr and Mrs Sydow's dining room looked like a costume place. There was many a time when I'm sure Mr Sydow couldn't sleep on a bed. The place was filled with rows and rows of material.

   Cecil Jacobs

Preparing stage décor in the Ochberg Hall.
PHOTO Cloete Breytenbach, 1965

I still remember May Abrahamse's dress, if there was anything wrong with it she would ask me to just patch it, make it right. Yes, because sometimes there's stitching that has to be done when things break. And then after that we will sort out now what's dirty and what's clean. And you know [Carmen] was never ashamed to walk through that big town with a bag – with the pillowcase with the washing. And I would carry one and I was becoming a teenager. I feel so shy, I don't want to walk with this now, you know? 'Auntie Gaya, moet ek nou loop met die sakkie?' 'Sheila, jy loop met die sakkie! Die wasgoed moet gewas word!' ['Aunty Gaya, must I walk with this bag?' 'Shiela, you walk with that bag! The washing must be done!'] Then we come home and she would take the washing and sort out. Each thing goes into a separate bucket to be washed. And when it's washed, then we would iron it and pack it nicely away until the next show.
Sheila Beukes

Mrs Sydow and her team made the most magnificent costumes ... costumes were recycled. I would rush home from school and get on the bus or the train, because the older members would do our hair, you know, and it was like make-believe. You put on makeup and you have your hair all done up and then you put on these gorgeous costumes, all recycled, by the way. From opera to opera, they recycled the costumes. Poor Mrs Sydow, don't ask me how she did it. And for me that was absolutely magical.
Virginia Davids

When I turned the garment upside down I said to my husband, 'This is what Mrs Sydow taught me, a perfect job, not an untidy job.' A dressmaker or a mess maker or, you know? And I treasure that up till today. I will never do anything that is not properly. She learned me what it is to be a housewife; how to clean a house, all, not just sewing and doing. And what I admired about her, you know, she would call me if she lay out the material and she said to me, 'Sheila, come stand here.' And she would tell me, 'No waste; you don't cut to waste, because then you're not a dressmaker.' And she would lay out the material and the patterns on the table and cut.
Sheila Beukes

The sewing ladies worked for very little money.

There was no other ladies [to help at that stage], but then she asked me to get two ladies. And I got Mrs Sodley and Mrs Muller to just help out, because there was too much sewing for Eoan. And they still said, 'Yô, ons werk vir tien rand 'n week.' ['Wow, we work for ten rand per week.']

Carmen Sydow in 1967.
PHOTO Eoan Group Archive

The sewing team in 1956.
PHOTO Eoan Group Archive

Because then they also got ten rand. Then there was a big argument with Mrs Sydow. She never came in the Friday, and because I was now in charge, seeing to everything, I went to the office girl and I said, 'The ladies want to go now. I just come to fetch the money.' And she said, 'Fine.' And she pay, she looked and she said, 'Oh my word! Do you only get a ten rand? But you're supposed to get a thirty rand.' She was a young girl who helped us in the office and she said, 'But you people are supposed to get thirty rand a week not ten rand.' And then Mrs Sydow got so upset with me. And she skelled me out [shouted at me] so bad. And she said to me I'm a snake. Because of that came out now, you know. But she said yes, she sometimes had to take the money to buy the materials and things like that. But our wages was thirty rand a week, not ten rand. Then she skel me out and she said to me, 'I don't need your service anymore,' because I'm a snake. I went home and I cried and I told my mommy, that we had to get thirty rand, not ten rand, thirty rand not ten rand. [Mrs Sydow] said to me she don't need my service anymore.
Sheila Beukes

Eoan employed ballet teachers to train dancers who performed mostly in the opera productions. But being a ballet teacher at Eoan was difficult at the best of times. Besides the long hours, the group often did not have the money to pay teachers, and employment elsewhere became a necessity.

The dancing was for me what was important, you know, the love of the art. That's why I'm still involved with it. Go to the extreme, you don't worry about travelling and money and that, because the one time the

Carmen Sydow (back) and one of the sewing ladies working on the costumes for Verdi's *Il Trovatore*.
PHOTO Cloete Breytenbach, 1965

Eoan Group never had money to pay us a salary for a couple of months and we went on teaching, you know, we went every day and we did it until Mr Sydow could get money again and then he paid us. But he couldn't even back pay us for the money that we lost and we weren't upset about it. Our hours were very, very long. We would start at 3 o'clock and end up half past 7, 8 o'clock, 9 o'clock. You see as people left the Eoan Group because of money, the Eoan Group couldn't pay people's salaries, a decent salary, I would say. You know, they left and then they did either teaching at the community centres, which was council-based, the municipality. So they earned a better salary there and eventually those little [Eoan] branches had to close down because there were no teachers.

I was sad to leave, but I also left due to money, you know, to salaries. Because I was teaching there, I was teaching every day for six days a week and then they had a modern dance teacher there, she came in twice a week for four hours – two hours per night. And she earned more than what I earned. So when I wrote to the executive and laid out my case, so they said but I don't work enough. So I said, well in that case I resign and then they tried to win me over again but then my mind was made up. Because if they couldn't pay me a decent salary, you know, what's the sense?

Lydia Johnson

The Eoan Group had their own teachers that they started training through Dulcie Howes [at UCT]. But why most of the teachers left was because the income was so measly. Full-time for Eoan, but there was never a pension or a medical aid. There was nothing. Now the branches are introduced for those who could not afford to pay the studio fees. The Eoan Group had a private studio, which was ten and sixpence per month for those who want and who could afford it. But for the children who could not afford lessons there was about ten to twelve branches and each branch in an area, and a teacher was sent to that branches. So we had Athlone, Landsdowne, Walmer Estate, Elsies River, Wynberg, we had Simon's Town, Somerset West, we had Bishop Lavis, you name it. All the different branches we had, but the teachers had to go to the branches. But the saddest part was from our salary we had to take our transport money. Now you can imagine if you're getting a measly salary, and you have to go and dance and be at rehearsals for opera, only near the end did the group give a little honorarium to our dancers when we danced in operas.

Cecil Jacobs

I think [rivalry between the sections] came about when the opera started and then the other departments tried to compete. You know, who could be the most high-brow, or the most popular or the most famous. And really the Eoan Group was quite a stifling organisation, because while they were a creative organisation, they never allowed the individuals to create. You always had to get permission, because when you join the Eoan Group, you're not allowed to dance outside, you're not allowed to teach outside. If you wanted to, you had to get permission from the board. The board were not very highly educated or qualified people, so they would always say no.

Merle Falken

Eoan's singers and dancers all had daytime jobs in order to make a living and pay the bills. In his book, *My Times*, David Bloomberg writes: 'It was difficult to appreciate that those who were attaining professional standards were by day ordinary workers in the city. While some were teachers, the majority were maids, messengers, labourers, factory hands and clerical workers, yet all were imbued with the same spirit – to give of their best and achieve excellence.'

I was working otherwise, yes. In 1956, I was still an apprentice at Heins Matthews, a chemical technician. I think it was in my third year when I came to the group. The Job Reservation Act came in, I think 1956. And that meant that as qualified as I was as a chemical technician I couldn't work

as a chemical technician. Although I qualified at Heins Matthews as pellet
tablet maker, I couldn't work as it – I had to work as a lab assistant and
that jobs were reserved for [whites].
  Gerald Arendse

Lionel [Fourie] did tailoring for six years, and then he came to Worcester.
When, after his six years in Worcester, he did a teacher's course at the
non-white college there. And there he sang in the choirs and conducted
the choir because he was older than all the other students. And then
he went to teach in Villiersdorp. He also studied German while he was
there. He had an aptitude for languages, so he studied German there,
under Dr Con de Villiers, who was in Stellenbosch. [Dr Con] was a great
musician. He spoke seven languages, and he had an amazing collection
of records, in those days, you know, all the little 78s and 45s. [He let
Lionel listen to those] and then he also encouraged Lionel that he
come to Cape Town to audition for Eoan. He was accepted, and then he
initially sang the *Elijah*, and in *Messiah*.
  Ruth Fourie

Izaak Hartzenberg het gewerk op die hawe, hy het gesê, 'Ek is 'n
bootskeper.' Hy kon nie maklik af kry nie. Toe het Manca gevra, 'Can he
get off for three hours. We will pay him that three hours.' Dan loop hy
van die hawe, kom sing hy klaar, dan gaan hy weer terug. Hy het meestal
nagwerk gedoen. Martin Johnson het met 'n fiets gery uit Athlone uit om
by te woon.
   Met die opvoerings nou moet ek so min as moontlik praat in die skool,
want die stem moet mos hou tot vanaand toe. Toe het ek dit so uitgewerk
dat meeste van daardie periode is aantekeninge. En ek rol toe die bladsye
af, dan is dit nie nodig dat meneer moet praat nie, meneer gee net die
bladsye uit. Daarvandaan af het dit baie beter gegaan. Maar nou waantoe gaan ek nou in die tussentyd? Want ek is half-drie in die stad in en
die opvoering begin vanaand agt uur. Wat doen ek in die tussentyd? Toe
besluit ek nee, ek gaan nou vra of ek maar binne in die stadsaal kan in.
Maar wat vir my komies was, hulle het mos daardie barriers gehad tussen
die blankes en die nie-blankes. Voor die ingang lees jy mos 'Whites only'.
Toe moet ek anderkant omgaan, vanaand is jy hoofsolis, maar in die dag
mag jy nie … Baie belaglik gewees. Ons het altyd besluit, julle is besig met
apartheid, wat ons gaan doen is: whenever we take a curtain call, it is first
to the coloured side of the hall and then to the other side. En iemand het
dit opgetel en toe verskyn dit in die koerant in. En toe sê Dr Manca, 'If we
still want the City Hall, then we have got to abide by the rules.' Hy was 'n
wonderlike man, Dr Manca was 'n vreeslike wonderlike man. Hy was baie
lief vir my en ek was baie lief vir hom gewees.

~ Izaak Hartzenberg worked at the harbour, he said, 'I am a boatsman'. He could not get off easily. Then Manca asked, 'Can he get off for three hours. We will pay him that three hours.' Then he walks from the harbour, does his singing, then goes back. He worked mostly at night. Martin Johnson rode by bike from Athlone to attend.

For the performances I had to talk as little as possible at school, because the voice had to last till tonight. So I worked it that most of those periods were for notes. And so I duplicated the pages, then it was not necessary for sir to talk, sir would just hand out the pages. From then on it went much better. But what was I to do during the in-between time? Because I was in the city at half past two and the performance begins tonight at eight. What do I do in the meantime? So I decided, no, I'm just going to ask whether I can go into the City Hall. But what was funny to me was that they had those barriers between whites and non-whites. At the entrance you read 'Whites only'. So I had to go around to the other side, tonight you are the main soloist, but during the day you may not ... It was truly ridiculous. We always decided, you want your apartheid, what we are going to do is: whenever we take a curtain call, it is first to the coloured side of the hall and then to the other side. And someone picked this up and it appeared in the newspapers. And then Dr Manca said, 'If we still want the City Hall, then we have got to abide by the rules.' He was a wonderful man, Dr Manca was really a wonderful man. He really loved me and I really loved him.
  Gerald Samaai

I worked in a factory called African Clothing Factory in [Zonnebloem]. And [my husband] knew after work I never used to come home. I had to go stage at the City Hall. And from there we used to do our operas and so on and come home quarter to twelve. And tomorrow night is the same procedure and that's why you see I'm so slender in the pictures, because I worked hard.
  Sophia Andrews

[Joseph Gabriels] was fortunate to have a good boss, Mr Tarshish, who always gave him time off to go out and rehearse or sing.
  Mabel Kester-Gabriels

We just asked for leave, you know [from our daytime jobs]. I think you know a lot of the folk, the bosses and things like that, they were very proud of the fact that their people are getting involved and so on. So everybody was very sympathetic. Ja, they got leave from their work. And I also when I was working I took leave sometimes.
  May Abrahamse

Gerald Samaai teaching in Bishop Lavis.
PHOTO *Sarie Marais*, 9 September 1970

Actually when I first joined the opera group I was in school and taking
piano lessons at the time and at my school we had performed in the
Eisteddfod, which gave me an appreciation for singing. My piano teacher
gave me a choice, he said I could not participate in school piano and
the [Eoan] Group and I could not drop school so I opted to stay in the
opera group and drop my piano lessons. Later on when I started work,
my employer was very accommodating when we went to Scotland for
the International Festival of Youth Orchestras. I guess you could say the
balance between work and the group was perfect.
  Anna-Maria Kuipers-Liliefeldt

I don't think I struck a balance. It was very difficult, because you know,
as an artist, I don't know if artists are all that balanced. I think we drive
ourselves up the walls and drive ourselves into hospital or drive ourselves
crazy. I think it's that type of temperament that we all have to deal with.
At some time or another we have a setback or sometimes you call it a
nervous breakdown or you're exhausted and so forth. I used to teach. My
programme basically was that I'd start the day off teaching. I'd start at
eight o'clock in the morning and I would stay at school till about half past
three, four o'clock to complete my task for the day. I would come home
and rest for about an hour, an hour and a bit. And by five o'clock, half past
five, I'd be going to rehearsals, and rehearsals would start either with the
répétiteur at six o'clock. Then after the répétiteur and the voice studies,
we would then start a rehearsal at half past seven o'clock and go through
until half past ten, sometimes eleven o'clock at night. So it was quite a
long day. And then get up in the morning and start at eight again. And
often we didn't get into bed before twelve, twelve thirty.
  Phillip Swales

Some of Eoan's singers made extra money by working in the entertainment
industry.

Then myself and Danny [Josephs] teamed up. We went out with the name
'Danny and Gerry'. We were a duet team and we used to do the nightclubs.
I earned more money doing the circuit at the nightclubs than during the
day, because the city council paid only 3.8 a week. And to complement
my salary there, I did what they call the weekend watch. Came on duty
weekends and scrub the floors, polish the desks, clean the windows of the
roads next to the traffic department – that all had to be done. But I would
earn double my salary for the week at the night clubs, all in town, the
Balalaika, the Three Cellars, Dominic's. This was all the so-called white

May Abrahamse on the cover of *Talk of the Times* in the *Cape Times* in 1956. At the time, May was employed in the 'cheque room' of the *Cape Times*.
SOURCE *Cape Times*, April 1956

clubs. They had to get a permit for us to perform. In 1959 I established myself as a one-man band and quickly acquired a reputation as a solo musician singer. I was able to play at sport clubs, dances, weddings, various birthdays and corporate functions over the last forty-six years.

Gerald Arendse

Gerald Arendse in 1970.
PHOTO Eoan Group Archive

5

Playing Roles

On stage, the Eoan Group excelled. The choir's first choral concert under Joseph Manca was held in the Cathedral Hall in Victoria Street, Cape Town in 1944, when Helen Southern-Holt was still at the helm of the organisation. Over the next twelve years the choir gradually expanded its repertoire to include religious works, like Martin Shaw's *The Redeemer* and other cantatas, and then operettas such as Alfred Silver's *A Slave in Araby* and oratorios like Mendelssohn's *Elijah* and Handel's *Messiah*. Even a royal performance was given during the South African visit of Queen Elizabeth II in 1947.

124

I said to Ms Southern, 'The concert is tomorrow night and I think we're going to make a hash of it.' She said, 'Don't worry, it will come right.' I thought to myself, 'Yes, you can talk, you're not singing in the choir.' So you know, this Saturday night, the orchestra performed and it was interval. Then the bell is rung and the orchestra members come in to their seats, and Ms Southern comes onto the stage and the audience comes into the hall. And we said to one another, 'What the hang is the woman coming to do here?' beautifully dressed in black. And she stands in front of the choir and she says, 'Close your eyes,' and we close our eyes. And she starts praying! In the City Hall! That the choir must sing properly, you know.

But the highlight for me was in 1947 when the royal family was here. The Bloombergs were mayor and mayoress at the time. I, together with Ms Southern of course, and Frank Lightdon and Harry Henry and Pat – I forget what Patty's surname was – we were the core of arranging [Eoan's performance at] Queen Elizabeth's twenty-first birthday at the Rosebank Showground. The last thing the choir did for the royal family was when they left the shores of South Africa, the Eoan Group stood on the docks, singing to the royal family as the boat was going out.

Tillie Ulster

Manca's ambitious vision became reality in 1956 when Eoan staged its first opera, Verdi's *La Traviata*, as part of Eoan's First Arts Festival. The soloists included May Abrahamse, Ruth Goodwin, Lionel Fourie and Ron Thebus. Manca conducted the Cape Municipal Orchestra and the production was directed by Alessandro Rota. *La Traviata* was to become the opera that the Eoan Group would be most associated with.

[In 1956] we did *Traviata*, and [Manca] made us realise it was a very big undertaking and a costly one. Because it would have to be properly costumed, otherwise there's no point in putting it on. So it had to be period costumed. The backdrops are going to be expensive. And he made it clear that this was a very expensive project. And, all right, the people

1 9 4 9

EOAN GROUP

Presents

"A Slave in Araby"

by ALFRED J. SILVER

Comic Opera in Two Acts

Produced by: BILLIE JONES

under the auspices of the

Cape Town Municipal Orchestra

Conducted by: JOSEPH S. MANCA

————::————

CITY HALL

Saturday, 13th and 20th August, 1949

at 8.15 p.m.

Castle, C.T.

The programme for *A Slave in Araby*, performed by Eoan in 1949.
SOURCE Eoan Group Archive

Eoan Group Arts Festival   Eoan Groep Kuns Fees

SATURDAY 10th, THURSDAY-SATURDAY 15th-17th and SATURDAY 24th MARCH, 1956
SATERDAG 10de, DONDERDAG-SATERDAG 15-17de en SATERDAG 24ste MAART 1956
GRAND OPERA

"La Traviata"
VERDI

Producer/Opvoerder: ALESSANDRO ROTA   Conductor/Dirigent: JOSEPH MANCA

THURSDAY 26th and SATURDAY 28th (Matinee and Evening), APRIL 1956
DONDERDAG 26ste en SATERDAG 28ste (Matinee en Aand), APRIL 1956
CHILDREN'S OPERETTA — KINDER-OPERETTA

"Mikado"
GILBERT & SULLIVAN

Producer/Opvoerder: MARJORIE HILL   Conductor/Dirigent: DANIEL ULSTER

SATURDAY 5th MAY 1956   SATERDAG 5de MEI 1956

"Johnny Belinda"

Producer/Opvoerder: JOHN PACKHAM

SATURDAY 2nd JUNE 1956   SATERDAG 2de JUNIE 1956
ORATORIA — ORATORIUM

"Elijah"
MENDELSSOHN

Conductor/Dirigent: JOSEPH MANCA   Organist/Orrelis: LESLIE ARNOLD, F.R.C.O.

THURSDAY 14th and SATURDAY (Matinee and Evening), 16th JUNE 1956
DONDERDAG 14de en SATERDAG (Matinee en Aand), 16ste JUNIE 1956

"Ballet"

Dance Director/Dansbestuurder: GWEN MICHAELS   Conductor/Dirigent: DANIEL ULSTER

MONDAY 30th JULY to SATURDAY 4th AUGUST 1956 (Matinee Saturday)
MAANDAG 30ste JULIE tot SATERDAG 4de AUGUSTUS 1956 (Matinee Saterdag)
MUSICAL COMEDY — MUSIEK BLYSPEL

"Zip Goes a Million"
MASCHWITZ AND POSFORD

Producer/Opvoerder: JOYCE BRADLEY   Conductor/Dirigent: JOSEPH MANCA

with   *met*
CAPE TOWN MUNICIPAL ORCHESTRA   KAAPSTADSE MUNISIPALE ORKES

Eoan's First Arts Festival in 1956 consisted of six works.
SOURCE   Eoan Group Archive

agreed that we would work, that within the branches we would work to try and help wherever we could. Because there were dancers and all that in it, as you know. Ms Michaels was then the dance director and then she used to get in touch with [Manca]. And he used to speak at that level with her, and tell her what dancing he wanted in the show. He would tell her that and that, and she would sort the girls out. And then that would become the dancing girls for *Traviata*.
  Alethea Jansen

Traviata … I can tell you it was a great success. May Abrahamse sang the lead, and she alternated with Ruth Goodwin and Abeeda Parker and Winifred du Plessis. They all alternated because the opera ran for months. It was a great success. Queues around the City Hall – I can still picture how the people came to see *Traviata*. Because [the public] couldn't believe people off the street singing Italian.
  Cecil Jacobs

Traviata is the first production I can remember. They repeated that every year. And Lionel [Fourie] was a dramatic tenor. And then, because they didn't have a baritone, they just made him a baritone, and that's how he sang Germont.
  Ruth Fourie

Traviata natuurlik, met Vera Gow. Sy was die ster gewees. Maar ek dink nie sy was die enigste een wat 'n ster was nie. Ek kan onthou dat die

Scene from Eoan's first production of *La Traviata* in 1956.
PHOTO Eoan Group Archive

OVERLEAF
A scene from Eoan's production of *La Traviata*, which became their signature opera. Shirley English is dancing the lead.
PHOTO Cloete Breytenbach, 1965

groepwerk was so goed. Daar was sangers wat kleiner rolle gesing het wat nie uitmuntend was nie, maar hulle was goed afgerig, hulle het goed ingepas, en dit is wat ek bedoel met die groepwerk. Ja, die koor was goed en miskien nie altyd wonderlike toneelspel gewees nie, maar jy weet, ek meen as jy dink die mense was almal amateurs.

~ Traviata naturally, with Vera Gow. She was the star. But I don't think she was the only one who was a star. I remember that the group work was so good. There were singers who sang the smaller roles who were not outstanding, but they were well trained, they fitted in well, and that's what I mean by the group work. Yes the chorus was good and the acting was maybe not always wonderful, but you know, I mean, if you think the people were all amateurs.

   Pieter Kooij

Met *Traviata* het ek dit baie amusing gevind – aan die einde sterf Violetta mos. Ek móét die stukkie vertel van die stoute Robert Trussell. Hy het die part gedoen van [die dokter]. Nou aan die einde as Violetta sterf, het Rota dit so uitgewerk, die sopraan beweeg al vorentoe, Violetta, dan loop ek al so agter, want ek besef iets is verkeerd en as sy val, dan val sy in my arms. Nou kom die dokter en hy voel net haar pols en skud hy net sy kop, en dan weet ons. Alles het pragtig uitgewerk. Opening night, standing ovation! Tweede aand begin Robert Trussell. Nou sing die sopraan vorentoe, Violetta loop vorentoe, ek agterna. Val sy in my arms. Robert Trussell moet nou vir my sê sy is nou dood. Sy rug na die gehoor toe, draai hy sy gesig op na my toe en sê, 'Gerry, sy's vrek!' Ek bars uit van die lag, dan lag ek en ek laat sak my kop. Manca kom by en sê, 'Very well done! Do it tomorrow night again!'

~ I found it very amusing with Traviata – as you know Violetta dies at the end. I must tell you this story about naughty Robert Trussell. He played the part of [the doctor]. At the end as Violetta is dying, Rota worked it out like this, the soprano moves slowly forward, Violetta, then I walk gradually backwards, because I realise something is wrong and if she falls, then she will fall into my arms. Then the doctor comes in and he feels her pulse and just shakes his head, and then we know. We worked everything out beautifully. Opening night, standing ovation! The second night Robert Trussell starts. Now the soprano sings to the front, Violetta walks forwards, I walk backwards. She falls into my arms. Robert Trussell must now tell me she is dead. His back to the audience, turns his face to me and says, 'Gerry, she's kicked the bucket!' I burst out laughing, I laugh and I lower my head. Manca comes round and says, 'Very well done! Do it tomorrow night again!

   Gerald Samaai

With each opera season Eoan presented from 1956 to 1975, their repertoire expanded. Manca conducted every opera the group performed, with either Gregorio Fiasconaro or Alessandro Rota directing and stage designs by Mario Bierti. In Eoan's Second Opera and Ballet Season in 1958 Mascagni's *Cavalleria Rusticana* was added to the repertoire.

My first role was Mama Lucia in *Cavalleria Rusticana*. Now imagine making a young girl up from sixteen to be a old lady. So I had a wig on, it was all grey and you know the makeup artists they put lines on you and you haven't even got the lines but the lines is there. And that was my first role. That was my first role that I sang. I wasn't even finished with my studies yet when I did Mama Lucia on the City Hall stage. And I must tell you I thank God.
   Sophia Andrews

I had to learn *Cavalleria Rusticana* in two weeks. I had nightmares about it, but I did it with [Gregorio] Fiasconaro standing in the wings, to prompt me. And Manca miming the words while I was singing and we got through it. I mean, I used to come home and get nightmares about it. I used to dream about it, being on stage and not knowing what to do next.

   [May Abrahamse as Santuzza] was a fantastic help on stage – she's got a fantastic stage presence. So I did it with her and of course one of the nights – I can tell you about this. One of the nights – I had false teeth – she was ready to curse me in *Cavalleria*. And I walked in the church and while I was singing my front teeth jumped out of my mouth. And I caught the teeth. And she's got to keep a straight face. Of course she cursed me. She tried to curse me with a straight face. Ja, that was one of the incidents. Then we had other incidents. I can't remember who the chorus girl was, one of the younger chorus girls who played the part of a widow. And she was an old maid. She said she was not going to play the part of a widow, because she is not married! Ha-ha! That was the thing we had to put up with!
   Gerald Arendse

Jy weet die koor ken als. Jy kan 'n rolletjie het en jy sing verkeerd, dan sing hulle dit vir jou. Toe kom, is dit Tassiem, ja? Toe kom die ou vorentoe en hy sê hy ken dit. Maar hy het nie so 'n wonderlike tenoorstem gehet nie, maar hy doen dit. Ja! En toe is hy een van die tenore, solo-tenore van die Eoan Groep. Toe sit hulle hom in nog 'n rol in *Cavalleria Rusticana*. Maar daar's 'n opening daarso, maar hy sê hy't nie daardie so goed gesing nie! Nou die gehoor het nie so lekker hande geklop vir hom nie. Toe staan Manca op uit die put uit en hy sê vir die gehoor, 'That was sung in the true

CAVALLERIA RUSTICANA

(RUSTIC CHIVALRY)

★

MELODRAMA IN ONE ACT

by

G. Targioni-Tozzetti and G. Menasci

Music by

Pietro Mascagni

Producer - - - - GREGORIO FIASCONARO
Conductor - - - - JOSEPH MANCA
Chorusmaster: Vincent Costello   Scenographer: Joseph Cappon

★

With

CAPE TOWN MUNICIPAL ORCHESTRA

★

CAST

Santuzza (a young peasant girl) - - - - - - - - - - - - - MAY ABRAHAMSE
Turiddu (a young peasant) - - - - - - - - - - - - - YUSUF WILLIAMS
Lucia (his mother) - - - - - - - - - - - - - - - SOPHIA ANDREWS
Alfio (a carrier) - - - - - - - - - - - - - - - BENJAMIN ARENDSE
Lola (his wife) - - - - - - - - - - - - - - - SHIRLEY SMIT
Peasants - - - - - - - - - - - - - - - - EOAN GROUP CHORUS
Villagers - - - - - - - - - - - - - - - -

The action is laid in a village in Sicily

CHORUS

LADIES			GENTLEMEN	
Matilda Theunissen	Patricia van Graan	Maggie Kloppers	Floris Arendse	Herman Strydom
Maggie Kampher	Ann Matthews	Anne Cloete	Michael Rousseau	Donald Brown
Irene Cupido	Rose Magolie	Sophia Jansen	Abraham Lewis	Henry Muller
Joan Cloete	Maureen Magolie	Jessie Matchessa	Stephanus Appolis	Charles Josephus
Marjorie Wiener	Mary Williams	Christine Julie	Samuel Amos	Michael Johnson
Francis Peters	Phoebe Cooke	Irene de Kock	Isaac Adams	Fred Forgus
Sheila Fransman	Vera Harding	Kitty Paulse	Richard Paulse	Cecil Muller
Lena Paulse	Grace Fisher	Marina Rushin	Peter Petersen	Henry Harding
Sabena Loubser	Nita Hamer	Magdalene Appolis	Arthur Abrahams	Jack Lockey
Sylvia Lindeboom	Rachel Abrahams	Kathleen Seconds	Mervyn Rinquest	David Alexander
Matilda Domingo	Annie Naidu	Jane Blythe	John Williams	Carl Preston
Winifred Lotter	Naomi Thebus	Edna Kemp	William Abrahams	Carl Ephraim
	Kitty Hinds		Martin Netta	Clifford Rinquest

The cast list for the performance of *Cavalleria Rusticana* in 1958.
SOURCE Eoan Group Archive

The chorus for *Cavalleria Rusticana* and *La Traviata* in 1958.

Sicilian language.' Toe dink die gehoor sjoe, en toe klap hulle hande.
~ *You know the chorus knew everything. You could have a small role and sing*
something wrong, then they sing it for you. Then up stepped, was it Tassiem?
Yes, the guy came up and said he knows it. But he did not have such a won-
derful tenor voice, but he does it. Yes! And then he was one of the tenors, solo
tenors of the Eoan Group. Then they put him in another role, in Cavalleria
Rusticana. *But there's an opening there, but he says he did not sing that so*
well! So the audience did not clap their hands too enthusiastically for him.
Then Manca steps up out of the pit and says to the audience, 'That was sung
in the true Sicilian language.' Then the audience thought, my goodness, then
they really clapped their hands.
> **Ronald Theys**

In 1959, the Third Opera and Ballet Season was held, with Verdi's *Rigoletto*
now included in Eoan's repertoire.

Well, I must say, I love Verdi. First of all, *Traviata* for me is a beautiful
opera, but when I did *Rigoletto*, I think it was amazing. I love the opera.
It's not only the music, but it's the story. The problem is, in most of these
operas, you always die ... I died so many times, I think that's probably why
I'm still alive, ja.

So Lionel Fourie, one night I was lying in the bag, as his daughter
[Gilda], who is now going to die … and he has to open the bag at the top.
The bag, a hessian bag, is tied in such a way that he doesn't … You know,
all he has to do, is just [untie it]. And I sort of help him inside the bag, but
the audience is not aware of that. But that night, Lionel, you know, he's
lying across the bag and he has to open the bag, but instead of opening
the bag at the top, he's fiddling at the bottom. And I'm lying in the bag
and I said: 'Lionel, you're at the wrong end!' You know those are all funny
things. It is true! We couldn't laugh at the time.
   Ruth Goodwin

In 1959, Lionel Fourie sang the title role in Eoan's first production of
Verdi's *Rigoletto* and became well known for the role. It is said that he once
proclaimed that no other Eoan singer would ever sing that role. He died
in 1963, and when the opera was performed again in 1971 it is believed that
a second, ghostly Rigoletto roamed the stage during the production. All
involved swear it was the ghost of Fourie. Subsequently, in a 'cleansing'
ceremony, the company members burned Fourie's costume.

Hoogtepunte was die aand toe ons gesing het in die ou Alhambra,
Rigoletto. Dit was vir my 'n groot hoogtepunt. Ek was nog taamlik jonk
in hierdie kunsvorm. En op hierdie aand, sweer ek, toe ek met die
Rigoletto sing, toe's daar twee Rigoletto's op daai verhoog. Die een was
soos 'n skim, en ek het so groot geskrik dat ek net ophou sing het. En
hier sit ou Manca in die pit en tick tick tick. Nou kyk hy ook en hy sien
ook twee. En toe moet hy die orchestra eers stop, toe gaan ons aan. 'n
Ou storie wat ná dit geloop het, het gesê dat een van die ou Rigoletto's
het altyd gesê niemand, selfs tot op sy sterfbed, niemand gaan weer
daai rol sing nie. En dit was een van die hoogtepunte, nie laagtepunte
nie, hoogtepunte: om twee Rigoletto's op een verhoog te sien.
~ *One highlight was when we sang in the old Alhambra,* Rigoletto. *For me
that was a great highlight. I was still fairly young in the art form. And that
night, I swear, when I was singing with Rigoletto, there were two Rigolettos
on that stage. The one was like a ghost, and I got such a big fright that I just
stopped singing. And there old Manca sat in the pit and tick tick tick. Then
he also looks and also sees two. And then he first had to stop the orchestra,
then we went on. An old story that did the rounds after that was that one of
the old Rigolettos always said, even on his deathbed, that nobody was going
to sing that role again. And that was one of the high points, not low points:
to see two Rigolettos on one stage.*
   John van der Ross

'RIGOLETTO'
OPERA IN THREE ACTS

☆

Libretto: M. Piave   Music: Giuseppe Verdi

☆

PRODUCTION: GREGORIO FIASCONARO

☆

SCENERY: JOSEPH CAPPON

CHORUSMASTER: VINCENT COSTELLO   CHOREOGRAPHER: JOAN BOONZAAIER

☆

THEATRE ORCHESTRA
Leader: Walter Mony

Conducted by
JOSEPH MANCA

☆

CAST

DUKE	JOSEPH GABRIELS
RIGOLETTO	LIONEL FOURIE
GILDA	RUTH GOODWIN
SPARAFUCILE	ROBERT TRUSSELL
MADDALENA	SOPHIA ANDREWS
GIOVANNA	SYLVIA LINDEBOOM
MONTERONE	BENJAMIN ARENDSE
MARULLO	GERALD ARENDSE
BORSA	SAMUEL AMOS
CEPRANO	ARTHUR ACKERMAN
COUNTESS CEPRANO	SUSAN ARENDSE
PAGE	PATRICIA VAN GRAAN

Place: Mantua

☆

CHORUS

WILLIAM ABRAHAMS	PETER ABRAHAMS
PETER PETERSEN	LIONEL PETERSEN
ABRAHAM LEWIS	STEPHANUS APPOLLIS
RICHARD PAULSE	FRED FORGUS
MERVYN RINQUEST	MICHAEL ROSSOUW
SAM VAN DER ROSS	
LAWRENCE HOSAIN	

DANCERS

Ladies	*Gentlemen*
JOAN BOONZAAIER	DANIEL JOSEPHS
DIDI SYDOW	PETER ABRAHAMS
PHILIDA HARRIS	LIONEL PETERSEN
PAULINE HENKEL	LAWRENCE HOSAIN
JEAN JOHNSON	
JEAN THEBUS	

The cast list for Verdi's *Rigoletto* in 1959.

Lionel Fourie as Rigoletto in 1959.
PHOTO Eoan Group Archive

Puccini's *La Bohème* was added to the repertoire for the Fourth Opera and Ballet Season in 1960.

> They didn't do enough in the repertoire, you see. Initially they only had *Traviata*. Then they brought, I think, *La Bohème* after that, and then *Rigoletto*, and then they do all that. But it was all the same voices. Like the bass for instance, Robert Trussell, sang in *Traviata*, he sang in *La Bohème*, he sang in *Rigoletto*. He was Sparafucile in *Rigoletto*.
> *Ruth Fourie*

> And my favourite opera, that must be noted, amongst all the operas, is *La Bohème*. I love the last scene when she's dying. I love it, and we did it so wonderfully. Your tears would run down your cheeks every time you see it. I used to have nights off when *La Bohème* was on – I don't take a night off, I go sit in the audience just to listen to it.
> *Sophia Andrews*

> Joey Gabriels en May Abrahamse doen *Bohème*, dit het ek nou nie self gesien nie, maar dit het wel gebeur, want ek het vir May uitgevra. Toe sê

A scene from Eoan's production of *La Bohème* in 1960.
PHOTO Eoan Group Archive

sy vir my, 'Yes, it happened.' Aan die einde sterf Mimi. Maar hulle het die
bed waarop Mimi sterf so op 'n skuinste gesit, want dan is dit maklik vir
haar asemhaling en al die goed wat daarmee gepaard gaan. Joey kom in,
gryp hy mos vir Mimi dan seg hy, 'Mimi, Mimi.' Toe hy vorentoe gaan om
vir May te gryp, toe skeur sy broek agter. Toe seg hy, 'Jes God, daar skeur
my broek, Mimi.' May sê, 'Imagine, I'm supposed to be dying! The bed was
shaking and everybody said it was touching the way you shook that bed.
You were really dying!' Vrolike momente wat ons gehad het.
~ *Joey Gabriels and May Abrahamse were doing* Bohème, *I did not see
this myself, but it did happen, because I asked May about it. And she said
to me, 'Yes, it happened.' Mimi dies at the end. But they were sitting at an
angle on the bed upon which Mimi dies, because that made it easier for her
breathing and everything that goes with that. Joey comes in, grabs Mimi and
says, 'Mimi, Mimi.' But as he stepped forward to grab May, his pants tore
at the back. And he says, 'Oh my God, my pants have split, Mimi.' May says,
'Imagine, I'm supposed to be dying! The bed was shaking and everybody
said it was touching the way you shook that bed. You were really dying!' Fun
moments that we had.*
  Gerald Samaai

But the highlight of ours, the *Bohème* in Durban. Now our props was tea
– red tea with a little honey or whatever, you know, to help the voice. But I
decided not to take the props on stage. I put a real bottle of sherry in the
basket on stage, right. And then, well, they open the sherry and the first
one to taste was Professor Roberto. When he tasted this it was the real
McCoy, you know what I'm saying. And then Bennie tasted. But Joseph
couldn't, because he was on our far side, left to the bed close to Mimi.
Mimi was about to die, you know what I'm saying, and the bottle started
moving, this is now not part of the act that we were supposed to do, but
our stage movements was now totally different, we were doing things but
which was beautiful. It didn't upset the performance.
Martin Johnson

In *La Bohème*, when there is supposed to be wine. Now I could never sing
with wine, you know, I could never. And of course they used to enjoy
themselves … Yes, sometimes there was real wine, you know, that type
of thing. Oh we used to have fun, very much. [Because they used to have
drinks backstage.] But it was always, if you didn't want to partake, it was
not necessary for you, but you allowed. Look it was also that they have so
many parties after the show, but we were never, I was never invited.
Benny Arendse

In 1962, the Second Arts Festival, which included Eoan's Fifth Opera Season,
was held. The new works in the repertoire were Puccini's *Madama Butterfly*,
Johann Strauss's *Die Fledermaus* and Verdi's *Requiem*.

In *Fledermaus*, when [the character] is supposed to phone the president,
nè, and so he called him 'Blackie'. So the following night it was out, you
understand, nè, because 'Blackie' was the [then] president [CR Swart],
you understand! And also, each one of us had his own way, that we take
curtain calls. I never take a curtain call to this bays or that bays, I always
take to the centre and up there.
Benny Arendse

Eoan's Sixth Opera Season in 1965 saw Verdi's *Il Trovatore* and Donizetti's
L'Elisir d'Amore added to the repertoire.

Ronnie Theys was doing the role of Manrico and I did the role of Ruiz [in
Il Trovatore]. And being so difficult, the timing was terrible because there
was nothing in the orchestra, no melody. And of course you know, if you
did it wrong you were called a 'poloni'. Then you've got to do it over. And

<table>
<tr><td>

Eoan Group - Peninsula Round Table
Arts Festival 1962

—●●●—

GRAND OPERA
MARCH / APRIL

MADAM BUTTERFLY · · · · · *Puccini*	
LA BOHEME · · · · · · *Puccini*	
LA TRAVIATA · · · · · · *Verdi*	

Producer: GREGORIO FIASCONARO *Conductor:* JOSEPH MANCA

CHILDREN'S OPERETTA
JULY

TRAVELLING MUSICIANS · · · *Martin Shaw*	
ALICE IN WONDERLAND · · · *Harvey Paul*	

Producer: MAVIS TAYLOR *Musical Direction:* NORMAN TAYLOR

DRAMA
AUGUST

AT THE LITTLE THEATRE

Producer: ROBIN MALAN

—●●●—

WITH CAPE TOWN MUNICIPAL ORCHESTRA

</td><td>

Kunsfees 1962
Eoan-Groep/Skiereilandse Tafelronde

—●●●—

ORATORIUM
AUGUSTUS

REQUIEM · · · · · · *Verdi*

Dirigent: JOSEPH MANCA

BALLET
SEPTEMBER

„THE SQUARE"

Musiek deur STANLEY GLASSER *Dirigent:* STANLEY GLASSER

Choreografie: DAVID POOLE *Besoekende Arties:* JOHAAR MOSAVAL

OPERETTE
OKTOBER / NOVEMBER

DIE FLEDERMAUS · · · · · *Strauss*

Regisseur: ROBERT MOHR *Dirigent:* JOSEPH MANCA

—●●●—

MET KAAPSE STADSORKES

</td></tr>
</table>

The programme for the Second Arts Festival in 1962.
SOURCE Eoan Group Archive

now Ronnie laughed. Now, it was tough but I eventually managed to do it.
I mastered it. Some years later at CAPAB, the lead or Italian tenor Franco
Bonisolli was brought in to do the role of Manrico. And Ronald Theys,
who laughed at me, did the part of Ruiz in the CAPAB production and he
battled. And he battled so much that he got Franco Bonisolli heading off
the stage and the curtain had to come down, because he was out. It's very
difficult, it's just one of those things which is just, just tough. It's not a
nice melodic thing where like, like you know, you have a lovely aria? Or
you sing the part of Gastone in *La Traviata*. No, this is awkward.

Trevor Pretorius

In Donizetti se *L'Elisir d'Amore* was James Momberg nogal baie goed, wat
'n uitstekende 'Una Furtiva Lagrima' gesing het, en hy't 'n mens eintlik
heeltemal meegevoer. Om hierdie stem, hierdie pragtige tenoorstem
te hoor wat jy nie geweet het wat hier is nie. En dan daar was nog ene
gewees, ja, Patricia van Graan het 'n baie goeie Adina gesing en ek het
ook hier [in 'n resensie] oor haar toneelspel gepraat wat baie goed was en
natuurlik Cecil Tobin.
~ *In Donizetti's* L'Elisir d'Amore *James Momberg was really quite good, he
sang an exceptional 'Una Furtiva Lagrima', and he actually swept you along.*

A scene from Eoan's 1962 production of *Die Fledermaus* with May Abrahamse, Faried Nardien and Cecil Tobin.
PHOTO Supplied by May Abrahamse

May Abrahamse as Cio-Cio San and Sophia Andrews as Suzuki in *Madama Butterfly* in 1962.
PHOTO Eoan Group Archive

To hear that voice, that lovely tenor voice that you did not know was here.
And there was another one, yes, Patricia van Graan sang a very good Adina
and I also spoke here [in a review] about her acting which was very good, and
naturally Cecil Tobin.
   Pieter Kooij

142

In the late 1960s, Eoan had a very successful period performing musicals.
In 1967, the New York producer Stanley Waren directed Eoan's (and South
Africa's) première of the Rodgers and Hammerstein musical *Oklahoma!*.
David Bloomberg's production of the duo's other well-known musical,
South Pacific, followed in 1968, and in 1970 the musical *Carmen Jones* was
performed.

Now why this was great, apart from singing the Rodgers and
Hammerstein, was to work with someone like Dr Stanley Waren, who
had a doctorate in drama. And he wrote it at an American university,
University of New York and a university in South Carolina. His wife
[Florence] was a well-known ballet dancer in her day. She appeared in
all the countries. So, I find I must mention this because here you have,
call it an amateur society, but the people, the members are coming into
contact with world-renowned producers, directors, ballet dancers. So
the exposure there, a lot did rub off. We learned a great deal from them.
   They were out here for short spells, Dr Stanley Waren and Florence
Waren, and they were very exacting. They would not put up with a little
'am-dram' society, if you know what I mean. The standard had to be
good enough for them to work with. They were not going to teach you
the basics.
   He did *Carmen Jones* as well, yes. So I had that exposure working with
them … worked with Bloomberg on his production. And of course, not to
forget Alessandro Rota, he was also outstanding. I don't think that people
remember that this man had a repertoire of fourteen leading roles at La
Scala. That was Sandro, Sandro Rota, as we called him.
   Trevor Pretorius

Toe beplan hulle *Carmen Jones*, die Amerikaanse weergawe van *Carmen*,
en hulle cast my as Joe, die tenoor José in *Carmen*. Nou's ek opgewonde,
oe *Carmen Jones,* nè. Daar gaat ek nou Saterdag rugby speel. Ek twyfel
nogal daardie dag, want daar is ouens, jy weet, net twaalf ouens daag op,
en jy moet jou vrek speel, nogal eerste span, en ek besluit ek smaak nie
vandag om te speel nie. Onse eerste skrum, daardie ou – ons het baie
baklei daardie tyd want daar was nie skeidsregter om te sien of die TV-
kamera nie. Die ou gee my 'n karate punch reg in my keel in. Aaa, sak ek

Sophia Andrews in *South Pacific* in 1968.

nou af. Dit het my nou nie gepla met my spelery nie, maar ek sê ek is 'n
sanger, gaan na my kaptein, toe ek loop. Hy sê, 'Waarheen gaan jy nou?'
Ek sê, 'Nee, hulle het my geslaat in my keel.' 'Ja, maar jy kan mos nog
hardloop.' Ek sê, 'Nee, wat!' Toe gaat ek af. Toe moet ek nou die dokter
gaat spreek en hy sê my die spiere in my gorrel, die larynx, as ek 'n top
noot wil sing dan buig hy en hy moet reguit wees, styf, jy weet soos 'n
vioolstring wat kan 'peng' maak, hy buig 'n kleine bietjie en daarom is
ek geaffekteer met daardie punch ... en toe seg hy ek moet vir omtrent
ses maande stilbly. Was treurig, saans dan huil ek om te dink nou dié
het gebeur nou. Manca het gehuil. Rota, hy is Italianer, hy het nou nie
gehuil nie, maar hy het darem nie lekker gevoel nie. Hulle was almal
teleurgesteld. Maar the show must go on. En toe kry hulle vir Martin
Johnson in. En nou wil ek graag betrokke wees in die ding – daar was 'n
Amerikaanse [regisseur] daardie tyd. Maar hy sê my hy't 'n karakterrol vir
my, ek is 'n photographer met daardie klein boks-kameras, man. Ek het
so die mense laat lag met die kamera. En ek kam my hare soos Charlie
Chaplin, en ek sit 'n snor aan en loop op die verhoog soos Charlie Chaplin.

Gerald Arendse as Joe in *Carmen Jones*.
PHOTO *Sarie Marais*, 9 September 1970

En die koor, hulle moet sing, hulle het skoon uitgebreek van lag. En as
dit kom by die gordynbuiging, dan kry ek nogal meer applous as die
hoofsanger! Maar dis 'n karakterrol – jy sê niks, jy sing niks nie. En elke
aand as ek opkom, dan gaan die mense mal.

~ Then they planned to do Carmen Jones, *the American version of* Carmen,
and they cast me as Joe, the tenor José in Carmen. *Now I'm excited, ooh*
Carmen Jones, *you know. Then I went to play rugby on the Saturday. I was
a bit hesitant that day, but there are guys, you know, just twelve guys pitch
up, and you must play frantically, first team you know, and I decide I really
don't feel like playing today. Our first scrum, that guy – we fought a lot in
those days because there was no referee to see or a TV camera. That guy
gives me a karate punch right on my throat. Aaah, I drop to the ground. It
did not worry me in my playing, but I said I'm a singer, went to my captain,
then I left. He says, 'Where are you going now?' I say, 'No, they hit me on my
throat.' 'Yes, but you can still run.' I say, 'No, I don't think so!' Then I went
off. Then I had to go and see the doctor and he says the muscles in my throat,
the larynx, if I want to sing a top note then it bends and it must be straight,
stiff, you know, like a violin string that can 'ping', it was bending a little and
that is how I was affected by that punch ... and he said I should remain quiet
for about six months. Was sad, in the evenings I cried to think that this could
happen now. Manca cried. Rota, he is an Italian, he did not actually cry, but
he did not feel good about it. They were all disappointed. But the show must
go on. And then they brought in Martin Johnson. And I very much wanted to
be involved in the thing, there was an American [director] at that time. But he
says he has a character role for me, I was to be a photographer with one of
those small box cameras, man. I made the people laugh so with that camera.
And I combed my hair like Charlie Chaplin's, and I put on a moustache and
walk on stage like Charlie Chaplin. And the chorus, they had to sing, they
just burst out laughing. And when it came to the curtain call, then I even got
more applause than the main singer! But it was a character role – you don't
say anything, you don't sing anything. And every night when I came on the
people went mad.*

   Ronald Theys

Vera [Gow] in *Carmen Jones*, the last act before I stab her with a plastic
dagger, I showed her a real one when I come to her room and says, and I
use explicit words, bad words, and I start an argument with her and I said,
'Tonight I'm using this thing and not this plastic.' And I dumped that
thing away, you know, and Vera's now very scared, because Vera gets upset
very quickly.

   Martin Johnson

Another opera, Rossini's *Il Barbiere di Siviglia*, was added to the repertoire in the Eighth Opera Season in 1969.

Met *Barbier van Seville*: Don Basilio, die sangonderwyser kom binne, nou staan ons op die verhoog. En [Jacobus Erasmus] vergeet sy woorde, dis resitatief. En hy sing niks, smile net. Ek loop by hom verby en sê [die woorde]. Niks gebeur nie. Patricia van Graan kom, sy smile saam met hom, hy smile net terug. Nou daai lyk soos 'n ewigheid al klaar al. Ek kan nie eens aangaan nie, want hy moet vir my sê. Ek reageer op wat hy gaan doen. En dit was klaar. En Patricia sê [sy woorde]. Hy smile net en Patricia smile net terug. Rota, wat hier in die vlerk staan, is sommer dadelik bewus van wat aangaan, hy laat val net 'n stoel daar agter en hy sê [die woorde]. Toe hoor jy duidelik: 'O gods!' Onmiddellik kry jy al die applous! Maar dis soos hy [Rota] opera geken het, nè. Hy't opera binnetoe buitentoe geken. ~ *With* Barber of Seville: *Don Basilio, the singing master, comes in, we are standing on stage. And [Jacobus Erasmus] forgets his words, the recitative. And he doesn't sing, just smiles. I walk past him and say [the words]. Nothing happens. Patricia van Graan comes, she smiles at him, he just smiles back. Now it already seems like an eternity. I can't do anything, because he must tell me. I respond to what he does. And it was finished. And Patricia says [his words]. He just smiles and Patricia just smiles back. Rota, who was standing in the wings, is immediately aware of what is going on, he just knocks over a chair at the back and says [the words]. Then you clearly heard: 'O gods!' Immediately you get all the applause! But that's how he [Rota] knew opera, you know. He knew opera inside out.*
Gerald Samaai

For Eoan's Ninth Opera Season in 1971, the group performed *Cavalleria Rusticana*, *Rigoletto*, *La Traviata*, and also added Ruggiero Leoncavallo's *I Pagliacci* to their repertoire.

The Tenth and Eleventh Opera Seasons followed in 1974 and 1975 before the group embarked on their tour of the United Kingdom. For the first time since they had begun performing grand opera, the opera group did not add a new work to the repertoire for the season. The last opera the group performed was *La Traviata* as part of the Eleventh Season.

We did our last performance, it's so strange, we started with *Traviata*, and throughout the years, now and again, it was performed every now and again. And our last opera we did again was *Traviata*. So you know, the first opera was *Traviata* and the last.
May Abrahamse

IL BARBIERE di SIVIGLIA
(The Barber of Seville)

Opera in Two Acts   ◆   Opera in Twee Bedrywe

Libretto by/Libretto deur: CESARE STERBINI

Music by/Musiek deur: GIOACCHINO ROSSINI

First produced at the Teatro Argentina, Rome on 20th February, 1816/
Eerste opvoering in die Teatro Argentina, Rome op 20ste Februarie, 1816

PRODUCER/REGISSEUR: ALESSANDRO ROTA
Repetiteur: Gordon Jephtas
Decor: Mario Bierti
Costumes/Kostumms: Carmen Sydow
Chorus trained by/Koor Afgerig deur: Dr. Joseph Manca

CAPE TOWN SYMPHONY ORCHESTRA/KAAPSTADSE SINFONIE ORKES
(Leader/Leier: Artemisio Paganini)

Directed by/Gederigeer deur: DR. JOSEPH MANCA.

CAST/ROLBESETTING
(in order of appearance/volgens verskyning)

Fiorello (Servant to the Count/die Graaf se bediende)	Baritone/Bariton	JAMES KALAMDIEN
Count Almaviva (Spanish Grandee/Spaanse edelman)	Tenor/Tenoor	GERALD SAMAAI
Figaro (Barber of Seville/Haarkapper van Sevilla)	Baritone/Bariton	MARTIN JOHNSON
Doctor Bartolo (Rosina's Guardian/Rosina se oppasser)	Comic Baritone/Komiese Bariton	CECIL TOBIN
Rosina (Dr. Bartolo's ward/Dr. Bartolo se pleegkind)	Soprano/Sopraan	PATRICIA VAN GRAAN
Don Basilio (A singing teacher/sang-onderwyser)	Bass/Bas	JACOBUS ERASMUS
Berta (Rosina's Governess/Rosina se private onderwyseres)	Mezzo Soprano/Mezzosopraan	JOSEPHINE LIEDEMAN
Officer/Offissier		JAMES KALAMDIEN
Notary/Notaris		RICHARD PAULSE

Chorus of Musicians and Guards/Koor van Musikante en wagte

Locale: Seville, Spain   Period: Seventeenth Century
Plek: Sevilla, Spanje   Tyd: 17de eeu.

The cast of *Il Barbiere di Siviglia* in 1969.
SOURCE Eoan Group Archive

Eoan held regular Gems from the Operas concerts, in which they performed arias and ensembles from their repertoire, but also popular opera tunes, like the sextet from Donizetti's *Lucia di Lammermoor*.

When we had evening of song, or the Gems, I would have a dressmaker make me a dress. And I would walk onto that stage and render my item and the choir is sitting at the back of me, most of them. And as I come up, those will comment: 'Wie kan vir haar klaarmaak?' [Who can beat her?] And every time I used to get onto that City Hall stage was for me the most important thing in my life, because there I would give to those to enjoy what I have.
Sophia Andrews

Daardie tyd was die Eoan Groep baie sterk, as ek nou dink aan tenore wat hoofrolle vertolk het. Daar was Joey Gabriels, en dan was daar Jimmy Momberg, myself en nog twee of drie ander hoofsoliste. Deesdae soek hulle een tenoor vir 'n opera. Ons het gehad vier of vyf in elke kategorie. Soprane was daar gewees May Abrahamse, Ruth Goodwin, Winifred du Plessis, Yvonne Jansen, Vera Gow. Maar daar is 'n grappie in verband met die sekstet. Ek en Jimmy Momberg, ons tipe stem was amper dieselfde, ons het nooit geweet wie gaan die lead sing in die sekstet nie. In die opvoering het ons maar net gekyk waar gaan Dr Manca vir ons plaas, staan jy aan die linkerkant, weet jy jy het die hoof. Al twee dele kon ons sing uit die sekstet uit.
~ At that time the Eoan Group was very strong, and I'm now thinking of the tenors who played the main roles. There was Joey Gabriels, and then there were Jimmy Momberg, myself and another two or three main soloists. These days they look for one tenor for an opera. We had four or five in each category. Sopranos were May Abrahamse, Ruth Goodwin, Winifred du Plessis, Yvonne Jansen, Vera Gow. But there's a little joke about the sextet. Me and Jimmy Momberg, our voice types were almost the same, we never knew who would sing the lead in the sextet. In the performance we just looked where Dr Manca was going to put us, if you were on the left, you knew you were the lead. We could sing both parts of the sextet.
Gerald Samaai

Eoan singers became well known for specific roles they performed on stage, and even group members had their favourite singers for certain roles.

Oh, what a voice! Sophia always impressed me. I started buying opera records, you know, and I listened to mezzo-sopranos and then I listened to Sophia and I said to myself Sophia's better than that recording. And

Gerald Samaai and May Abrahamse performing in *I Pagliacci* in 1971.
PHOTO Supplied by Gerald Samaai

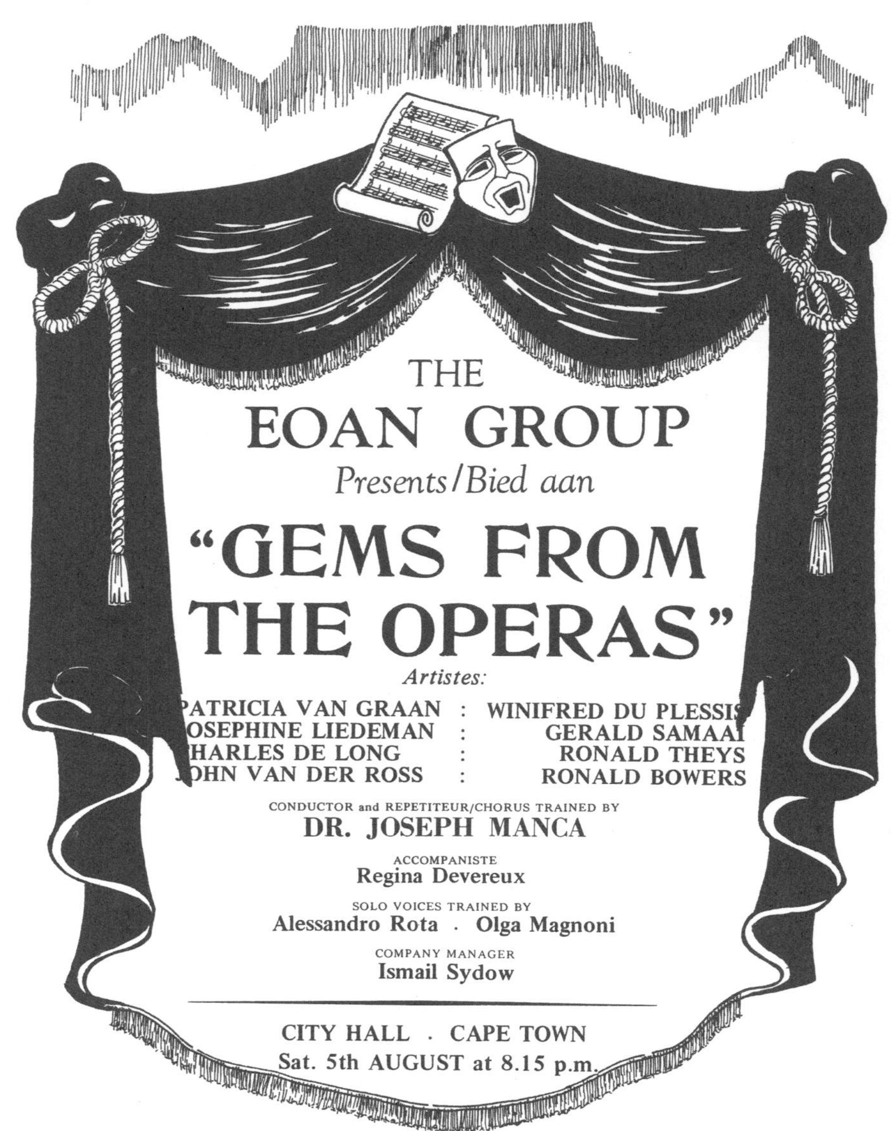

The programme of one of Eoan's Gems from the Operas concerts in 1971.
SOURCE Eoan Group Archive

I listened to another recording and I'd say, no, Sophia's better. I will always remember May as Mimi, because she played Mimi very well. I've heard recordings of Renata Tebaldi singing Mimi, *La Bohème*, and then I always used to listen to May and listen to Renata when I listened to the recordings at home, and here again, maybe I can be wrong, but to me May was still better. And *Butterfly*. May could also move on stage so beautifully when she did *Butterfly*, Cio-Cio San. And that, to me, was May's highlight.

There's a lot I can talk about Jimmy [Momberg] – when he opens up his mouth, it comes out naturally.

Martin Johnson

Robert Trussell, the bass was really marvellous. Many people – I remember there was an Afrikaner man who was the principal of a school in Bellville – every night he was there, and I asked him, 'You have seen this opera, and you are at the matinee performance again?' He says, 'I must tell you, that bass, I've never heard a bass like that!' And that was Robert Trussell! He was amazing. And then of course, Lionel Fourie, he had the most amazing baritone voice. I think when you do an opera, you must know what you're doing. You must let people feel that she's now telling him she's in love with him. The audience must feel that, they must hear it in your vocal production.

Ruth Goodwin

The leading opera singers of the Eoan Group who started a career there: May Abrahamse, who did many leading roles in little operas. When I was a young child, certain of the solo singers only did solo work. And that is how I remember May. I remember May in *I Pagliacci* and I also remember some of the solo singers who had been in the operas, then you don't see them for the next few months and then they came back again and that was a lifestyle; they came and they gone. And one of the Eoan Group's best opera singers, also a woman with a very, very beautiful voice, was Abeeda Parker. Abeeda Parker today lives in Canada. She was one of the top-class singers the Eoan Group also had, and did a few productions for the Eoan Group. And it was always the solo singers like May and Ruth [Goodwin] and them who took care of us. Yes, May Abrahamse, Vera Gow, Patricia van Graan, Sophia Andrews, what we would call the divas at the time. As a younger singer and being on tour with them and going here and going there, they always took great care of us as the younger singers and we could ask them questions. They liaised with us, they showed us the ropes. And it's with the Eoan Group that I learned all the ropes in the art of opera. They were lovely singers to work with.

Fuad Sawyer

They did great work with very little, great voices who all had to leave the country to go and make careers elsewhere, I think of Evan Jansen, Fred Martin, Patricia van Graan … I mean, Sophia, a mezzo-soprano, a quality that you wouldn't find easily. You know, Vera Gow sang everything, and that is the thing, Vera sang everything and anything and nobody else got any opportunities, but what an amazing voice. But people had to leave or you had to kill that fire, because then it became hard, people couldn't go on doing things for free. If things had been different, I'm sure people like Vera would have had different lives. I mean Jimmy Momberg had such natural talent, he could have sung in La Scala if he wanted to, but Jimmy couldn't read a note of music and Jimmy just sang, you know, who cared what came out, you know. There was somebody like Charles de Long, he went overseas.

Virginia Davids

Singers also had their favourite arias and roles.

I liked the Easter Hymn [from *Cavalleria Rusticana*]. I like the dramatic songs. You know, I need to express myself when I'm hurt. I suppose because at that stage I was going, how can I say, going through a troubled marriage. So then you feel a little bit, your emotion, I mean you get into those love scenes, things that really carry you there. And then most of my songs that I really did there were, how can I say, with a lot of expression and dramatic things like that.

Judith Bailey

Ek dink my hoogtepunt was definitief met *Die Barbier van Seville*. Want ek sal sê toe Manca vir my sê,'I want you to do *The Barber of Seville*, the part of Count Almaviva,' toe gaan ek dadelik na Hans Kramer, hy't mos die winkel gehad met plate. En ek luister daarna, this is what I'd like to do. I always looked for a challenge. En ek het net gevoel die stem het 'n ligte aanslag, en ek behoort dit te kan doen. En reg aan die begin het ek gesê, 'I'm going to work so bloody hard, they'll marvel at it.' En dis nou nie ter spog nie, maar ek kon maklik twee, drie *Barber of Sevilles* per dag sing, en dan nie moeg voel nie. Waar toe ek *Rigoletto* gesing het, as die tweede bedryf kom, dan dink ek, hel, wanneer kom die laaste bedryf nog? Dit was die groot verskil. Dit was definitief vir my 'n hoogtepunt gewees. En natuurlik het almal met *L'Elisir d'Amore* gewag vir die 'Una Furtiva' – as jy begin met 'Una Furtiva' dan hoor jy mense sê, 'Here it comes!'
~ *I think a highlight for me was definitely with* The Barber of Seville. *Because I tell you when Manca told me, 'I want you to do* The Barber of Seville, *the part of Count Almaviva,' I went straight to Hans Kramer, he*

had that record shop. And I listened to it, this is what I'd like to do. I always looked for a challenge. And I felt the voice had a light touch, and I should be able to do it. And right at the beginning I said, 'I'm going to work so bloody hard, they'll marvel at it.' And I don't want to boast, but I could easily sing two, three Barber of Sevilles *per day and not feel tired. Whereas when I sang* Rigoletto, *by the time we got to the second act I was thinking, hell, when will we get to the last act? That was the big difference. It was definitely a highlight for me. And naturally in* L'Elisir d'Amore *everyone was waiting for the 'Una Furtiva' – as you start with 'Una Furtiva' then you hear people say, 'Here it comes!'*
  Gerald Samaai

With a limited number of soloists at Eoan's disposal, singers sometimes had to sing roles that they should otherwise not have sung, because these were not in their *Fach*.

The big question that was coming up in my own mind was how much actual skill was there? How much vocal abuse was happening? Were people doing things that their voices could do? Or are people switching to falsetto and they get away with it? There is Ronnie Theys singing 'Di Quella Pira' from *Il Trovatore* and he pulls it off! But Ronnie is nowadays a baritone, so was he a tenor? You had the wonderful, absolutely wonderful Vera Gow, who had a pitch problem. My God, she had a pitch problem. She was wonderful, she was stunning, she was the closest thing to Leontine Price that I ever heard, she was an amazing woman. So she worked with no nonsense, and she did, *Trovatore*. Even a better job in *Traviata*. That was her one we could not wait to hear.
  Peter Voges

I did Verdi's *Requiem*, also the alto part. I hated the alto part, because I knew I wasn't an alto. Just because I had a deep voice and a strong voice, they used me.
  Sophia Andrews

With Dr Manca, if you had the voice he'd begin to train and train and then put you into bigger roles. And sometimes you would do nothing but Italian songs and Italian opera, it was quite demanding. He pushed the voice quite a bit, yes, he was pushing the voice, because he had his aspirations to produce the Italian opera. There were a couple of people who actually were not happy with being pushed so far. And some of them just left and went to do other things as well.
  Phillip Swales

153

Robert Trussell during a rehearsal in the Cape Town City Hall.
PHOTO Cloete Breytenbach, 1965

The world of opera has its divas and divos, and Eoan's opera company was no exception.

Well, you know the men always related very well to each other. But the women: divas. You could see Ruth [Goodwin] and May [Abrahamse], being on the outside, you could see that they didn't [get along]. I'm not saying they disagreed in any way. But there was something, you never saw them talking to each other. And they sang in different operas. Or they shared the same opera but they were never at rehearsals together. You know what I mean?
Ruth Fourie

Ruth and I we were never like friends, you know. She had her own group of friends and things like that. And I, you know, the chorus people were my friends, because we were at the Eoan Group as part of the beginners, they were my friends. And Ruth and I, we weren't actually friends. And then Ruth – no, I mustn't say anything – but I'll tell you this, Ruth seemed as though she didn't worry about the chorus people, she was only with the principals. And we have sometimes more male principals from the group. So when we got to Port Elizabeth, I think this was the first stop, her first tour. And then we were in a hotel there. Usually Manca told us what was going on. And then he said, so and so is in this room, and so many people are in that room, and so on. And then apparently he had arranged for Ruth and I to share a room. And I often think about it. You know, nothing was said, nothing. But anyhow, so I remember I was in the room and I was unpacking my things and Ruth came into the room too and she started unpacking her things. And I thought to myself, now whose going to say hello first, because we never, never ever had a chat together. I don't know why. Anyhow, and so I was busy unpacking my things and I thought, oh well you know, we're going to be together. And then she left the room without saying anything. And then I had a message that Manca wanted to see me. And we had a woman who was in charge, Mrs Williams. And so there was Manca sitting and Mrs Williams and Ruth, too. And Manca said to me, 'Now May, what is the problem?' So I said, 'About what?' So he said, 'Well, I don't know about you two.' And I never ever had any altercation. So then he said, 'So where am I going to put you now?' And I said, 'But Dr Manca, I didn't complain, I'm quite happy where I am.' And then Mrs Williams said, 'Ja, Dr Manca she didn't complain'. And so I had the room and they brought in another friend to come in. I mean, that was the only altercation we ever had. I can't even say, we never even had arguments. Ruth always just kept herself with the principals. She was just one of those people. I don't blame her, because she didn't know the chorus people and I knew them all these years.

May Abrahamse

The only one I fought with was Joey Gabriels. Because when I got my write-up in Johannesburg, they said he had to come up to my standard to keep going. And that's what he didn't like, because I tell you, he was busy with rather big shots that was going to send him overseas. And he wanted the praise so that they could send him. And after the first night, the second night came and he refused to get on the stage with me. 'It's your opera, take it! I'm not singing with you!' So I say, 'I didn't do the write-up. I didn't, somebody else did it!' End of that. So here we're waiting for the curtain to rise on my scene and he's at the back. Manca had to get off the [podium], go to the back and said to him, 'If you don't get onto that stage, I'm gonna send you home under police escort because you signed a contract. And if you don't get on the stage, I'm gonna send you out home in this case.' And I'm crying out to Manca, 'What did I do?' So here I come on stage and there's certain moves that we've gotta make. He's moving all over the place, confusing me. I thought to myself I must just get finished with this scene, because he's now in for it, wanna put me off and the orchestra's playing. So off he goes, first scene. I go to the back, I said, 'Mr Sydow, I'm not getting back onto that stage with that man! That man is walking, he's walking all

Ruth Goodwin in 1956.
PHOTO Eoan Group Archive

May Abrahamse in 1956.
PHOTO Eoan Group Archive

over the stage. I don't know where I am.' 'Okay Sophia, okay Sophia, you just do your bit.' I said that was the worst night that I experienced on the stage with Joey Gabriels. We were always fighting.

Sophia Andrews

Of Joseph, I remember one night when we did a concert in Johannesburg and he had laryngitis. Or it was a cold or something, but he couldn't go on stage that night. And I sang 'Largo al Factotum' from *The Barber of Seville* – standing ovation that I got at that concert. When we got back to the hotel, Joseph shouted, because my room was next to his room, and his wife, Mabel, was with him and she said, 'Joseph roep jou' ['Joseph is calling you']. En ek sê, 'Wat het ek nou weer gedoen?' [And I say, 'What have I done now?'], you know. And as I walked in, he was lying on the bed, and he said to me: 'Jy dink jy's 'n "tweet tweet" star, nè?' ['You think you're a "bleep bleep" star hey?'] Cause the information came so quick to Joseph that I got a standing ovation, that Joseph was upset now.

Martin Johnson

They were all so full of themselves. Mind you, Bennie Arendse, he was a baritone, he was ag, he was a real lovey-dovey and so on. Uhm what's the name? Joseph Gabriels. He was a typical artist, typical temper, gets 'moeilik' [difficult] about everything. We did *Fledermaus* together. And he was cross with me about something, I don't know what it was. And so we were doing one of our scenes and I'm walking around with a key or something singing. And he's trying to get the key from me for some reason, I can't remember the story anymore. And I had a long train. And every time the bugger would tramp on my train, you know.

May Abrahamse

Eoan's opera seasons were highlights on the music calendar in Cape Town, with crowds queuing to buy tickets outside City Hall. Often, extra performances of their operas had to be scheduled. Their country-wide tours were equally popular, and Eoan singers became the opera stars of South Africa.

Opera was suddenly a novel thing for South Africans because there were no performing arts boards. So they all attended this. It was a great success. Let me also go back to that first *Traviata*, which was done when the Separate Amenities Act was in place already ... the government of the day must have realised they'd slipped up, that they had attended these performances while the Separate Amenities Act had come into operation.

Trevor Pretorius

Patricia van Graan and Martin Johnson rehearsing Donizetti's *L'Elisir d'Amore*.
PHOTO Cloete Breytenbach, 1965

I cannot remember that the Eoan Group ever played to an empty house.
It was always full, extra productions had to be put on. Because if they
had six productions they had to put on four more. You see people queing
around the City Hall at the time. The Eoan Group played to capacity
houses. I mean every member of the Eoan Group was an important
member … we all became distinguished through a chorus part, a minor
part, a little any part that was given to you. I cannot remember that
the Eoan Group had ever played to an empty house, despite what was
happening on the political side around us.
  Fuad Sawyer

Yes, most of them were full houses. And they extended the season always.
Every year they would extend by a week, sometimes two weeks. We were
going to get married the December, and I got mumps, so we couldn't get
married. Then the opera season came up, so we were going to get married
in March, but they extended the season, for two weeks! And we eventually
got married, on the fourth of April. And that was during performances.
We got married, he [Lionel Fourie] did a performance, a *Traviata*
performance, and at night he did a *Rigoletto* performance.
  Ruth Fourie

The audience loved them, they were stars. They are still today. May is
still a star. You know, these people still talk about May. These were the
stars that people related to. People went especially to see Vera Gow. They
heard May was singing and they worshipped the ground that they walked
on, because those were their stars and they were what the youngsters all
aspired to. You would love to be like Vera, or love to be Frieda Koopman.
And Phillip Swales singing Sparafucile. It was just, you know, I was so in
awe of them. And Ronnie [Theys]. These people were the idols, you know,
you wanted to be like them.
  Virginia Davids

Die produksies self was partykeer wisselvallig. Die koorlede, jy weet,
as 'n mens dit nou vergelyk met die mees professionele koorlede van
byvoorbeeld Kruik, soos ons in die goeie jare gehad het, dan was hulle
natuurlik 'n bietjie stokkerig en jy kan dit verwag, dis mense wat gewerk
het, wat tyd moes opoffer, maar die koor self het goed gesing. Hulle
bewegings was partykeer nou nie so professioneel nie en ek dink as ek
dit vergelyk met die beste operas wat ons nou in Kaapstad gehad het,
soos byvoorbeeld *Tristan und Isolde*, dan is dit nie op dieselfde vlak nie,
want daar het ons die beste mense van oorsee ingevoer wat die dekor en
produksie gedoen het en dit was die mense wat in die Met beroemd is.

Vera Gow as Violetta in *La Traviata* in 1969.

Eoan was die enigste mense in daardie tyd wat opera gedoen het. So ek meen, dit moes getref het en dit hét getref. Ek meen, ons almal het altyd graag gegaan. Dit was aangenaam om te gaan, maar natuurlik, jy weet, ek hou van musiek en ek hou van opera. So dis maklik, jy weet. Maar ek dink ook die musiekmense wat ek geken het, hulle het baie dieselfde indruk gehad. Wat 'n wonderlike groep mense doen hier musiek wat ons nie self gedoen het nie.

~ *The productions themselves were sometimes of varying quality. The chorus members, you know, if one compares this with the most professional chorus members of CAPAB, for example, as we had in the good years, then they were naturally a bit stiff and you could expect that, they were working people who had to sacrifice time, but the chorus itself sang well. The movements were sometimes not so very professional and I think if I compare this with the best operas that we have had in Cape Town, such as* Tristan und Isolde, *for example, then it was not on the same level, because there we imported the best people from overseas that could do the décor and the production and they were people who were famous in the Met.*

Eoan was the only group at that time that did opera. So I think it must have had an impact and it did have an impact. I mean, we all always went

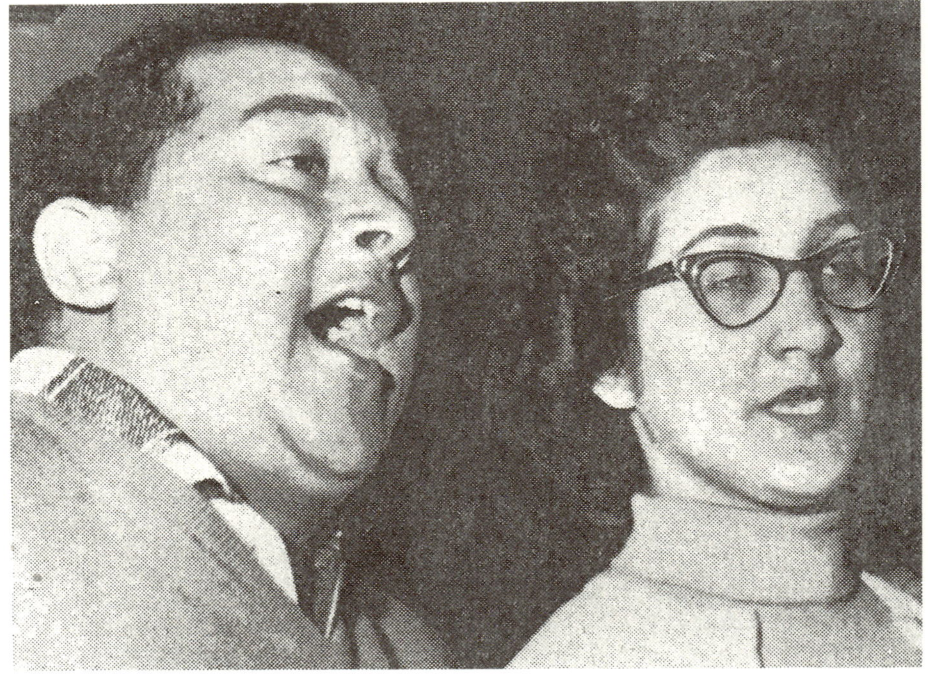

Joseph Gabriels and May Abrahamse in rehearsal.
PHOTO *Daily News*, 22 July 1960

gladly. It was pleasant to go, but naturally, you know, I like music and I like
opera. So it's easy, you know. But I also think the music people whom I knew,
they had much the same impression. What a wonderful group of people is
making music here, which we did not do ourselves.
   Pieter Kooij

Nou luister ek na 'n paar opnames … na die Eoan Groep-koor. Sjoe, dit was
nie so kwaai nie, omdat ons die eerste kleurlinge gewees wat gesing het,
verstaan, het die mense mal gegaan! Hulle sing Italiaans, ons het sommer
'tamatie' gesing, 'komkommer tamatie', jy weet sulke goed in plaas van
Italiaanse woorde. Ons het dan somtyds as ons gaan toer het hier in die
platteland of so, dan sê hulle die mense sing opera, nou wil ons wys ons
kan Italiaans praat. Nou praat ons sommer 'n lyntjie van *Traviata*. Dan sê
hulle: 'Wow, die hotnotte[1] kan darem lekker Italiaans praat!'
~ Now I listen to a few recordings … to the Eoan Group chorus. Goodness,
it was not so good, because we were the first coloureds who sang, you
understand, the people went crazy! They sing in Italian, we just sang
'tomato', 'cucumber, tomato', you know, things like that instead of Italian

---

1   Skeldnaam vir bruin mense.

*words. Sometimes when we went touring in the more outlying areas, then
they say the people are singing opera, and we want to show that we can talk
Italian. So we just say a short line from* Traviata. *Then they say: 'Wow, those
hotnotte² can talk Italian nicely!'*
   Ronald Theys

Eoan's dance section performed ballets and other dance pieces during the
Eoan seasons. Apart from performances like Stanley Glaser's *The Square*
(South Africa's first indigenous ballet), dancers were used in the operas and
musicals.

The last one I did with them was *Carmen Jones*. The production was
done by Stanley Waren and his wife. It was not a popular production.
I think they lost heavily, but the losses were always made up by the
Coloured Affairs Department. We did not know all this. And they made
a lot of money and were very specific and, as I learnt recently, some of
the principles got some of the takings. And of course there was that
odd production of *La Traviata*, so when it was on you became a Spanish
dancer. And you get Spanish dance lessons with Deanna Blacher and I
learnt very quicky so I could do many things. It is the only production
that I know of where there is dancing in.
   Peter Voges

Through the opera the State had no alternative, they had to give us
subsidies. But for the opera, not for dancing. And there we sat and at that
time the ballet section was introduced with different teachers. So if the
chairlady says, 'Mr Jacobs, I'm afraid that tonight you will have to stay
here, you were here the whole day, I'm emptying my dining room but
you'll have to rehearse the girls for that number,' then Mr Jacobs would
just have to stay. Poor Lydia and myself, we had to kill ourselves at that
branch, Wynberg and Landsdowne. We had a three-act ballet to do with
about 400 children. That was the branch. We were putting on a show at
the Landsdowne Civic, or the Luxarama. While the luck's around, you
have to stay here and rehearse these children. So the children go home
and the chairlady would give us a meal and go back into that room and
rehearse. Till 8 o'clock. But when the branch shows come, that's the
biggest headache. If that's a two-hour show and there isn't two hours,
Cecil Jacobs must dance with Lydia. We had to then work out a number
with the two of us, so the programme can stretch for two hours. So you
must know it wasn't an easy thing. And then from all the branches, the

---

2   Derogatory term for coloured people.

Ballet dancers of the Eoan Group.
PHOTO Eoan Group Archive, 1960

best children were selected to come to the Ochberg Hall. That was like a special bursary that we gave to the best children from each branch, and they do ballet and tap and a bit of everything.

Cecil Jacobs

From the 1950s to the 1970s, when Eoan's opera section flourished, drama, like dance, took a back seat, though a number of performances were given.

[The drama section] performed many plays around the town. A modern version of Jesus Christ in modern dress. I was Mary Magdalene. We didn't perform on a stage. The audience sat in a circle around us. Very interesting. *Behind the Yellow Door* by Flora Stohr in 1963. I was Sanna. Performed at the Little Theatre or the Labia Theatre in Government Avenue. There were many other plays I don't remember. There were always write-ups in the press, and I won a trophy for the best director for *Behind the Yellow Door.*

I then started learning to do stage makeup and working with the opera section doing the makeup of the main characters. This was wonderful because I made people ugly and I made them beautiful; I made them old and I made them different. Most of all I met and married my husband, Joseph. I met him with *La Bohème* and I was twenty-four years old when we got married [when they performed] *Madama Butterfly.* I was the makeup artist on one of the tours around the country.

Mabel Kester-Gabriels

For those involved in Eoan's opera, drama and dance productions, the theatre provided a magical world away from their everyday lives.

You know, I would rush home from school and get on the bus or train because the older members would do our hair, you know, and it was like make-believe. You put on makeup and you have your hair all done up and then you put on these gorgeous costumes – all recycled, by the way, from opera to opera. For me, that was absolutely magical. And then we also did performances in the old Alhambra Theatre. These old theatres, they held such a charm. You know, the really old theatres, the charm and the smell of makeup and the bustle, and the bitchiness in the dressing room, because we were young and all these old ladies … We would be intimidated by all these old ladies … the chorus ladies. They were so nasty to each other, and I loved all of this, because it was like intrigue, drama. It was so exciting. How stupid one can be when she is a child, hey. And it was really for me like stepping into this fairyland everytime I went on stage. There were a few down sides. I don't think they liked us much,

Sophia Andrews preparing her makeup for *South Pacific* in 1968.
PHOTO Supplied by Sophia Andrews

the old ladies … because they always said to me, 'Julle kinders wil alweer vir julle slim hou!' ['You children are trying to make as if you are clever again!' Because I could read music; I could read music and I could count.]

You know, we didn't know much about what was going on backstage. You just brought your own makeup along and do your hair, because nobody dresses you. And that one helped with that one's hair and you pulled up that one's zip and things like that. There weren't dressers running around. So it was very much everybody helping themselves. When I went in there for the first time, I went in as a young starry-eyed teenager and it is only when one is actually in it that you start seeing the flaws, the ugliness, but that is like that with everything. I always said to people, don't think it is a glamorous profession, it is plain hard work. And if everybody thinks it is glamorous, you put on your lashes and your makeup and everything and your hair and this glamorous dress and then, of course, once I was in it and the hard work and things like that, so [the glamour] was stripped a bit, but I enjoyed it.

Virginia Davids

Johaar Mosaval danced the lead role in Eoan's 1962 production of the ballet, *The Square*.
PHOTO Eoan Group Archive

And just talking about makeup, nowadays people use the readymade makeup which the ladies use, but in those days people used this type of thing – these came in boxes and what you used was a number five which was terrible. Number five which gave you some colour and your eyes were highlighted. And of course under the lights on the stage you really perspired like a dog. To get it off is a major job. You couldn't just go running off after a performance. You had to wipe your face with liquid paraffin. And you got number five off and number nine.
Trevor Pretorius

The Eoan Group was known as an amateur company because artists where not paid a professional fee. Throughout their existence, this has been a painful issue as Eoan's singers and dancers increasingly demanded the right to be treated and paid as professionals. The establishment of the provincial arts councils in 1963, providing professional opportunities to white artists only, did not make matters easier.

Joseph Gabriels said, 'Look, I'm not going to sing for nothing, you'd better start paying me!' I think he got something initially, but ah, we were not paid anything.
Ruth Goodwin

You know the Eoan Group was regarded as being an amateur society, amateur strictly to the name because we did not get paid. You know that makes the difference when you talk amateur and professional. So, we were amateur but the height and the standard [of our singing] was totally, totally professional.
Trevor Pretorius

During performances we got two and six for supper, everybody, twenty-five cents. We would go to the local takeaway – opposite the City Hall there was a place called Ferns. We could get quite a little bit of food for twenty-five cents there. This is late sixties, early seventies and then at the Alhambra there was another takeaway up on the corner, they knew that close to a 150 people are going to buy at two and six food, so they adjusted. You got that every night and you got transport home. You didn't get it to the theatre, but you got it home. We didn't get paid. [But for you as a performer it was about] them making money and them putting on productions. We were just a vehicle. But you went into this because there was no such thing in your life. To be performing on the City Hall stage was a big, big status.
Peter Voges

An Eoan member preparing costumes for a production.
 Cloete Breytenbach, 1965

We young ones were not really interested in the politics and why we can't
perform here or why we can't perform there. We were there to enjoy.
I mean if you think of why did we join the Eoan Group. It's a cultural
organisation. You don't get paid, so why would we join then. If it was for
the love of money, we wouldn't be there.
  Valerie Johnson

Ek het so gelag vir Mario Bierti, die *stage designer*. Ek staan een middag,
ek sê, 'Mario, are you paid well?' Hy sê, 'Well enough to buy another
drink.' En so was dit met almal wat by die Eoan Groep gewerk het. Ek weet
byvoorbeeld van die balletdansers, Henry Paulse, Achmed Okkerts, wat
maande sonder geld gegaan het, want daar was nie 'n bron van inkomste
vir die Eoan Groep nie. Maar hulle was bereid om dit te doen. En vanaand
as die gordyne oopgaan, dan het hulle met 'n wye glimlag daar gestaan,
asof hulle almal miljoenêrs is.
*~ I laughed so at Mario Bierti, the stage designer. I was standing around
one afternoon and said, 'Mario, are you paid well?' He said, 'Well enough
to buy another drink.' And that's how it was with everyone who worked with
the Eoan Group. I know, for example, of the ballet dancers, Henry Paulse,
Achmed Okkerts, who went for months without money, because there was no
source of income for the Eoan Group. But they were prepared to do this. And
tonight when the curtains open, then they were standing there with broad
smiles, as if they were all millionaires.*
  Gerald Samaai

A lot of time had been devoted [to opera but] you got nothing financial to
show for it. Maybe the soloists got paid, I don't even know. I don't think
so though. And I remember Jimmy [Momberg] and I, we worked close
together, and there came a time that Jimmy was without work and I asked
my dad don't you have a job for Jimmy because everybody had to have a
day job. Now just imagine, having a day job and singing *La Traviata* in
the evening or something like that. Having a family to feed and you were
working the whole day, whether you are a bricklayer or a street sweeper
or what. At the end of the day, at night, you put on your tails. It was also
a very leveling factor, nobody cared the hell whether you're the school
principal and whether you are a street sweeper or whatever. At night, you
go on the stage, dressed up and you're all even. And I remember singing
a lot with Cecil Tobin, he was a school principal and he sang a wonderful
Rigoletto, but there was Jimmy singing the Duke and I don't even know
whether Jimmy had passed standard eight. But we sang, we sang.
  Virginia Davids

Mario Bierti preparing scenery.
PHOTO Cloete Breytenbach, 1965

6
Magical Halls

During the early years, the Eoan Group operated from the Isaac Ochberg
Hall in Hanover Street in District Six, Cape Town. However, fifteen additional
branches had been established throughout the Cape Peninsula by the mid
1950s, offering a range of activities including ballet, folk dance, speech,
drama, singing, painting and sewing.

174

> The Eoan Group had dance schools in various areas like Salt River,
> Cape Town, Hanover Street, Maitland, Kensington, you know, all over
> the show. And they were called branches. And then on a Saturday the
> various branches in the areas had to come to a Saturday class, which
> was at Zonnebloem College [in District Six]. There we were trained to do
> examinations and the other dance forms. You know we had to do a bit
> of Greek dancing, Spanish, tap, modern dancing, all the different fields.
> If you were in Woodstock, like Salt River, then our main venue was the
> Woodstock Town Hall. Every year we had our concerts, our annual
> concerts at the Woodstock Town Hall. So that was a regular thing too.
> *Lydia Johnson*

In 1950, the Group Areas Act that consigned racial groups to different
residential and business areas was passed in parliament. Apartheid
legislation was rolled out in the subsequent decades, resulting in the
loss of freedom of movement for the Eoan Group and the coloured public
that supported them. Not only were many forced from their homes
and relocated kilometres away from the city centre, the group was also
increasingly denied entry to performance venues where they had been
performing for many years.

Eoan presented their annual opera season in March 1960 in the Cape
Town City Hall, and from June to September of that year undertook their first
tour of the country, presenting full seasons in Port Elizabeth, Durban and
Johannesburg. Going on tour with a large group that had to be housed every
night, and that performed in white areas, posed many challenges. At the
time of this tour, however, the effects of the Group Areas Act seemed to be
less tangible than during the group's second tour five years later.

> In those days [1960], if I remember correctly, [skin] colour didn't come
> into it. I remember specifically the Market Theatre. We performed there.
> Now those people organised it. And I don't know whether they had to get
> a permit, but the audience was mixed everywhere we went. I remember
> the last performance that we did in Johannesburg, it was a concert in the
> Johannesburg Town Hall. We did *Cavalleria*, amongst other things, and
> as far as I can remember, there wasn't a problem, but like I say, we were
> performing …
> *Tillie Ulster*

The Isaac Ochberg Hall in Hanover Street, District Six, was the Eoan Group's home from 1949 to 1969.
PHOTO *Africa Media Online*

> The Feathermarket [in Port Elizabeth] was interracial. In Durban,
> we performed in their City Hall, and it was interracial. We went to
> Johannesburg, everybody could come to the university Great Hall, that's
> where we had our performances. But then, people wanted more of the
> opera: 'Sorry, the hall is booked out.' The university hall was booked out.
> I mean they didn't foresee that, they had to perform more. And then I
> remember Dr Manca coming to us and saying, 'The people want us to
> sing more, and we can't go to perform at the university Great Hall.
> **Ruth Goodwin**

The 1960 country-wide tour was a financial and artistic success and
newspaper critics in the various cities wrote as many positive reviews as
Eoan held performances. They received numerous letters expressing sincere
thanks, appreciation and good wishes to Manca and the group, many
indicating that no consistent or quality opera productions were available in
their own cities at the time.

The 1960 tour group in Port Elizabeth.
PHOTO Supplied by Patricia van Graan

I enjoyed the tours that we had, which also was a lot of work. We had to go and sing in different places, Feathermarket Hall and the City Hall in Joburg and so on. We travelled. But we didn't mind because we were spreading the word: 'Give us a chance, then we can show you'. That is what Manca's motto was: 'Give them a chance, then they will show you what they can do'.

Sophia Andrews

Manca was very strict [on the tours]. And also we always had somebody in charge. A man would be in charge of the males and a lady would be in charge of the ladies. After performances the guys want to go somewhere, they want to go party and all the rest like that. You know, you're supposed to go and sleep and what not in a hotel. And you sit around and then sometimes, 'Come to my room and we have a few doppies [drinks], hey?' and things like that, you know. So they got up to a lot of mischief. You are so worked up, you can't just go along and sleep, no, and if you just sit around and chat and laugh and have a drink and so on, you know. It was nice, I really enjoyed it.

May Abrahamse

Eoan's principal singers in front of the City Hall in Port Elizabeth while on tour in 1960. From left to right: Joseph Gabriels, Ruth Goodwin, Sophia Andrews, Robert Trussell, Winifred Domingo, Gerald Arendse, Lionel Fourie, May Abrahamse and Benny Arendse.
PHOTO Supplied by Benny Arendse, 1960

178

The Eoan Group's performances of ballets, dramas, choral concerts,
operettas and grand opera were mostly held in the City Hall in Cape Town.
For most artists, the City Hall remained their venue of choice. The Ochberg
Hall in Hanover Street, District Six was bequeathed to the group by the estate
of Isaac Ochberg, a Cape Town businessman, philanthropist and Zionist who
was born in the Ukraine and came to South Africa in 1894. The Ochberg Hall
functioned as the Group's administrative base and rehearsal hall.

Initially, no permits were needed for the group to perform in the Cape Town
City Hall. From the 1960s onwards, however, not only did they have to apply
for permits, but separate seats, entrances and amenities were allocated for
whites and coloureds.

In 1973, the Cape Town City Council informed the Eoan Group that the
City Hall was to be renovated to its original design of 1905. The implication
was that the venue would, after renovations, no longer be suitable for staging
operas or musicals. For Eoan, this meant that the City Hall was out of
bounds for any future opera productions. The Nico Malan Theatre on Cape
Town's Foreshore was a whites-only building and Eoan had to go elsewhere
to perform their operas.

The Cape Town City Hall in the 1960s.

G.C. 188

REPUBLIEK VAN SUID-AFRIKA.   REPUBLIC OF SOUTH AFRICA.

Lêer No.
File No. 32/1/4584/4

DEPARTEMENT VAN GEMEENSKAPSBOU.
DEPARTMENT OF COMMUNITY DEVELOPMENT.

PERMIT.

06352

[Artikel 18 van die Wet op Groepsgebiede, 1957 (Wet No. 77 van 1957)].
[Section 21 of the Group Areas Act, 1966 Act No. 36 of 1966.

Uitgereik op las van die Minister/Minister se gedelegeerde* handelende ingevolge 'n delegasie van bevoegdhede
Issued by direction of the Minister/Minister's delegate acting under a delegation of powers in terms of section twenty-two of*
kragtens artikel *negentien* van die Wet op Groepsgebiede, 1957 (Wet No. 77 van 1957).
the Group Areas Act, 1966 (Act No. 36 of 1966.

1. Uitgereik aan
Issued to

   MEMBERS OF THE COLOURED GROUP AS INDICATED IN PARAGRAPH 4.

2. Doel waarvoor uitgereik **to lease and occupy on 26th.27th & 31st August,1968;**
Purpose for which issued
   1st. 3rd. 7th to 10th, 16th to 18th, 21st 22nd. & 30th September 1968;
   1st. 3rd. 5th to 13th, 16th to 31st October,1968; 1st & 2nd Nov. 1968,
   for the purpose of rehearsing and presenting three operas during the
   Eoan Group's 1968 Opera Season.

3. Beskrywing van grond of perseel
Description of land or premises

   CITY HALL, CAPE TOWN.

4. Voorwaardes waaraan hierdie permit onderworpe is
Conditions to which this permit is subject

   (a) The number of Coloureds that may be admitted to the operas each
   night shall not exceed the number of seats allocated to those
   Coloureds who attend the Municipal symphony concerts;

   (b) The seats allocated to Coloureds who attend the Municipal
   symphony concerts shall be used by the Coloureds who attend the
   operas.

   (c) Separate entrances, exits, ticket boxes and toilet facilities
   shall be used by Whites and Coloureds.

5. In die geval van 'n verkryging van onroerende goed of die okkupasie van grond of 'n perseel verval hierdie permit
In the case of the acquisition of immovable property or the occupation of land or premises this permit will lapse if the
as die betrokke onroerende goed nie verkry of die grond of perseel nie ingevolge die permit geokkupeer word binne
immovable property concerned is not acquired or the land or premises occupied in terms of this permit within

vanaf die datum hiervan nie.
from the date hereof.

Plek
Place

Datum

Gemagtigde Uitreikingsbeampte.
Authorized Issuing Officer.

*Skrap wat nie van toepassing is nie.
Delete whatever is not applicable.

DEPT. VAN GEMEENSKAPSBOU
DIE STREEKVERTEENWOORDIGER
PRIVAATSAK/PRIVATE BAG 9027
27 -5- 1968
KAAPSTAD/CAPE TOWN
THE REGIONAL REPRESENTATIVE
DEPT. OF COMMUNITY DEVELOPMENT

A permit issued to the Eoan Group in 1968 for their opera season which was to be held in the Cape Town City Hall.
SOURCE   Eoan Group Archive

nou 'n konsertsaal wees. So in die operas het hulle altyd gordyne makeer, ek dink dit was die rede. En toe sing ons in die Sea Point stadsaal, en daardie was nou nie rêrig vir opera nie. En ons het eens op 'n tyd in die Alhambra gesing, en daar het ons 'n musical gedoen, *South Pacific*. Dit was 'n groot geleentheid om daar te sing, want dis mos nou modern en al die tipe goeters is daar, jou kleedkamers en almal daai.

~ In those days the City Hall, how does one say, they also took the City Hall away from the Eoan Group. Not because of the apartheid, there were curtains there, then they took down the curtains, and they said it was now going to be a concert hall. So in the operas they always needed curtains, I think that was the reason. And then we sang in the Sea Point town hall, and that was not really meant for opera. And at one time we sang at the Alhambra, and there we did a musical, South Pacific. *It was a great occasion to sing there, because it's so modern and all the different kind of equipment stuff is there, your dressing rooms and all.*

    Ronald Theys

The Eoan Group then moved to the Alhambra, but it became whites-only, and then to the Luxorama. And then the Joseph Stone was built, so they went with that and opened in Athlone. But that did not work very well, because people did not enjoy going there, they enjoyed going to town or to Wynberg. It was a strange place, it was not very welcoming. Suddenly the world changed for me. I made the decision to maintain contacts with white performers, where I was not treated differently at all, and made conscious contact all the time. But we made contact with them, the dancers, singers, actors whatever they were, I did that.

    Peter Voges

Until 1969, the Eoan Group's activities were central to Cape Town's cultural life. Not only did the group perform annually in venues in the city, but rehearsals took place in either the Ochberg Hall in District Six or Delta House in Bree Street in the city centre. On 21 November 1969, the Eoan Group Cultural Centre – consisting of the Joseph Stone Auditorium, several studios, practice rooms and offices – was inaugurated. The Cape Town Municipality donated 3.25 acres of land in Athlone and the main financial contributors to the building of the centre were the South African Government (R120 000), the Joseph Stone Foundation (R100 000), The Bernard van Leer Foundation from the Netherlands (R34 000) and the Eoan Group (R33 000), bringing the total cost of the building to R287 000. Two years later, in 1971, the Nico Malan Theatre, a whites-only building, was built at a cost of R11 million, fully funded by the government.

The move to Athlone is indicative of how the forced removal of people under apartheid could and did disempower them culturally. Moving away from the city centre also meant moving out of the centre of Cape Town's cultural activities.

182

I remember George Manuel was a journalist, he wrote about all these things. The two of us were sitting in that hall, at the opening night, we were invited. And I looked at this place and I didn't like it. The Joseph Stone, oooh I don't like it! That's for the coloured people!
   Ruth Goodwin

Oh I hated [the Joseph Stone], I think we all did. Going to a prison down there, that building, I think it's a horrible building, I don't like it very much. It's so dismal and dull and awful. Then we lost a lot of our followers because they turned against us because when we moved away from the City Hall, because all those years it was like our home, you know. We performed there all the time. We looked upon it as our home, the City Hall.
   Patricia van Graan

It was nice to be [in the Joseph Stone Theatre] and to go from your studio straight to the stage and do your productions. You know, it was a very professional theatre. It had everything that a professional theatre had, so it was something new and exciting and we didn't mind to stay hours there and work.
   Lydia Johnson

Well, that Joseph Stone is part of my bricks that I worked for. I was glad in a way that we had a home that we could go to. If there was no other venue for us, we could play boss in our own place. So therefore I was happy with the Joseph [Stone]. I didn't mind where I used to sing, although they tried to make that hall almost like the City Hall, with the orchestra pit. We have got a orchestra pit and everything. I didn't mind, we had our music, our rooms where we could go and practice in and it didn't really matter to me. As I say, we were all very happy when we had a home that we could call a home, because drifting from one place to the other is not a good thing. We had a stage where you could practice on, we had an orchestra that you could bring in. There was everything for us there.
   Sophia Andrews

That is our building. It's a community building, ja. And the schools have their annual concerts and they have gospel concerts, that kind of thing. I

EOAN GROUP
CULTURAL CENTRE

INCORPORATING
JOSEPH STONE
AUDITORIUM

MESSAGE FROM THE EOAN GROUP TRUST

Outstanding progress has been achieved since the Trust was formed early in 1964, in establishing the Eoan Group as a natural focus for the further cultural advancement of the Republic's Cape Coloured Community and the first major complex of the Group's new Cultural Centre at Athlone incorporating the Joseph Stone Auditorium is to be handed over for the Group's use shortly after the end of their present Opera Season. The complex will operate as a teaching, training and experimental centre for Opera, Ballet, Music and Drama.

The Trust, thanks to all who have donated so generously to capital funds, has been able to finance all but a small amount of the R305,000 required for the building and equipping of the present Athlone complex.

Concurrently the Trust is seeking to build up the level of its Endowment Funds which if firm promises are included, now total about R110,000.

The cost of staffing and administering the New Cultural Centre and of expanding their performing arts activities will be high and the Trust is seeking to increase the Endowment Fund to the R150,000 level. This is a significant challenge to all who have the well-being of the Group at heart.

R40,000 are needed to make up the final amount. Will you assist?

BOODSKAP VAN DIE EOAN GROUP-TRUST

Sedert die Trust vroeg in 1964 gestig is, is uitstekende vooruitgang gemaak in die pogings om die Eoan-groep daar te stel as 'n natuurlike brandpunt vir die voortgesette kulturele bevordering van die Republiek se Kaapse Kleurlinggemeenskap, en die eerste vername kompleks van die Groep se nuwe Kultuursentrum te Athlone, waarin die Joseph Stone-auditorium behels word, sal kort na die einde van hul huidige operaseisoen vir gebruik deur die Groep oorhandig word. Die kompleks sal dien as 'n onderrig-, opleiding- en eksperimentele sentrum vir Opera, Ballet, Musiek en Drama.

Danksy al diegene wat so mildelik bygedra het tot die kapitaalfonds, was die Trust in staat om alles, op 'n klein deeltjie na, van die R305,000 vir die bou en toerusting van die huidige Athlone-kompleks te finansier.

Terselfdertyd poog die Trust om die stand van sy skenkingsfonds op te bou en, met beloftes van firmas ingesluit, beloop dit tans R110,000.

Die koste om die nuwe Kultuursentrum van personeel te voorsien en dit te administreer en ook die uitvoerende kunsbedrywighede uit te brei, sal hoog wees en die Trust poog om die skenkingsfonds tot 'n vlak van R150,000 op te stoot. Hierdie feit bied 'n betekenisvolle uitdaging aan almal wat die welvaart van die Groep op die hart dra.

R40,000 word benodig om die finale bedrag te bereik. Sal u hierin help?

The Joseph Stone Auditorium became Eoan's home in 1969. The group is still housed in this building.
SOURCE Eoan Group Archive

The former Nico Malan theatre, now Artscape.
PHOTO Hannes van Heerden, 1971, Documentation Centre, JS Gericke Library, Stellenbosch University

think a lot of it had to do with Shafiek [Rajap's] ethic, which is that this is
a building for the community. So that was a big turnaround from what it
used to be to what it is today, and yes, that building is theirs.
  Jocylyn Liedeman

The Joseph Stone became the centre point of activity, that is out in
Athlone. Again, very often when we drive through there and elsewhere
and we would say, 'Oh that pocket was for these people and that pocket
for that people.' It suited the kind of thinking of the government of the
time of that day. Because they would say, 'Put a building there, by the
people for the people.' So many people were within walking distance of
the Joseph Stone and they did attend, yes they did attend. But the big
performances was when they went to the City Hall. We did not get into
the City Hall that time. Later on there was the Nico Malan – that was
no-go. I mean you could walk past the Nico Malan, the building which
is now Artscape, but there was no way that they could perform there,
because of the restrictions.
  Ronnie Samaai

When I left [the Joseph Stone Theatre] it was still a new building,
everything was intact and for me it was so charming, everything was

Eoan's soloists were often invitied to present operatic concerts in cities further afield. They travelled to places such as Port Elizabeth and Johannesburg, but also sang in bigger towns in rural areas such as Oudtshoorn. In 1970 they presented a concert in the Cango Caves, organised by the Minister of Coloured Affairs, Dr ID du Plessis. From left to right: Martin Johnson, Jimmy Momberg, accompanist (name unknown), Dr ID du Plessis, Patricia van Graan, Ismail Sydow, Benny Arendse, Yvonne Jansen, Gerald Samaai and Cecil Tobin in the Cango Caves in 1970.
PHOTO Eoan Group Archive

so enchanting, when you switch on the lights for your makeup, you know. It was difficult to go back and to see the way it had deteriorated there, the upkeep was zilch and because that was actually a wonderful little theatre, it has everything. It has dressing rooms and I remember I said to Sidwell [Hartman] I don't have the courage to see that place alone tonight. And we went together and I was very, very sad. Lots of memories, good memories, but also sadness about the place, about what it could have been.
Virginia Davids

When they opened up the Nico Malan for all races, I didn't go. I said I'll go when I feel like it. You know, there are some people who have resisted going there up to this day. If I think how much they are missing.
Dirk Alexander

Having been denied access to professional performance opportunities in South Africa, some of Eoan's artists pursued training and performing opportunities abroad. Among them were Joseph Gabriels, Gordon Jephtas, Patricia van Graan, Vera Gow, Fuad Sawyer and Charles de Long.

If [Joseph Gabriels] didn't go, he would not have been able to sing. And that's where he stayed. His family was there, his family is still there [in Italy], his wife. And he used to come back to South Africa every year for a holiday. But he came one year, and he says, 'Ruth, I've been down there to the Nico Malan, and I've asked them whether I could perform. And they refused.' You see? And that really hurt him, because by now he was a trained singer, and he had this magnificent voice.
Ruth Goodwin

On 5 February 1971, Joseph Gabriels made his debut at the Metropolitan Opera House in New York as Canio in Leoncavallo's *I Pagliacci* and became the first South African to sing in this prestigious venue. This was, however, his only performance there. The advertisement in the *New York Times* called him 'the South African Caruso' – Gabriels's uncanny physical likeness to the short and rotund Caruso, who made this role famous, is indeed striking.

Then they got him, through contacts, a performance at the Met, as Canio in *Pagliacci*. And you know, I said to the Smiths [they are] digging his grave, he cannot sing Canio at the Met, at the standard that it is. Because don't forget, it is a tradition from Caruso down, all the great tenors. And you put a somewhat inexperienced, I'm sorry to say it, little Cape coloured

Joseph Gabriels in costume for his performance as Canio in *I Pagliacci* in 1971.
PHOTO Supplied by Mabel Kester-Gabriels

"Singing has done me the world of good and it should be encouraged more in schools, not just on secondary level but also on primary level," Joey said in an interview to Alpha. Despite

★ ★ ★ ★ ★

Joey Gabriels: His particular blend of talent and

Newspaper clippings about Joseph Gabriels's performances abroad.
source Mabel Kester-Gabriels

who was very fat, that's why they gave him that role [because of his physical resemblance to Caruso]. He really was a lyric tenor, he was not a dramatic tenor anyway. You are killing him! Because he will never, ever have another chance, because he's not up to it. Why don't you rather help him in the smaller way to come out, to get experience, but you cannot launch somebody at the Met. And of course, it was just as I was saying. They thought I was being nasty. Well, I was just telling the truth!

The Smiths, the [South African] consul [were pushing for that]. He was the friend of an agent in Milano, and this agent was a friend of Rudolph Bing's [of the Metropolitan Opera], and through this agent who was a friend of Bing's they nagged him: South African coloured, also politically, slightly pushed a chance. So he said, 'All right, I'll give him one performance of *Pagliacci*.' I said to him, 'You are doing the wrong thing, you're not helping him, you're doing absolutely the wrong thing.' I don't know if they thought I was being bitchy or nasty or something, but I was just telling the truth, because I by that time had been in the business a long time and I knew exactly what the set-up was. And I knew that wouldn't work. He sang it, and he left. And nobody ever gave him another chance. Nothing. Nothing. He went back to, I think to Germany. His contract was not renewed, and then, I don't know what happened.

Emma Renzi

I left the country and I went to England. My friend Jenny Major, who played the violin in the Cape Town orchestra, she's an English girl, and when all this apartheid started, she said, 'Patricia you have to leave and go overseas, you'll have more opportunity over there and get some proper good training.'

The apartheid was awful, having to perform to separate audiences, at the time you wanted people to be together, you know, people are people, not segregated and so she started me off, started the ball rolling and spurred me on and we ran lots of concerts to gather some money together. Dr Manca tried to talk me out of it. He said, 'Patricia why'd you have to go overseas when you can be a big fish in a small pond? There you'll be a small fish in a big pond.' So I said, 'Dr Manca I want to go 'cause I feel this is my destiny, my chance to go now and I've always wanted to travel.' So anyway, they couldn't persuade me, so off I went, and I won a British scholarship actually. I had to audition in Stellenbosch, it was somewhere, I forget where, it's a long time ago.

Patricia van Graan

When I was in London [in 1975] I met Claudio Abbado, and he encouraged me to go for a scholarship. And when Gordon Jephtas came down to

Judith Bailey in Drury Lane, London in 1975.
PHOTO Eoan Group Archive

South Africa a couple of months or a year or so after we've done the tour in London, I was also on the verge of divorcing. And then Gordon encouraged me to go and at least go away for a year and go and get experience. I went for an audition in La Scala. The Italian Consulate they got me there. And then at La Scala they said that I could come back, but I must first go to the conservatoire there at the Giuseppi Verdi. And then after a while I can come back [to La Scala]. Because I suppose they wanted their way of teaching and things like that. I liked it in Italy. Just for one year to study over there. [The teaching] wasn't much different from what we had here. Because Alessandro Rota was a good teacher and the other difference was that most of their work was all in Italian. So you were forced to learn Italian.

When I came back from Italy I went to CAPAB. Then they said I could join. But I explained to them that I'm a Seventh Day Adventist, I'll be prepared to do any other shows during the week, but not shows on a Saturday and Friday night shows. Then they didn't accept me as a soloist, had to go into the choir, which I didn't have a problem with, 'cause you start crawling anyway first. You know what was very disappointing was that I explained to them, I explained to them and I said but you have Manuel Escorcio who is also Seventh Day Adventist. So I said it to Christine Reynolds. She was very, very upset. She was very sad, because she was also one of my [teachers], she was very upset that CAPAB wouldn't accept me.

And then Ronnie Theys also used to say, 'Judith, hoekom kom jy nie?' So I said, 'Jy wiet ek het my geloof baie lief.' [Judith, why don't you come?' So I said, 'You know I love my faith very much.] And until they can make provision I'm sure the Lord will help me, because I'm standing up for Him. But it would've cost me that I would practice at night and what would happen to my sons? I'm a parent alone. And things like not having a car, going to live in Mitchells Plain, travelling. There was a time when the train is travelling late at night from town to Mitchells Plain. I had about three or four rehearsals with them until they said, no they can't accept me anymore, because of my religion I'll not be able to practice. So I said, 'Well, I'm available anytime.' So, there were times when they required my assistance.

Judith Bailey

I've had a good career in this country and I chose to stay. And [my singing students said] 'but Ma,' they call me Ma, 'why didn't you go?' And I said, 'Well, if I had gone, you wouldn't have been here.' If I'd gone, they wouldn't have been here and yes, it was very hard for me. But you know, standing in the wings, I knew the operas by heart, I knew every note,

because we played them on the old LPs, cracking on a Sunday afternoon
and it was just magical. As I say, at that stage I always thought that I would
leave the country, but I didn't think I would make a career and it took
somebody like Valerie du Toit, who said to me, 'You know, you can make a
career.' And I said, 'How, where, what in this country?'

     Virginia Davids

Gordon Jephtas, Eoan's répétiteur, left South Africa in 1966 to pursue a
successful career as a répétiteur in Europe and America, working with artists
like Renata Tebaldi, Plácido Domingo and Elena Suliotis. He also assisted
various conductors, among them James Levine and Nello Santi, for opera
companies such as the Chicago Lyric Opera and the Metropolitan Opera in
New York. He often visited South Africa for short periods during which he
poured much of his energy into the Eoan Group, training individual singers.
On 3 March 1979, Jephtas and May Abrahamse presented a lieder recital in
the Nico Malan Opera House. In the programme notes to this performance,
he wrote about his experience as musician abroad:

> If I had not worked with the Eoan Group in the operas *Traviata*, *Rigoletto*,
> *Cavalleria*, *Butterfly*, *Bohème*, *Trovatore*, *Carmen* and *L'Elisir d'Amore*, I do
> not think I could have survived the brutality one encounters entering the
> international field.

In August 1975, Eoan was invited to participate in the International Festival
of Youth Orchestras and Performing Arts held in London and Aberdeen,
Scotland. Since it was a Youth Festival, the members chosen to travel had to
be younger than twenty-six years of age. The full company consisted of forty-
two people, of which Manca selected a choir comprising twenty-six young
singers, four guest singers (Ronald Theys, Gerald Samaai, Vera Gow and
May Abrahamse), six dancers and six administrative staff, including Manca
and his wife Minke, Ismail Sydow and his wife Carmen, Eoan's voice trainer
Alessandro Rota and Eoan's accompanist Regina Devereux.

> Whilst being in the festival we made friends with so many other people.
> Today there is a world famous conductor that we performed alongside,
> Claudio Abbado – he's a conductor. Simon Rattle, who today is Sir Simon
> Rattle, and those were all the people that we met. And the audience
> was jam-packed. As we arrived back in South Africa it was a complete
> new world, besides just looking at the aspect of music. Coming out of
> political South Africa where one race went the one way and the other
> race went the other way, coming there and seeing white people sweeping

Gordon Jephtas in 1979.
PHOTO Eoan Group Archive

The group departing South Africa for their tour of the UK in 1975.
PHOTO *Rapport Ekstra*, 21 September 1975

the streets, this was foreign to us. We practically grew used to the idea
after three weeks. We had lots of free time, we rehearsed very well. We
also performed in Glasgow and at His Majesty's theatre and the Prince of
Wales theatre where at the time some of the very top dignitaries that we
had met was. And what we had seen was the Queen Mother, even if she
just passed us by, but we were sort of face to face, and that was a great
opportunity. Well for myself, just being very young at about nineteen
years old where most of the things was absorbed and out by the other
ear. Thirty years later we think, wow, but we were there. So as a young
person and as an opera singer the world was opened with that tour of the
Eoan Group.

    Fuad Sawyer

Dit was nogal 'n groot geleentheid en dit was 'n eer, man. En nou reis
ons eerste Bloemfontein toe, om daar ook 'n konsert te gee. Nou moet jy
weet, nou is dit net Afrikaners, jong, ons is mos nou in die apartheidsera.
Maar dit was iets nuuts vir ons om nou in 'n hotel te wees – baie van
ons was nog nie in 'n hotel nie. En ons vreet ons dik en ons word geskel
ons moenie so baie eet nie. Ons is nie gewoond dit nie. Ná daardie toe
reis ons op Pretoria toe, na die ambassadeur se huis en ek kan al sê,
daardie tyd was ek 'n groot drinker gewees en dis mos nou verniet! Jy
weet as iets verniet is, dan oordoen jy jouself. Ja, maar ons het dit geniet.
Daarvandaan toe gaan ons Engeland toe. Toe stel hulle my aan om die
opening van die fees te doen. Jy weet, daar was mense van verskillende
lande gewees. Wat so snaaks gewees het, as ons by die ontbytplek kom,
dan staan al die verskillende lande in hulle lyne. Nou kyk jy rond dan sien
jy daardie is mos Chinees, jy sien daar is nou Ghananians, hulle lyk soos
Mexikaans, hulle lyk soos Japannees. Nou kyk hulle vir ons aan. Ons het
die hele United Nations! Want die ouens vra waar is ons dan vandaan, jy
weet? En wat is so lekker gewees, ons kan met wit girls praat, man. En jy
kan 'n wit girl uitgeneem het, en dis nou iets groots vir jou, joe! Jy kan dit
nie glo nie!

    Almal daardie dinge was kwaai gewees. Ons was geneem na die South
Africa House, 'n De Wet-ou was die ambassadeur gewees, en het ons
boerewors geëet en gebraai daar. Maar jy loop daar, dan staan daar nog
altyd 'Whites', 'Non-whites'. Ja, jy kan nie braai by die whites nie. Toe reis
ons af van Skotland, per trein tien uur ry jy na Londen toe. En toe ons in
Londen kom, toe ontmoet ons 'n ou, Rolf was sy naam, ja, hy't sommer
nou kennis gemaak met ons. Saans dan sit ons so en drink en dan vra
hy ons vrae en dan maak hy Suid-Afrika sleg, man. 'Don't you think this
and don't you think that?' Sommige van ons was uitsprekend gewees, en
sommige het maar net hulle monde gehou. En twee dae later, toe verdwyn

hy sommer en toe dink ons hy was 'n spioen daarso om vir ons dop te
hou en uit te vra. En toe ons eendag kom toe protesteer daar so mense
teen Suid-Afrika by die konsertsaal, toe praat die Suid-Afrikaanse media
met ons en sê, 'Sê vir die mense dit is nie so nie, dat hulle sê nou ons is so
behandel in Suid Afrika.' En nou sê ons nee ons sê maar niks …

*~ It was a great occasion and an honour, man. And so we travelled first
to Bloemfontein, to give a concert there too. And you must realise, there
it was just Afrikaners, I'm telling you, this is the apartheid era. But it
was something new for us to be in a hotel – many of us had never been in
a hotel. We stuffed ourselves with food and we were scolded not to eat so
much. We were not used to this. After that we travelled up to Pretoria, to
the ambassador's home, and I can tell you I was a big drinker in those days
and it was all free! You know if something is free you overdo it. Yes, but we
enjoyed it. From there we went to England. Then they appointed me to do the
opening of the festival. You know, there were people from different countries.
What was so funny was, when we came to the breakfast place, then all the
different countries were standing in their queues. You look around and see
those are Chinese, you see there are Ghanaians, those look like Mexicans,
they look like Japanese. And they look at us. We had the whole United
Nations! Because the guys asked us where we're from, you know? And what
was so nice, we could talk to white girls, man. And you could take a white girl
out, and that was something big for you, I'm telling you! You can't believe it!*

*All those things were intense. We were taken to South Africa House, a
De Wet guy was the ambassador, and we had South African sausage and
barbeque there. But you walk around, there are still 'Whites', 'Non-whites'
signs. Yes, you could not barbeque with the whites. Later we travelled down
from Scotland by train, ten hours to London. And when we got to London we
were met by a guy, his name was Rolf, yes, he just got to know us just then. In
the evenings we would be sitting and drinking and he would ask us questions
and he would run South Africa down, man. 'Don't you think this and don't
you think that?' Some of us were outspoken, and some just kept their mouths
shut. And two days later he simply disappeared and we think he was a spy
there just to keep an eye on us and ask us questions. And one day when we
arrived there were people protesting against South Africa at the concert hall,
then the South African media spoke to us and said, 'Tell the people it's not
like that, that they are saying we are treated like that in South Africa.' And so
we said no we're not saying anything …*

Ronald Theys

Wonderlike ondervinding, want eerste ding wat ons opgelet het toe ons
nou by Heathrow land, toe's ek verstom om te sien dat mense met 'n baie
ligte vel is besig om vensters te was en so aan. Ons was nooit daaraan

The Eoan Group Choir with soloists, conducted by Joseph Manca, in one of their performances
in the UK, 1975.
PHOTO Eoan Group Archive

blootgestel nie en dit was die heel eerste ding wat ek opgeneem het. Ek
het ook ontdek dat in die vliegtuig self, was dit heel anders, want kyk,
ons het grootgeraak diep, diep in die apartheid-era. En vir my was dit net
anders. Ek hou nie daarvan om terug te blik na wat gebeur het nie. Ek is
iemand wat wil vorentoe beweeg, maar toe het ons in Engeland gekom,
posh hotel, die Penta Hotel, een van die groot hotelle, vyfster hotelle in
Londen. Ons het darem al met 'n mes en vurk geëet by die huis, maar dit
was nou luuks, ek meen ons was nie gewoond aan daai tipe behandeling
nie. Mense van die anti-apartheidbeweging in Engeland het probeer om
met ons in aanraking te kom en so 'n bietjie politiek te praat, maar ons
was gewaarsku om nie in daai rigting te gesels met enige persoon nie.

Die bestuur van die Eoan, wat saam met ons was – dis nou natuurlik
Manca en Sydow en Rota-hulle – het vir ons gevra om nie enige
kommentaar te lewer oor onse land nie. Voor ons Suid-Afrika verlaat
het, was ons by die konsulaat se huis, Sir James Bottomley, waar ons ook
uitgevind het dat die jeugorkes, Suid-Afrikaanse jeugorkes, gaan saam

met ons en toe moes ons eers meng hierso en later toe voor ons weggaan,
want Sir James Bottomley sê, 'Julle gaan nie na my land toe 'n gesplete
geselskap nie. Julle gaan saam wees as een, almal Suid-Afrikaners.' En so't
ek baie mense ontmoet, trompetspelers en vioolspelers wat saam met my
daar was.

*~ Wonderful experience, because the first thing we noticed when we landed
at Heathrow, I was astounded to see that people with very light skins were
busy washing windows and so on. We were never exposed to that and it was
the very first thing that I observed. I also discovered that it was very different
in the plane itself, because look, we grew up deep, deep in the apartheid
era. And for me it was just very different. I don't like looking back on what
happened. I'm someone who wants to move on, but then we arrived in
England, posh hotel, the Penta Hotel, one of the big hotels, five-star hotels
in London. We had eaten with a knife and fork at home, but this was now
luxury, I mean, we were not used to that type of treatment. People from the
anti-apartheid movement in England did try to get in touch with us to talk
politics a little, but we were warned not to let the talk with any person go in
that direction.*

*The management of Eoan that was with us – which was naturally
Manca and Sydow and Rota – asked us not to make any comments about
our country. Before we left South Africa we were at the home of the consul,
Sir James Bottomley, where we also found out that the youth orchestra,
the South African youth orchestra, was going with us and so we first had
to mingle here and later before we left, because Sir James Bottomley said,
'You are not going to my country as a split company. You are going together
as one, all South Africans.' And I met so many people, trumpet players and
violinists who were with me there.*

   John van der Ross

7
Supporting Roles

Tracing the trajectory of the varying support levels the group enjoyed over the years is a telling representation of its history.

[My mother] always took an extra shirt or two along because if he [Manca] would get terribly wet he would change, yes. He perspired quite a lot when he was conducting and he would change. She looked after him, incredibly supportive wife, an incredible mother. My mother loved my father very much. And so this was his life, so it was her life and we all had to fall in. It is the way it worked.

Ruth Grevler-Manca

Charles [my husband] was a great lover of music. The interest that he had in what I was doing was wonderful. He was always there for me. So I must say thank you to him also.

[He used to go to] rehearsals and transport everybody home. We had no cars, I think Charles was about the only person who had a car, and after rehearsals take them home. But ah, he did it for the love of it. At the time when I performed in the City Hall, everybody could come. Black, white, we had Italians, we had Afrikaners, who are great lovers of opera. And the Jewish people. And you know, there was never place in that City Hall, that place was packed out every night. It ran for very long and it had to be extended. So [in the early days], everybody could come. Fine, we go and perform in Port Elizabeth. That was wonderful, the people they've never experienced coloured people singing grand opera the way we did. I mean, you must read some of the write-ups, of all these people, what they wrote about the singers and so on.

Ruth Goodwin

I was nervous to tell my parents that I had decided to join the Eoan Group. I came from a religious household and most of what we did revolved around the church, so my announcement that I had joined a secular group did not go down very well. But I could not see what harm I was doing, so I accepted the reprimands, but did not back down. They finally came to accept it.

Joan Watson

My husband was interested in the group, and he didn't belong to any branch activity, but he was interested in the group, and he would take me to wherever I had to be. And when we had a show, the costumes had to come to my home, they couldn't remain at the City Hall. Then we used to bring the rails at one, two o'clock in the morning after the show's over.

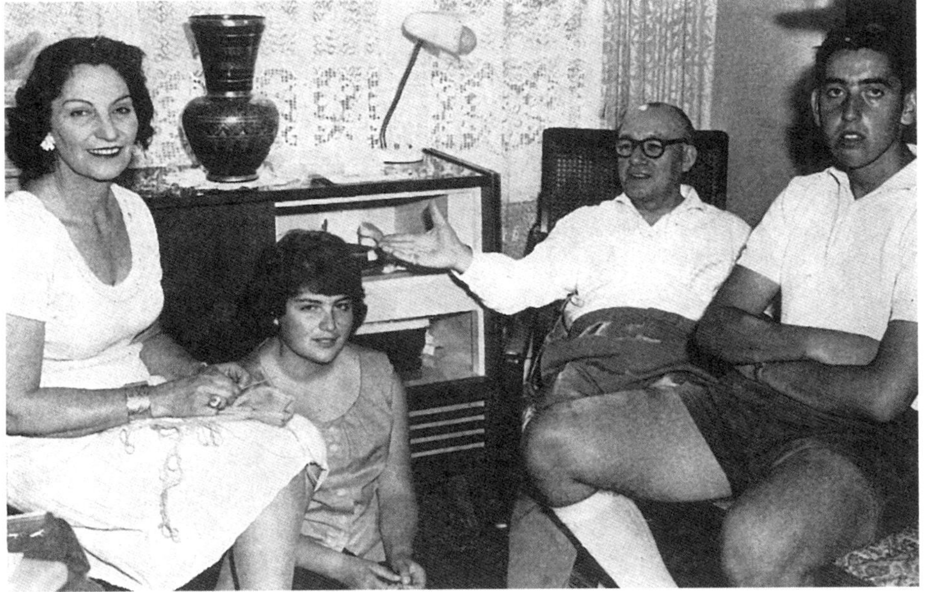

Joseph Manca and his family in 1962. From left to right: Minke Manca, Ruth Manca (15), Joseph Manca and Leonard Manca (16).
 Supplied by Ruth Grevler-Manca

Bring it to my house, and it stays there and that sort of thing. So he was always very helpful.
Alethea Jansen

Ek sê altyd my groot sukses was die omstandighede waarin ek opgegroei het. Ek het twee broers wat albei in musiek gekwalifiseerd is. As ek probleme gehad het, kan ek altyd hardloop, ek sê, 'Ronnie just play this phrase for me. I'm struggling with the top Cs. Give me a couple of scales there.' Of ek hardloop oor na my oudste broer toe – ons sê hom 'Boeta' – en meeste van die tyd as ek kans gekry het, ons bly almal naby mekaar, het ek maar saam met hulle ook gewerk. So ek was een van daardie bevoorregtes op daardie gebied.
~ I always say my great success was the circumstances in which I grew up. I have two brothers who both have music qualifications. If I had problems I could always run to one and say, 'Ronnie just play this phrase for me. I'm struggling with the top Cs. Give me a couple of scales there.' Or I could run to my oldest brother – we call him 'Boeta' – and most of the time when I had a chance, we live close to one another, I also went to work with them. So I was one of the privileged ones in that respect.
Gerald Samaai

Ja, so opera is my eerste liefde. My vrou sê somtyds vir my, 'Jong, hoe lief is jy vir my?' Dan sê ek, 'Luister, laat ek jou gou vertel: dis God eerste, dan musiek en dan jy en die kinders en die honde en die katte en so gaan ons aan.' Maar musiek is my voorliefde. Jy kon nie net daar aansluit by die Eoan Groep nie. Dit was soortvan 'n prestasie om te behoort aan so 'n organisasie. Daar waar ek grootgeraak het in Kensington was ek so te sê die enigste operasanger. Ek moes Saterdae rondhardloop seker drie tot vier kerke om te gaan sing vir troues. Sonder geld en dan moet jy nog op tyd wees. En al wat jy kry is natuurlik 'n uitnodiging dat jy kan kom eet in die aand. Dit was maar so, geld was nooit die kwessie nie. Ons het een keer so 'n vraag gevra in 'n groot vergadering. Wanneer word ons dan betaal om opera te sing? Dit was Dokter Manca, en ek haal aan, wat gesê het, 'Die dag as julle gaan sing vir geld, dan gaan die liefde vir musiek by die venster uit.' Ek het dit nogal ondervind, want ek het ná daai vir 'n hele paar streeksrade gaan sing, professioneel, en ek het eendag so stilgesit en, 'Ai, die is maar net nog 'n werk, nog 'n job', en toe onthou ek wat hy gesê het.

~ Yes, so opera is my first love. My wife sometimes asks me, 'But tell me, how much do you love me?' And I say, 'Listen, let me tell you straight: it's God first, then music and then you and the kids and the dogs and cats and so one.' But music is my first love. You could not just decide to join the Eoan Group. It was a kind of achievement to belong to such an organisation. Where I grew up in Kensington I was so to speak the only opera singer. On Saturdays I had to run around to probably three to four churches to sing at weddings. Without pay and you had to be on time too. And all you get is naturally an invitation that you can come and eat in the evening. That's the way it was, money was never an issue. We once asked this question in a big meeting. When will we be paid to sing opera? It was Dr Manca who said, and I quote, 'The day you sing for money, the love of music flies out the window.' And I actually experienced this, because I afterwards went to sing for a few of the regional councils, professionally, and one day I was just sitting there and thinking, 'This is just more work, just a job', and I remembered what he said.

John van der Ross

In the 1950s I [was going to do] Violetta, it was great excitement. My late husband then promised Mr Manca I would be here, but he wouldn't take me out. And, of course, two weeks after the wedding, it was 'No', you know. And May [Abrahamse] then stepped in. Like I've said to you, that moment is like now. It was just, 'No, they'll have to find somebody else.' May stepped in and she excelled. She did beautifully. But it was something that was taken from me, that I don't think I've ever forgotten.

Elizabeth Engelbrecht-April on her wedding day in 1960. Joseph and Minke Manca are seated left, Dulcie Howes is seated in the middle.

I wasn't even allowed to go back to the Eoan Group. [Initially] he attended every function I sang at, he was at every rehearsal, if need be to see me home. There was never any question about [me not taking] part, which is difficult to understand. But going back to a marriage counsellor afterwards about it, the priest had said one simple word to me, he said to me I had never made him feel first in my life.

Elizabeth Engelbrecht-April

There's nothing he [my husband] could really do. He didn't like it at all, but there's nothing he could do about it. That was the problem all the time. That's why eventually we parted. And then of course we remarried again. And then people said, 'You're crazy, how can you marry the same man?' And I said, 'Rather the devil you know than the devil you don't know.' And then I divorced him again. No, he didn't like the Eoan Group. He didn't like Manca, he used to say Manca was my God. It's not that, you know it's not that. But you know, you must love music to appreciate it. And he wasn't actually interested in classical music.

May Abrahamse

Sophia Andrews and her husband Solomon van Rooyen in 1962.
PHOTO Supplied by Sophia Andrews

[My husband] joined me even in the church choir, he joined in *South Pacific*, he joined in with *Il Travatore* as one of the soldiers and never said a word, even when I went on tour he never said, 'You're not going anymore', and so on. He left me to enjoy the life that he found me. He knew I was a singer and he knew you don't touch that. I'll do everything, I was a good housewife, I did practically everything for him and we worked beautiful, we were married forty-two years and we worked together as hand and glove. We'd have a argument here and there, little tiffs and stuff, but not much. But uh, most of the time what he desired in life, I desired. And if he knows I'm going to sing somewhere he would never say, 'You're not going.' He would say, 'Go, bokkie, go!'
  Sophia Andrews

My wife was nineteen [and we] had two boys, baby boys. But I was singing, I was going out late at night singing. Thank you to my wife. But it's not always that she appreciated that, because there was times that I had to be with her too. But she sacrificed her social time for me to sing.
  Martin Johnson

Martin Johnson in 1971.
PHOTO Eoan Group Archive

My father had to bring [my mother] through to town. And he and I would sit on the parade and wait for her while they were rehearsing. And he objected then, so she had to leave the group. I was about sixteen years old, we had a shop in Mamre, my mom and I ran the shop.

Well, when my mom went back the second time, it was she and I, cause then we were moved from the mainframe family. My father was pretty removed from it. The only thing that concerned him was the inconvenience of having to bring my mom through to town. And when he objected, she obviously couldn't travel that distance. But for instance, like Gerald Samaai, he travelled to Paarl.

Jocylyn Liedeman

How many times I have wasted my family life? Even when they needed me, I wasn't there. Certain things happened, even my father when he died, I wasn't there. You understand? So, they sacrificed a lot. But God gave me a very good wife. A wife that really understands, you know, everything and stood by me. But even Dr Manca, there is a man, his family, his friends, his home! Because remember we used to go to his home. It was an open house for everyone, you understand? Even the same thing applies to Mr Sydow, all their homes were open for each and every one.

Benny Arendse

For many years the Eoan Group was an active part of the cultural life of Cape Town, where the group had a large support base, comprising members of the white and coloured population groups. Up until the establishment of the provincial arts councils in 1963, the group was the only organisation that consistently brought Italian grand opera to local audiences. Despite the increasing political difficulties as well as Eoan's compromised political situation – because they accepted money from the apartheid government – public support and admiration remained high throughout the 1960s. Filling venues to capacity never seemed to be a problem.

Die operaliefhebbers het graag gegaan omdat hulle goeie opera gehoor het. Al was dit nie altyd in alle opsigte so goed nie, dit was in elk geval lekker om opera te hoor. En ek dink daarom was die gesindheid van die regte musiekliefhebber welwillend.

~ The opera lovers were keen to go because they heard good opera. Even though they were not always so good in all respects, it was pleasant anyway to listen to opera. And I think this is why the attitude of the real music lover was one of goodwill.

Pieter Kooij

You take your *La Traviata* and you associate it with your great opera houses overseas. And here you have in South Africa a small group who tries also to sing that. They had the admiration of a great part of the community. But, as I said, a portion of the community embraced that, another portion of the community said, 'No, no, my political convictions are stronger.' So there was this mixed feeling about that too. I know that Dr Manca was at that time almost a household name, because he did wonders with untrained voices, and some of that voices came from all walks of life.

Ronnie Samaai

There were audiences and [the venues were] filled to capacity, but I think the Group Areas Act, everybody being shifted out to the outskirts of Cape Town, drove away the audiences. I say to you that City Hall was packed. The Alhambra was packed, there was never a problem with an empty house and I say, where had all these audiences gone? It is an era gone missing. The people just loved the art form, people just came for the plain, pure enjoyment of coming to the opera. I go and people didn't question it. It was so different then, or maybe I was just young and I wasn't aware of all the things. People enjoyed coming to the opera and it was such a treat. You know, I remember going to Pretoria to talk about the Eoan Group and to Bloemfontein and people talked about the Eoan Group. They drove far and wide to come see the Eoan Group, to come listen to the operas, because the standard of singing was very high.

Virginia Davids

Yes, when they performed *La Traviata*, many, many people were so impressed and I know still today some of your so-called white friends would say, 'You know, I went to that performance where your brother [Gerald Samaai] sang Alfredo.' And I play dumb and say, 'What do you mean, Alfredo?' 'In the City Hall that time.' I say, 'I don't remember.' 'No, the Eoan Group, you know they did fantastic work.' I say, 'Well, that was that time, can you imagine if all the avenues were open for them to go to technikons, to go to universities to make a decent study of it.' 'No, Ronnie please don't go there.' But there was that admiration there and people realised, hey, here we have so much to tap from, but within limits. What Eoan also did was, many people who went to the performances would – I am talking about in my age group, maybe younger – they would listen to the radio and say, 'Oh yes, that comes from *La Bohème*, that comes from *Il Trovatore*, we saw that hey! We saw it forty-five years ago. Eoan sang it.' And I am talking about ordinary people who can't read a single musical note. So there was an advantage in that, there was a degree of education that took place, which in my mind was good for people also to enjoy it, because music is universal and should be enjoyed by each and everyone.

Ronnie Samaai

Ek het *L'Elisir d'Amore* gedoen en een Saterdagmiddag gaan ons vir 'n middag vertoning. Soos gewoonlik, het ek van Paarl geryloop om in die stad te kom. En hier stop 'n blanke vrou met 'n dame langsaan haar, stop om vir my nou 'n lift te gee. My eerste gedagte was, ek alleen bruin man, met daardie twee blanke vrouens, is dit nie nou 'n setup, of wat gaat aan? En ek staan toe maar net doodstil en ek sien hier kom die kar effens terug, reverse hy en sy sê, 'Where are you off to?' Ek sê, 'I'm off to town'. Toe sy nou Engels praat, toe voel ek heeltemal tevrede. Toe weet ek nee dis nie die sogenaamde hiërargie nie. Ek klim toe daar in. Maar toe ek in die motor inklim, sien ek hier lê die Eoan Groep se program. Sy's ook op pad na die opera toe. En sy vra vir my, 'Are you interested in classical music?' Ek sê, 'Yes.' 'Do you know any of the Eoan Group?' Ek sê, 'Yes, I have heard of them. I know some of them.' Sy sê, ' I am going to see this little tenor, a brilliant …' Sy begin praat … oe, ek is lateraan so embarrassed. Ek kan nooit vir die vrou sê ek is die een van wie jy nou praat nie! Sy laai my toe af. Nee, toe ons by Oswald Pirowstraat kom, sê ek, 'It's somewhere around here. I've still got to look for this place.' Daar laai sy my af. Toe ek daardie ent stap na die stadsaal toe … Na die eerste bedryf kom sy na my toe, vra sy of sy vir my kan sien. Ons het so 'n skeiding daar gehad, blankes mos eenkant, nie-blankes anderkant. Nou wonder ek mag ek na daardie kant toe gaan? Maak hulle so op 'n skrefie oop, sy sê vir my, 'You little bastard, you've got a lift back home.'

Eoan was die eerste wat 'n vollengte opera Paarl toe gebring het, met die orkes. In die jare sewentig. Ons het twee aande gehad in die gemeenskapsaal, en 'booked out!' Terloops die Eoan Groep se Juwele uit die Operas was altyd booked out. Ons het natuurlik die voordeel gehad, wanneer ons opvoerings gehad het, dan het hulle vir ons gesê, 'Bookings open Monday.' Maar Sondagaand weet ons al en het ons kaartjies gekry. En die sogenaamde blankes het ook uitgevind, maar hulle kan vir ons nader vir kaartjies voor die tyd. Dan kom die mense Maandag om kaartjies te kry, dan sê hulle, 'Only thirty seats available. Booked out.' Ons het baie trots gevoel. Dit is nou een ding waarop ons staat gemaak het, ons het geweet die gehoor gaan vir ons teruggee wat ons moet opoffer. En dit vir ons was baie belangrik gewees.

~ I was doing L'Elisir d'Amore *and one Saturday afternoon we were going to the matinee performance. As usual I hitchhiked into the city from Paarl. And a white woman with another lady next to her stops to give me a lift. My*

Gerald Samaai in 1969.
PHOTO Eoan Group Archive

first thought was, I'm a solitary coloured man, with those two white women, is this a set-up, or what's going on? And so I just stood there dead still until I see the car reversing and she says, 'Where are you off to?' I say, 'I'm off to town.' When she spoke English, I felt completely satisfied. I knew then it was not the so-called hierarchy. So I get into the car. But when I got into the car I see the Eoan Group's programme lying there. She's also on her way to the opera. And she asks me, 'Are you interested in classical music?' I say, 'Yes.' 'Do you know any of the Eoan Group?' I say, 'Yes, I have heard of them. I know some of them.' She says, ' I am going to see this little tenor, a brilliant ...' She starts talking ... and I am eventually so embarrassed. I could never say to the woman I'm the one you are talking about now! She then dropped me off ... No, when we got to Oswald Pirow Street I said, 'It's somewhere around here. I've still got to look for this place.' She dropped me off there. Then I walked that bit to the City Hall ... After the first act she comes to me, asks if she can see me. There was a kind of barrier there, whites on the one side, non-whites on the other. Now I wonder whether I'm allowed to go to that side? I open the barrier a little, she says to me, 'You little bastard, you've got a lift back home.'

Eoan was the first to bring a full-length opera to Paarl, with the orchestra. In the seventies. We had two evenings in the Community Hall, and 'booked out!' Incidentally, the Eoan Group's Gems from the Operas was always booked out. We naturally had an advantage, whenever we had performances, then they said to us, 'Bookings open Monday', but we knew Sunday night already and got our tickets. And the so-called whites also found out that they could approach us for tickets before the time. Then the people come to get tickets on Monday, then they say, 'Only thirty seats available. Booked out.' We felt very proud. That was one thing we knew we could depend on, we knew the audiences would repay us for what we had sacrificed. And that was very important to us.

Gerald Samaai

Ek onthou baie spesifiek, daardie tyd was dit natuurlik apartheid, mense moes apart sit, maar dit was hoofsaaklik 'n wit ondersteuningsbasis gewees. Daar was ook bruin mense teenwoordig, maar dit was hoofsaaklik 'n wit ondersteuningsbasis. Van voor tot agter, dit was iets gewees. Daar was 'n blanke meerderwaardigheid gewees oor bruin dinge asof dit minderwaardig sou wees, maar nie teen die Eoan-operagroep nie. Want dit was gewoonlik vier aande gewees en dit was altyd, altyd goedkoop. En jy moet taamlik gou jou kaartjies kry. So ek het die meeste van daardie operas met die openingsaand en gewoonlik die laaste aand weer gesien.

Dis van my aangenaamste herinneringe. Dit was ook vir my baie belangrik gewees, want dit was apartheid. Ek het hier gewoon, in hierdie

omgewing, ek het nie bruin mense geken nie – ek het net bruin mense
geken in 'n ander soortvan huishoudelike verband en ek kon daarnatoe
gaan en mense daar leer ken op, wat my betref, op 'n gelyke voet. En
dit het vir my verskriklik baie beteken. En baie van die sogenaamde
vooroordele wat 'n mens dan sou hê, het vir my net opgeskort geword as
gevolg van die kontak. Dit was vir my besonder aangenaam. En die mees
uitstaande dinge vir my was in 1956, die *La Traviata*, dit is tot vandag toe,
ek kan amper nie na 'n ander *La Traviata* luister nie, dit bly vir my die
footprint van my *La Traviata.*

*~ I remember very specifically, that was naturally the time of apartheid,
people had to sit apart, but it was primarily a white support base. There
were also coloured people present, but it was primarily a white support base.
From front to back, it was something. There was a white sense of superiority
about things from the coloured community, as if they were inferior, but not
about the Eoan opera group. Because it was usually four nights and it was
always, always inexpensive. And you had to get your tickets fairly promptly.
So I usually saw most of those operas on the opening night and usually the
final night as well.*

*These are among my most pleasant memories. This was also very
important for me, because it was apartheid. I lived here, in this area, I did
not know coloured people – I only knew coloured people in another sort of
domestic context and I could go there and get to know people on, as far as
I was concerned, an equal footing. And this meant an enormous amount to
me. I had many of the so-called preconceptions that a person would have at
that time, were simply set aside for me as a result of the contact. This was
particularly pleasant for me. And the outstanding thing for me was in 1956,
the* La Traviata, *to this day I can hardly listen to another* La Traviata, *for
me that remains the footprint of my* La Traviata.

Amanda Botha

Some of the Eoan singers even had personal admirers …

Jack Hawkins, he was a window dresser for a very big firm. He heard me
sing one evening while he was doing the foyer in the City Hall and then he
stayed for the show. He was there every night. The first night he brought
me a bouquet that I would never see again with these two eyes, I'd never
see it again. He had it presented to me on a stand when we took the
curtain call. Somebody came walking in, put the stand down and then put
the flowers down. It was a *My Fair Lady* hat with almost twenty dozen red
roses in it. And he was there almost every single night that I sang. 'I just
can't get away from you. I can't skip one matinee when you are singing.'
And that man used to bring things to me.

In the course of the 1960s, the Eoan Group was gradually edged out of the centre of Cape Town's cultural life. Not only was District Six zoned for white occupation, but legislation also increasingly enforced racial segregation and by 1969 the group was relocated to the Joseph Stone Theatre in Athlone. This move seemed to be a watershed moment for the group as from this time onwards, white support diminished. Furthermore, support from their own community dwindled due to the politically compromised situation the group was in.

The group was well aware of the fact that, at the time, some prominent white opera singers took notice of their performances.

Sophia Andrews in 1968.

> Well, via the grapevine we heard that [Mimi Coertse] said, 'Oh no,
> we can't sing', you know, that kind of thing. At that stage she was very
> against any involvement. But then she was the best in her time as a
> coloratura overseas. So maybe she could make that in passing, that kind
> of statement. But she never got involved until she came back to this
> country. And there she's training people [today].
> *Ruth Fourie*

The Eoan Group had long received financial support from local authorities, which enabled them to continue their activities. In 1956, when Eoan performed Verdi's *La Traviata* for the first time, funding structures were already in place. At this time, government officials reminded the group that, should they continue to accept money from government, they would have to conform to legislation with regard to performing to racially segregated audiences. In the same year, the political activist, Alex la Guma, wrote to the group as follows:

> Allow us to congratulate you on your magnificent performance of 'La
> Traviata'. You have shown that, given the opportunities, Coloured people
> can excel in the realms of culture on par with all other peoples.
>
> It [was] rumoured for some time that your group was financially
> supported by the government through the Coloured Affairs Department.
> However, Dr. du Plessis now appears to be sufficiently bold as to have
> arranged for the Group to put on a 'Europeans Only' show, and this in
> the face of the mounting opposition of the Coloured people against
> Apartheid ...
>
> People can also conclude, therefore, that the Eoan Group supports
> Apartheid. In fact, the whole idea reminds one of the slave period when
> the farmers hired Coloureds to perform for them, their masters. Today
> in the 20th Century we do not recognize the white man as our master.
> This is the land of our birth and we demand government support for ALL
> cultural movements. BUT WITHOUT APARTHEID STRINGS.

From 1956 to 1965 Eoan was able to continue with opera and other activities without government funding. However, as the group's financial needs increased due to the demands of a burgeoning opera company, their financial situation worsened. By 1965, when the group was artistically at its peak, they had to decide to apply for funding in order to continue their activities, or face bankruptcy. It was decided to make use of government funding, a decision that came at a hefty price. In the end the compromise cost them their reputation within their own community, and Eoan's artists experienced this on a very personal level.

C

<u>SOUTH AFRICAN COLOURED PEOPLE'S ORGANISATION</u>

Chairman: Alex La Guma,   Secretary: R. September,
          13 Louisvale Rd.,   35 Ravenscraig Rd.,
          Gleemoor, Athlone.   Woodstock.
          Phone 693085.

Dear Friend,
              Allow us to congratulate you on your mag-
nificent performance of "La Traviata". You have shown
that, given the opportunities, Coloured people can excel
in the realms of culture on par with all other peoples.
              It has come to our notice, however, that
your group arranged a special performance of the opera
for 'Europeans Only' on Tuesday night, 20th inst. In fact
Dr. Du Plessis, head of the government's Coloured Affairs
Department had sent out invitations for this special
performance. Among those invited were the Cabinet Minist-
ers and Members of Parliament whose attitude towards the
Non-Europeans are well known.
              Since its birth the Group has rendered
invaluable service to the cultural well-being and advancement of our community and country, and managed to
remain independent of the government until the Coloured
Affairs Department took an interset in its affairs.
              In spite of official silence, it was
rumoured for sometime that your group was financially
supported by the Government through the C.A.D. However, Dr. Du Plessis now appears to be sufficiently
bold as to have arranged for the Group to put on a
'Europeans Only' show, and this in the face of the
mounting opposition of the Coloured people against
Apartheid.
              People can also conclude, therefore, that
the Eoan Group supports Apartheid. In fact the whole
idea reminds one of the slave period when the farmers
hired Coloureds to perform for them, their masters. Today in the 20th Century we do not recognise the white
man as our master. This is the land of our birth and
we demand government support for ALL cultural movements.
BUT WITHOUT APARTHEID STRINGS.
              The eyes of the world are on you, and
we can safely say that all advanced and progressive
people bowed their heads in shame when you performed
followed the footsteps of your slave forefathers, and
performed for a 'Europeans Only' audience.
              We realise however for you to have refused
to perform would have required great courage, but that
is surely what we-- who respect you as artists-- have
a reasonable right to expect. True art, surely belongs
to ALL the people of our land.
              We hope that, when the same situation
arises in the future, you will consider it in the
light of this letter and be prepared to uphold the
dignity of our people struggling for emancipation.
              With very best wishes for the Future,
              Respectfully yours,

        CHAIRMAN.   SECRETARY.

        [signature: [signature:
        Alex La Guma]   R. September]

Protest letter from the South African Coloured People's Organisation.
SOURCE Eoan Group Archive

But it is the government that gave the Eoan Group a grant with certain conditions. That after a while they were also the downfall of the Eoan Group. You know, if you withdraw financial support, you must eat, you must drink, you must live, and if you cut down that supply you might as well close down shop. That is what happened.

Ronnie Samaai

So nou en dan moet hulle aanvaar die Kleurlingsake se borge man, en daarvan het ons kleurlingmense nie van gehou nie. En baie van hulle het nie bygewoon ons operas nie en ons konserte nie. Ons het somtyds by sale gaat sing en dan is daar maar net drie mense in die gehoor. Maar dan het die Kleurlingsake vir daardie aand miskien R10 000 gegee, jy weet, vir die hele aand nou.

~ Every now and then they had to accept the Coloured Affairs sponsorships, man, and some of us coloured people did not like that. And many of them did not attend our operas and our concerts. We sometimes went to sing in halls and there were only three people in the audience. But then Coloured Affairs gave maybe R10 000 for that evening, you know, for that whole evening.

Ronald Theys

Ek het gevoel dis okay dat die Eoan Groep geld van die staat gevat het. Ek bly dan in 'n huis wat gesubsidieer word deur die staat. Waarom kon die kunste nie geld kry nie? Ek was heeltemal okay met dit. Ek was nie okay met dit wat die onderwysers en skoolhoofde gedoen het om anti-Eoan Groep te raak nie. Daarmee was ek nie tevrede nie. Want ek was bereid om vir hulle ook te challenge en vir hulle te vra waar kry hulle hulle geld vandaan.

~ I felt it's okay that the Eoan group took money from the state. I live in a house that is subsidised by the state. Why could the arts not get the money? I was completely okay with that. I was not okay with what the teachers and school principals did to become anti-Eoan Group. That I was not happy about because I was prepared to challenge them too and to ask where they got their money from.

John van der Ross

Omdat hy die groep laat vertoon het voor gedeelde – op rassegebied – gehore. Daardie deel van jou bruin gemeenskap wat redelik gesofistikeerd was, het nie daarvan gehou nie. Hulle het dit geboikot, nie almal nie, maar party. Maar Manca het gesê, 'Maar kyk, julle is nie die wat opera ondersteun nie, my ondersteuning, my gehoor kom van wit mense.' Ek dink nie dit was heeltemal waar nie, maar miskien die grootste gedeelte

GP-S—(F)—8

Telegramadres:
Telegraphic Address:
"KLEURSAKE"   Kaapstad
              Cape Town

Pos: Privaatsak, 9008 Kaapstad
Post: Private Bag,   Cape Town

Tel. 45-5641

Navrae: Mnr.
Enquiries: Mr   J.R. Young.

Geliewe in u antwoord te meld
In reply please quote................ 7/41/17/1/D. 29.

VR-L I

REPUBLIEK VAN SUID-AFRIKA—REPUBLIC OF SOUTH AFRICA

ADMINISTRASIE VAN KLEURLINGSAKE,
ADMINISTRATION OF COLOURED AFFAIRS,
ROELANDSTRAAT 37,
37 ROELAND STREET,

KAAPSTAD.
CAPE TOWN.

8 -9- 1970

The Chairman,
Eoan Group,
P.O. Box 55,
ATHLONE.

Sir,

APPLICATIONS FOR FINANCIAL ASSISTANCE : 1970/71 FINANCIAL
YEAR : EOAN GROUP.

With reference to the applications for financial assistance submitted by your Group in respect of the above-mentioned financial year, I have pleasure in informing you that grants-in-aid to a maximum of R31,000.00 have been approved, in principle, in favour of the organisation.

The grants are awarded for and must be utilised –

(a)   as assistance towards the costs of training
      in ballet – R1,000.00;

(b)   to meet the shortfall on the Group's 1968
      opera season – R2,061.00;

(c)   as assistance towards the Group's Admini-
      stration expenses in respect of its financial
      year ending on the 31st March, 1971 – R10,000.00;
      and

(d)   to cover the loss, if any, in respect of the
      Group's 1970 opera season – a maximum of R17,939.

Payment of the grants is subject to the conditions set out in the schedule attached hereto in duplicate, which conditions should be accepted by your organisation and signed by yourself and/or the secretary on behalf of the management committee. It is a further requirement that the grants, on

2/...

A letter from the Coloured Affairs Department confirming financial support to the Eoan Group in 1970.
SOURCE Eoan Group Archive

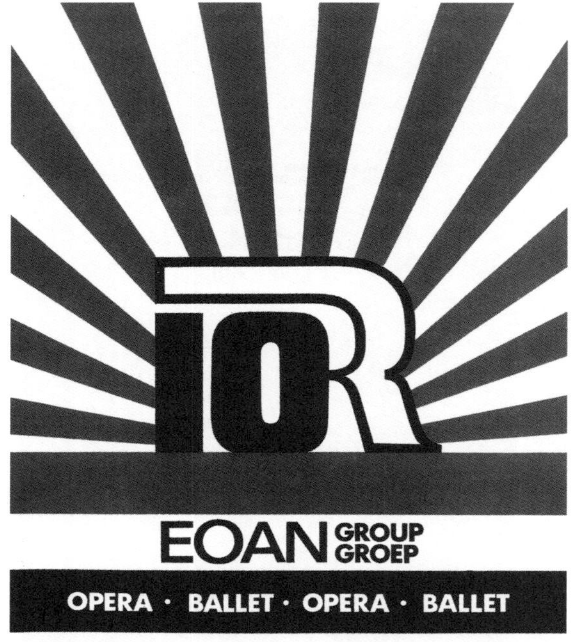

The programme brochure for the 1971 Republic Festival, where Eoan performed at the request of the government as part of the 10-year anniversary of the South African republic.
SOURCE Eoan Group Archive

daarvan. En toe was daar 'n beweging om dit te boikot, sekere mense het. Ek het nie, nee, laat ek dit so stel ek hou nie van die woord boikot nie, maar ek het weggebly van daardie verdeelde vertonings. En geleidelik het die groep in onguns geraak met die bruinmense.

~ Because he allowed the group to perform before divided – racially segregated – audiences. That part of your coloured community that was relatively sophisticated did not like that. They boycotted them, not everyone, but some. But Manca said, 'But look, you are not the ones who support opera, my support, my audience comes from white people.' I don't think this was entirely true, but perhaps the largest section. And then there was a movement to boycott them, and some people did. I did not, no, let me put it like this – I don't like the word boycott, but I stayed away from those segregated performances. And gradually the group fell out of favour among coloured people.

   Richard van der Ross

[They ostracised Manca] because we were taking the grant from the
Coloured Affairs Department and people didn't want us to take that grant
at all. They felt that we should do without the grant and still perform,
little knowing what it costs to put an opera on stage. They said we were
accepting people's money just to perform and that there are thousands
and thousands of people without jobs and things like that. They always
brought in the political side of things. We had to take the grant, otherwise
we couldn't have performed anything. That's the way we felt, here. You
either take it or you leave it. And they knew about it, they knew that
should you not take it, then it's a slow death.

Toe wil die mense mos weet waar kry die Eoan Groep die geld om 'n
produksie op die planke te bring. En hulle het dan nie geld nie. So we had
to tell them we are getting a grant from the Coloured Affairs Department.
Toe sê hulle mos, julle het nou gebou hiersa in Athlone, gee net die erkenning vir Coloured Affairs ook. En nou is die gebou, julle het dit gesien
Committee Coloured Affairs. Nou vandag nog as mense inkom, hoekom
moet dit daar sit, min wetend dat as ons dit nie gedoen het nie, dan het
ons nie die geld gekry nie.
~ *Then people wanted to know where the Eoan Group gets the money to stage
a production. And they don't have any money. So we had to tell them we are
getting a grant from the Coloured Affairs Department. So they said, you now
have a building in Athlone, also acknowledge Coloured Affairs. And now the
building, you saw it Committee Coloured Affairs. To this day when people
come in, why does it have to be there, little knowing that if we did not do
that, then we did not get the money.*
   Gerald Samaai

There was also a lot of controversy about [the grant]. Because you have,
they all got letters about the political side and why they receiving the
money from the government, you know. There was subsidy at one stage,
so they were sponsored by the government and then that ceased, but I
think they took it up again when they went to the Joseph Stone. There was
people who had fled the country, for instance, and wrote from overseas.
And then at the time [there was] the Unity Movement, a group of non-
white politicians who watched out for this kind of thing. And you were
not allowed to send your child to a white school or a Catholic college
or any of those things. You know those days the Catholics took in non-
white students. There was the Christian Brothers College and there was
a school in Athlone that was also run by the monks, the Irish monks, but
it was mixed and children, non-white children, were allowed to go there.
And those people were victimised. In sport, if your child went to a white
school, like, there was a group, a sport group, then you were not allowed

to play sport. If you belonged to a cricket club, for instance, and you went
to an international match, then you were actually not allowed to play in
the cricket club.

Ruth Fourie

There was a lot [of controversy in the coloured community], which came
from various people. They felt that basically we were sell-outs, you know
we [were] doing things we shouldn't be doing by subjecting ourselves to
this situation where we got to perform for segregated audiences, they felt
it shouldn't be. There were a lot of people anti the group at that stage,
yes. Some of my friends were, too. They couldn't give us an alternative.
'Cause everything that they would've wanted to do was still subject to
government rules and regulations. If they wanted to form a body, it was
going to be a segregated body. They couldn't perform to the people who
would appreciate it. One must accept the fact that much of the coloured
people weren't that well educated and versed in the arts to accept opera as
such. So, the audience who would have paid them, had to come from the
white side.

Leon Dreyer

I remember in the old days the Eoan Group also participated in one of the
festivals that was given during the apartheid time. And that also had a big
issue, you know, with people protesting and, because they thought that
we were a so-called non-white group. Why you performing there? But let's
face it, the government at the time, we cannot run down them all the way.
There was the good out of it. Every year a budget of money was given for
production work and things had to be done. Most of the teachers that we
had were white people, qualified, trained, ex-opera singers who had sung
overseas with the international experience, so they became our teachers.

Fuad Sawyer

**Dr ID du Plessis, the Minister of Coloured Affairs, was closely involved
with the fund applications of the group. In later years, he also served as
government representative on the Eoan Group Trust.**

Nou aanvaar ek dat toe die Eoan Groep begin 'n opgang maak het,
die subsidie wat hulle gekry het, het van sy kant af gekom, dat hy dit
geïnisieer het. Dit is nie vir my toevallig, met dit wat ek van ID du Plessis
geweet het, dat hulle in daai tyd begin het om 'n subsidie te kry van die
staat nie. Maar onthou nou, dis in die sestigs. En daar was nie 'n Maleier
wat in ons kantoor ingekom het nie wat nie vir Dr Eye-Dee geken het nie,
soos hulle dit uitgespreek het, ja.

Dr ID du Plessis, director of the Coloured Affairs Department.

~ Now I accept that when the Eoan Group started becoming successful, the subsidy they received was due to him, that he initiated it. For me it is not a coincidence, given what I knew about ID du Plessis, that they began to get a subsidy from the state at that time. But remember, this is in the sixties. And there was not a Malay who came into our office who did not know Dr Eye-Dee, as they pronounced it, yes.
  Phil Pienaar

Destyds het die Administrasie Kleurlingsake – die digter, ID du Plessis, was die direkteur – en hy was hulle uit die aard van die saak goed gesind. Hy het 'n baie goeie profile by hulle gehad vanweë sy betrokkendheid by die Maleiers en toe het hy bewerkstellig dat hulle R20 000 'n jaar subsidie gekry het. Daar was 'n groepering van bruin mense wat nie direk aan die Eoan Groep verbonde was nie, wat daarteen gekant was: 'Ja, hulle is nou sell-outs.' Jy weet, daar was 'n hele gevoel daaromtrent gewees – ook 'n seksie wat gesê het hulle boikot dit nou.
~ At that time the Administration Coloured Affairs – the poet, ID du Plessis, was the director – and he was naturally well disposed towards them. He had

*a very good profile among them because of his involvement with the Malays
and he then arranged that they get a subsidy of R20 000 a year. There was
a group of coloured people that was not directly associated with the Eoan
Group who were directly opposed to this: 'Yes, you are now sell-outs.' You
know, there was quite some feeling about this – also a section that said they
would boycott them now.*
Amanda Botha

As the political situation in the country worsened, the coloured community
increasingly viewed the Eoan Group as a government puppet. By the 1980s
the resistance movement, the South African Council on Sport (SACOS),
declared the group a 'banned organisation', thereby asking the coloured
community to boycott the group's performances.

The main reason was that the Eoan group was involved with the
showcasing of productions for the government. And then politically it
became an issue in our community where people were banned from
coming to the Joseph Stone. For me and my mom, my school didn't
allow anyone to come to the Joseph Stone at the time.
Shafiek Rajap

There were times when there was very little children to teach. Because
then the community said the Eoan Group is getting funds from the
government. And so I'm not sending my child there. It was hard. We had
to have studio shows instead of performances on the stage, because the
amount of children were so few. We had people not wanting to come here
and teach. Not wanting to step into the Eoan Group because, 'Sorry, I'm
not with you guys, I'm on the other side.'
Abeedah Medell

Well, the Eoan Group was a banned organisation. And at that time, I had
my first job, which was for the Metalworkers Association in Athlone. And
they knew that I was doing dance. And I was actually called into a board
meeting to say that my affiliations were frowned upon, it is a banned
organisation. I said fine, so where do I dance, because there is no other
dance tuition for coloured people in Cape Town and nobody teaches
modern at the Eoan Group? And then they said, well, they were prepared
to give me a bursary to go to the UCT Ballet School. I said I don't do ballet,
I do jazz and they don't teach jazz [at UCT] and then I had to make a
choice and then I resigned. So I lost my job [because of] the Eoan group.
     The schools were also very politicised, you couldn't belong to the
Eoan Group. So a lot of people had double lives because the kids that had

talent, they weren't allowed to do ballet and they wanted to do jazz and
they wanted to sing opera, but they couldn't, otherwise they would be
victimised and they couldn't perform in their school's supporting body.
Because we got a government supplement.

Merle Falken

Even today, support for the Eoan Group remains problematic.

In the new South Africa, to say that we are not black enough, I think it is
maybe a true statement. It is not something that you would like to believe
and to broadcast to the rest of the world, but that is the situation. I have
spoken to many of the arts and culture people, I have actually had a visit
from two of them a couple of weeks ago. And they asked me why I haven't
applied for funding and I said I don't want your money. You can't give us
crumbs and expect us to be happy. We are an organisation that has been
around for over seventy-five years and if you don't recognise what we do,
then keep your money. Younger organisations and institutions receive
a lot more money without application, and I know the process, I have
spoken to a lot of people that can guarantee me money if we complete our
funding proposals right, but I don't want money like that. And we can't go
back to full-scale operas, because we don't receive that type of money.

Shafiek Rajap

Final Curtain

The Eoan Group stopped producing formal opera after Joseph Manca left in 1977, but group members have divergent opinions on the demise of the activities of Eoan. The management of the group continued to be hampered by infighting and divisions, alienating its members. During the 1980s, dance and drama became the renewed focus of the group and these continue to be practiced today.

Ek was baie spyt dat Manca die Eoan Groep gelos het, baie spyt. Want dit was, ongeag die streeksrade, was dit altyd vir my 'n beginpunt van enige kunstenaar, sanger in die Wes-Kaap. Ek het altyd die Eoan Groep gesien as 'n broeikas vir die groter teater. Ek sien dit nou nog as 'n broeikas vir die groter teater. En ek wens net ons kan miskien op beter voet kom en ophou baklei oor die Eoan Groep. Daar's 'n bietjie baie bakleiery wat nie saamgaan met waarvoor die plek daar is nie. Ek is een van dié, ek sal sê van die oulede, ja, van die Eoan Groep. Maar ek voel altyd ek het 'n plek daar om terug te ploeg. Ek wil nie na die Eoan Groep toe gaan om 'n posisie te kry nie of om gesien te word nie. Die Eoan Groep, vir my, het die reg om te bestaan. Die Eoan Groep vir my is voorgangers, pioniers van klassieke musiek in die land en Eoan lê baie, baie na aan my hart. En as ek dit sê dan sê ek dit met baie eerlikheid. Ek het altyd gevoel dat musikante moet daai afdeling van Eoan self oorneem en self hanteer. Die musiek afdeling. En wanneer daai opset beter is, dan kan ons weer gesels met die owerhede, die huidige owerhede. Ek gaan nie 'n kraan regmaak as ek nie 'n loodgieter is nie. So, ek voel en ek weet ek gaan gekruisig word vir wat ek sê, maar ek voel dat musiekmense vir die musiek afdeling van die Eoan Groep hanteer. Dan gee ons nie om – ek is een van daai mense wat dit sal doen – dan gee ons nie om wie is aan die hoof van wat nie. Los die musiekmense om die musiek te bevorder.

~ I was very sorry that Manca left the Eoan Group, very sorry. Because it was, despite the regional arts councils, it was always the starting point for any artist, singer in the Western Cape. I always saw the Eoan Group as an incubator for the wider theatre. I still see it as an incubator for the wider theatre. And I just wish we might be able to be on better terms and stop fighting about the Eoan Group. There's a little too much fighting that does not go with what the place stands for. I am one of those, shall I say one of the old members, yes, of the Eoan Group. But I always feel I have a place there to plough back something. I don't want to go to the Eoan Group to get a position or to be seen. For me, the Eoan Group has the right to exist. For me, the Eoan Group is the predecessor, pioneer of classical music in the country and Eoan is very, very close to my heart. And when I say this I say it with great honesty. I always said that musicians should take over that section of Eoan themselves and run it themselves – the music section. And when that set-up

Joseph Manca rehearsing with the Eoan Group Choir shortly before he retired.
PHOTO Amanda Botha, 1976

*is better, then we can talk again to the authorities, the current authorities.
I am not going to fix a tap if I'm not a plumber. So, I feel, and I know I'm
going to be crucified for saying this, but I feel that music people should be
managing the music section of the Eoan Group. Then we don't care – I'm one
of the people who will do this – then we don't care who is the head of what.
Leave the music people to promote the music.*

John van der Ross

As far as my memory serves me, the disputes came along when certain
members used to feel that they were not getting enough financially. And
I remember a few of the members starting like a social club in which
they wanted to raise funds and give money, and get extra money. And I
remember one of those very concerts at the Eoan Group at the time. It
didn't flight because of poor management, I would say, but because the
Eoan Group had their own board of trustees and their management.
And I think that was the time when Dr Manca just got fed up, to put it
point blank, that's what I remember. And then Dr Manca's exit at the
Eoan Group at the time, I wouldn't say it was a very happy one, but rather
disappointing. But to come to a conclusion on that, I'm not sure what the
argument was. All I know, he just walked out and never came back again.
But he, Dr Manca, had the reins of opera and the connections at the tip of
his fingers, he could plug all over. Like any organisation I say, sometimes
the workers think you can run the organisation. But if the main body falls
away, you think those people are gonna be your friends, and it doesn't
work. But as far as I can remember, with all due respect to members of the
Eoan Group at the time, that was one of the things that happened.

Fuad Sawyer

The Eoan Group had been through a lot of upheaval. The old Eoan
Group, if you will say it like that, a lot of them left. And the Eoan Group
went down politically, financially, the organisation shrunk in a big way
and we always wanted to connect to the now and the then. And it was
always difficult. I remember when we spoke to the lady at the District Six
Museum, she said she'll never step foot inside the Joseph Stone ever.

I see the Eoan Group as one, even though I know there is little factions
all over the place that believe that they are still the Eoan Group. And the
focus on the opera, I don't have a problem with that. That is the Eoan
Group. That is where the Eoan Group started, created their fame. The
opera, I supported completely, especially what the Eoan Group have done,
when I've read up on the achievements, it gives you goose bumps. So if you
think that you can just put it aside, it is impossible, it is totally impossible.

One of the main reasons why I am doing this [interview], is so that I can teach the kids of today that is currently in the Eoan Group, what the Eoan Group meant in the bigger picture. A lot of them don't know half of the history of what the Eoan Group has achieved in the past. A lot of people think, 'Oh, you're doing a great job at the Eoan Group.' And I said to them, 'I don't think we are anywhere close to where the Eoan Group used to be – full-scale operas all over the country – we are not anywhere close to that.' We'd love to believe that we are going to get back there, and if this is a stepping stone to get there, then surely we should highlight this.

> *Shafiek Rajap*

Well, there were factions and I know that Phillip [Swales] was one of them who was involved. I get the impression that he wasn't fond of Manca. But then, he was an angry young man. But he came from Natal, which is totally different culture from Cape Town. You know the Cape culture is really something else. And people here didn't, at that stage, didn't feel that they were owed anything, like they do today.

I think there was some money, monetary, things that happened there, you know, where for instance that somebody donated a car so that the people could be transported and Mr Sydow claimed the car and so. And then finances, they had an accountant by the name of Ross. I know that there was trouble with the money and when they moved to the Joseph Stone then there was this group of people, Cecil Tobin was one of them, Phillip Swales, these guys approached certain of the groupers to ask them to join up. Cedric Adamson was one, Ronnie Theys, Martin Johnson. Now they were a group, they tried to get Manca and Sydow out. And I think that was the start of something. Alright, he was a good age already, but it was politics of the day as well.

And getting some credit for themselves, people did want to get credit for themselves. Not like the oldies who didn't worry about that kind of thing. So, because of the culture that we came from, so it was difficult for them to demand things from [Manca] when they knew that he was not getting rich from what he was doing. At least he didn't appear to be, I didn't think so anyway. But there was also the previous faction that got rid of Ms Southern-Holt.

> *Leon Dreyer*

The problem of administrative and artistic succession plagued the group for years, and remained unresolved when Manca and Sydow resigned. Manca wanted Gordon Jephtas to take over as artistic as can be seen in a letter written by Sydow to Manca after Sydow's visit to Jephtas in London in 1967:

Dear Brother Yusuf,   London
                                                       29th June 1967
                        so for ~~Gayar~~
Dudu, John, & Gordon & myself are all ~~~~
in the Very best of health hoping it is
the Same with you mrs manca Ruth and
Leonard, first I must tell you that everything
as for as the Groups future is concern
seems Very bright although one thing did
not come out the way I wanted that is
for Gordon to come with me but God
knows best he alone will give us
Gordon at the right time Gordon is
going to be to you what you want
him to be to you and the Group, ~~~~
in the meantime for a year ~~~~
~~~~ We will have to be Patieant and
wait I assure you that you will have
your greatest wish because Gordon
will come with a Vast knowlege
that will bring the Group up to a Very
high standard not that it is not high already
but he will be able to help you ~~~~
to build it So that it will be ~~~~ ready
for arts council the arts council will
be for you & Gordon I cant explain
to you in writing but please have
faith an Trust in me as you

Ismail Sydow's letter to Joseph Manca.
SOURCE Eoan Group Archive
~~~~

Gordon Jephtas and Ismail Sydow in London in 1975.

Dear Brother Yusuf,
I must tell you that everything as far as the Group's future is concerned seems very bright, although one thing did not come out the way I wanted. That is for Gordon to come with me, but God knows best, he alone will give us Gordon at the right time. Gordon is going to be to you what you want him to be to you and the Group. In the meantime for a year we will have to be patient and wait, I assure you that you will have your greatest wish because Gordon will come with a vast knowledge that will bring the Group up to a very high standard. Not that it is not high already, but he will be able to help you to build it so that it will be ready for the Arts Council. Please believe me when I say that you will get everything that you wish for the group, only be patient and let us wait one more year.

However, many of the group members are of the opinion that there was no contingency plan at all – younger singers were not given chances and Manca and Sydow would not loosen their grip of the functioning of the organisation.

That was Dr Manca's plan [to have Gordon Jephtas succeed him] but it was not Gordon's plan. Gordon wanted to come into something fresh and new.

Eoan members socialising together during their 1975 tour to the UK.
PHOTO Eoan Group Archive

Gordon had expertise, the most unbelievable expertise. Now don't forget his very first assignment or engagement was to accompany Renata Tebaldi on the Royal Albert Hall stage, now that's very far. He was not the amateur that Manca was. Manca went in as a chorus master, not a conductor. He became a conductor.

Peter Voges

I think after Dr Manca left, the opera really deteriorated, because he was like the major force, holding the opera together and putting on the performances. I don't think he really had any succession planning. He never empowered the opera singers with directing and producing the operas. At the time of Dr Manca, he did everything. He did everything, he trained the chorus, he conducted and okay, Mr Rota did the productions, I just felt if Dr Manca said, alright, fine, maybe you can be the chorus master, you know, or you can be the coach, you know. When he left, I think that's sort of when things fell apart. Because he was so passionate about it, but I think in him being so passionate about it, nobody else got a chance really to get in there and I just felt I could have had a lot to offer them but as I said to you, it was almost held against me that, or against the people that could have sort of helped themselves.

Virginia Davids

En toe Manca padgee, toe kan jy sien, stukkie vir stukkie hou dit op.
Ons het almal gehoop dat Gordon Jephtas sou oorvat, want hy was die
aangewese persoon vir daardie posisie. Maar wie kon hom betaal vir
die geld wat hy wou verdien? Oorsee het hy gewerk met Pavarotti, hy het
gewerk met Mirella Freni. Hier moet hy kom werk met die Eoan Groep.
Wat kan ons hom betaal? Daar was geen bron van inkomste nie. Die bron
van inkomste was maar net uit die Joseph Stone, die saal wat verhuur
word. En daarmee moet die Eoan Groep aan die lewe gehou word.
*~ And when Manca left, then you could see, bit by bit it stopped. We all hoped
that Gordon Jephtas would take over, because he was the designated person
for the position. But who could pay him for the money he wanted to earn?
Overseas he had worked with Pavarotti, he worked with Mirella Freni. Here
he must come and work with the Eoan Group. What could we pay him? There
was no source of income. The only source of income was the Joseph Stone, the
hall that is rented out. And with that the Eoan Group must be kept going.*
   Gerald Samaai

Despite administrative turmoil and the demise of Eoan's opera company,
former group members nostalgically remember the camaraderie they
enjoyed as a result of the time and hard work they invested in their art. For
many, Eoan was a second home.

Ja, I always loved to act. I kind of felt that when you're on stage you're not
yourself, you're someone else, aren't you? You're just someone else, you're
living a dream for a thing. I loved it, I really loved it.
   Patricia van Graan

The music was a comfort for me and I grasped every opportunity at the
Eoan Group. The Eoan Group was like a home and being a very young
singer, the older ones used to like you and they gave you tea and biscuits
and they gave you this and that. I absorbed every minute. At the same
time whilst doing my musical career, I was a jeweller but I also felt at
the time I could get up from that bench at any time and say goodbye.
My musical career enhanced me such a lot because all I thought, I slept
and ate was music. So that is how much the Eoan Group meant to me.
I've learned a lot of music from the Eoan Group. I grew with them, and it
was a second home for me and that is how much I loved the Eoan Group.
Like any other group they had their bits of problems, their ups and the
downs, but people still stuck towards each other, and became very good
family friends.
   Fuad Sawyer

It was such a happy crowd of people, everybody just wanted to sing, this is what it was all about, everybody wanted to sing. I mean, we were like one big, happy family and everybody who wanted to be involved was involved. Everybody looked after each other, it was a wonderful, wonderful feeling. I mean, this was our life. We all loved singing, there was no bickering, it was just happy moments with everybody. We were all big family.
Elizabeth Engelbrecht-April

These people lived, breathed, ate, dreamed, everything, Eoan Group. I must tell you they would bitch and moan and 'he did that', 'he didn't want to do that' and 'Mr Sydow this' and 'Mrs Sydow that', but they went back every time. I think it was passion for the music. They got a chance to live themselves out, to live their love for music. They got a chance to live that [dream]. There was that vehicle of the Eoan Group, there was Dr Manca who was willing to cultivate this in the people. With the demise of the music department, some of them went to CAPAB. I remember Jimmy Momberg started singing jazz. Some of them joined the Coons. But many of them didn't and that was the end of that era for them. That was also the end of their music. But this is what I'm saying, they lived for their passion, they lived for that. Nothing else mattered. That was the gap they could get, so they would take that gap. Sad, sad situation.
Jocylyn Liedeman

We were like a very vibrant artist community, whether it was musicians or dancers or singers or visual artists. But it was a hub even through the apartheid era. It was like a home and a haven where we would feel safe and secure and we could just be ourselves, you know, and express our art and be safe, you know. And even though people were saying we were a banned organisation and we shouldn't go there and whatever, it was a home to a lot of us.

We would take off the costumes, put it out on the floor and sleep over. It wasn't a bad thing, and it was really a home. It was our second home away from home, you know, Achmat and Dickie would make pots of food on the Saturday and the Sunday and we would rehearse the whole day. You know, because he would come in there and say, 'You're not leaving till this is done.' So it was really a home, a second home and that's what I like to remember about that place. And also the lasting friendships, you know, we're still in touch today, across all the genres. But as for the institution itself, I think it left a bad taste in a lot of people's mouths. And a lot of people will deny to the bitter end that that's where they started with what they did and I think that for me is sad, because the Eoan

Group is an organisation that's recognised by many people, nationally
and locally, and I think we should at one stage be proud to just stand up
and say that we are from the Eoan Group.
Merle Falken

What I miss the most about the Eoan Group is the children and having
worked there with the children, the talent that got lost in the Eoan
Group, the productions we did. The Eoan Group to me was one big family,
singers, actors, dancers, you name it, even with the admin with Mr Sydow
and them, it was just one big happy family.

I was extremely happy. You know, I even worked on Saturdays, we
even stayed there on a Saturday till 6 o'clock. And then we would come
in on a Sunday for rehearsals, you know, that was like a second home
to us. And then after Mr Sydow left everything just declined, everything
just changed.
Lydia Johnson

I got on well with people, even the chorus people, because you depended
a lot on them. Where you feel tonight you're not so good, then they make
it up. You know they are around you, they encourage you and things like
that. I can say that about all the principal singers that I performed with,
there was never a quarrel, there was nothing bad about it. When you
performed with May Abrahamse, boy, she was good, because she give it
to you and you give it back to her. Yes, that is right, she was not a selfish
person on stage.
Benny Arendse

I ate, slept, everything, at the Eoan Group. I only came home to come and
sleep. Because from work, I used to go straight to the Eoan Group. And
especially when the operas were on, at night for me to be there, go help
with the makeup and with the dressing. But we wanted to be there all the
time. It was wonderful in those days.
Winifred du Plessis

And over the years things grew so much that the Eoan Group to me was
a second home. I actually enjoyed me more in the Eoan Group than in
my own home. And up till today. Although the Eoan Group might not
function as what it used to be, but certain of the older members still get
together. And we have, like, little social parties and we help each other,
there was all that communication that was there. Many of the members
are deceased by now, so there is a good few that is still left, and we still
make the best of it. Although I'm not at the Eoan Group at present, the

Eoan Group is still part of me. I will still pop in at the group and see the happy memories and whatever I can do, I do.
    Fuad Sawyer

We struck up a friendship immediately. May [Abrahamse], of course, May was like a mother to all of us. Ag, it was, you know, I was like an easy-going person always, and I got on with everybody. So, I had no problems with anybody.
    Winifred du Plessis

And we never had a situation where there was any ugliness, you know? We were a great bunch of people. If I tell you, I mean, we would rehearse on a Sunday afternoon and people would come in their Sunday attire. With hats and bags and real dressed up. So it wasn't a jeans and T-shirt affair.
    Jennifer Wheatley

Those days are never going to come back, but that is where they are. It's important to them because it's what holds them together, look at the old photographs ... They were trapped in this 'time warp'. That 'time warp' is a reality, it is not gone yet and what is it thirty years later?
    Peter Voges

I was more in the mix with the chorus people than with the principals. I came out of the chorus to do my principal part, so I related [to the chorus singers]. I could hear them have problems and so on. And I used to listen to them and I used to love being with them. We had a lot of fun. You know, we were a family, we were a family that never, how can I say, fought with one another.
    Every performance for me was, was a milestone. Just to get on there and sing amongst ... just to sing over that orchestra. It's something that you cannot give to nobody and that you live with for the rest of your life.
    I have nothing to show of what I worked for all these years and I worked twenty-one years with the Eoan Group and I haven't given up my membership, I'm still a member of the Eoan Group, but I've got nothing to show. Then I say to myself if you go into the rugby boys' houses, like the captains, and see all the trophies and all the medals that they've got. My poor display cabinet is full of [dolls and other stuff], there's not one medal in there. There's nothing to show. I want to say to the Eoan Group today, thank you for giving me a chance to show off my talent, or to give you back what I have within me to make this world a better place. One thing I must say, the Eoan Group was my life.
    Sophia Andrews

Eoan Group members sharing a fun moment in Aberdeen in 1975.
PHOTO Eoan Group Archive

Timeline

1933   The Eoan Group, a cultural and welfare organisation, is founded in District Six in Cape Town by Helen Southern-Holt, offering classes in speech, literature and drama. Activities are later extended to include ballet and singing. Various branches are gradually established throughout the Cape Peninsula.

1935   The ballet section is launched under the leadership of Southern-Holt's daughter, Maisy.

1937   The first Dance Display is held with the Cape Town Municipal Orchestra in the Cape Town City Hall.

1938   Two of Eoan's dancers, Bertha October and Myrtle Martin, take part in the Royal Academy Dance Examinations in London.

1940   A thousand children take part in an open-air physical education display. From this year onwards the ballet section performs annually with the Cape Town Municipal Orchestra.

The Eoan Group Choir is started by the brothers John and Dan Ulster.

1943   Southern-Holt invites Joseph Salvatore Manca to join Eoan as choral conductor. During the following thirteen years he develops the small choir into an amateur opera company.

1944   A choral concert is held in the Cathedral Hall in Victoria Street in Cape Town.

1946   Eoan performs Martin Shaw's *The Redeemer* for organ and a choir of a hundred voices.

1947   The children's cantata *Sherwood* by Christopher Edmund is performed with the Cape Town Municipal Orchestra.

1948   The musical *The Rose and the Laurel* by Herbert Walter Wareing is performed.

1949 A costumed version of Martin Shaw's *The Redeemer* as well as the group's first production of an operetta, *A Slave in Araby* by Alfred Silver, are staged at the Cape Town City Hall with the Cape Town Municipal Orchestra.

May Abrahamse stars in her first principal role.

The Eoan Group acquires the Isaac Ochberg Hall in Hanover Street in District Six. The building remains their headquarters until 1969.

1950 The light opera *Hong Kong* by Charles Jessop is performed with the Cape Town Municipal Orchestra.

1951 Eoan performs Harold Fraser-Simson's musical comedy *The Maid of the Mountains*.

Helen Southern-Holt formally retires as leader of the group but continues close co-operation with the group until 1958.

1952 The Jan van Riebeeck Tercentenary Celebrations are held throughout the country. The Eoan Group joins the coloured community's boycott of this festival.

1953 Felix Mendelssohn's *Elijah* is performed by over a hundred singers with organ. Performances of the operetta *The Gipsy Princess* by Emmerich Kalman are sold out and later this year the choir performs excerpts from George Frideric Handel's oratorio *Messiah* and John Henry Maunder's cantata *Bethlehem*.

The Separate Amenities Act is passed. This law is soon dubbed 'petty apartheid' as it introduces segregation into all public spaces, including entranceways, seating and ablution facilities in concert halls.

1954 The musical comedy *Magyar Melody* by George Posford and Bernard Grun is staged with the Cape Town Municipal Orchestra.

1956 The First Arts Festival opens on 10 March with Eoan's historic performance of Giuseppe Verdi's *La Traviata* in the City Hall. This production proves to be a major success and marks the beginning of two decades of consistent opera production. The opera is performed to multi-racial audiences. Other productions at the Festival include a children's version of Gilbert and Sullivan's *The Mikado*, the musical comedy *Zip Goes a Million* by George Posford, Felix Mendelssohn's oratorio *Elijah*, the play *Johnny Belinda* by Elmer Harris, Greek and classical ballet, a massed physical education display and flower exhibitions. Eoan receives funding from the Department of Coloured Affairs and the Cape Town City Council. A special performance of *La Traviata* given for government dignitaries sparks unhappiness in the coloured community and some members leave the group due to its perceived ties with the government.

After a protracted legal battle between government and civil rights groups, coloured people are removed from the voter's role. Racial segregation is introduced on public buses.

1957   Eoan decides not to apply for government funding
        as the conditions for accepting funds stipulate that
        the group must abide by apartheid legislation. In
        practice this meant that they have to play to racially
        segregated audiences. However, they continue to
        receive an annual grant of R2 000 from the Cape Town
        Municipality.

1958   From 10 to 22 March 1958, the Second Opera and Ballet
        Season takes place, presenting Giuseppe Verdi's *La
        Traviata* and Pietro Mascagni's *Cavalleria Rusticana* as
        well as Leo Delibes' ballet *Spring Song.*

        Helen Southern-Holt emigrates to Canada with her
        daughter, Maisy.

1959   The Third Opera and Ballet Season takes place in
        March during which Giuseppe Verdi's *Rigoletto* is
        added to the Eoan repertoire.

1960   The Fourth Opera and Ballet Season is presented
        in March and Eoan performs four operas: Pietro
        Mascagni's *Cavalleria Rusticana*, Giuseppe Verdi's
        Rigoletto and *La Traviata* and Giacomo Puccini's *La
        Bohème,* as well as two short ballets. Eoan undertakes
        its first tour of the country from June to September,
        visiting Port Elizabeth, Durban and Johannesburg.
        Throughout the tour they perform to packed houses
        and earn many glowing reviews.

        **On 21 March, in the Johannesburg township of
        Sharpeville, 69 protesters are killed by police during
        a march. This signals the start of armed resistance
        against apartheid in South Africa, and leads to the
        anti-apartheid movements the African National
        Congress (ANC) and the Pan Africanist Congress (PAC)
        being banned by the National Party government.**

1961   Eoan's music section moves to the third floor of Delta
        House in Bree Street in Cape Town.

1962   The Second Arts Festival, which includes Eoan's
        Fifth Opera Season, is held in collaboration with the
        Peninsula Round Table. New works include Giacomo
        Puccini's *Madama Butterfly*, Johann Strauss's *Die
        Fledermaus* and Giuseppe Verdi's *Requiem*. Eoan
        stages the first full-length South African ballet *The
        Square*, composed for the group by Stanley Glasser.
        The story depicts gang life in District Six and features
        local ballet star Johaar Mosaval, dancing for the Royal
        Ballet in England at the time.

        Eoan's leading tenor, Joseph Gabriels, wins The
        Mimi Coertse Singing Competition, but organisers
        will not allow the prize to be awarded to him
        because of his race.

1963   On 28 June, Joseph Manca is awarded an Honorary
        Doctorate in Music by the University of Cape Town.

        Ballet dancer Didi Sydow (the daughter of Ismail
        and Carmen Sydow) leaves for training at the Royal
        Ballet School in London. Apart from dancing ballet
        scenes in the operas, the ballet section becomes less
        prominent during the following decade.

        Eoan's star baritone, Lionel Fourie, passes away in
        December.

**The performing arts councils, creating job
opportunities for white artists only, are established
in the four provinces of South Africa as well as the
former South West Africa (Namibia).**

1964   The Eoan Group Trust, consisting of well-to-do
        (white) citizens, is launched with the aim of providing
        financial stability for the group.

**Nelson Mandela is sentenced to life imprisonment for
treason.**

**A number of Cape Town suburbs such as Wynberg,
Constantia, Kenilworth and Rondebosch are declared
white residential areas. Thousands of people,
including many Eoan members, are forcibly moved out
of these areas.**

1965   The Sixth Opera Season takes place in March and
        April. Works include Giuseppe Verdi's *Il Trovatore* and
        La Traviata, Gaetano Donizetti's *L'Elisir d'Amore* and
        Giacomo Puccini's *La Bohème*. Despite the existence
        of the provincial arts councils, the group continues to
        be the only opera company in the country consistently
        producing grand opera at this time.

        Eoan undertakes its second tour of the country from
        June to August. Although an artistic success, the tour
        is plagued by difficulties that plunge the group into
        a financial crisis. As a result the group, after nine
        years of financial independence, decides to reapply
        to the Department of Coloured Affairs for financial
        assistance.

1966   Eoan's production of Giuseppe Verdi's *La Traviata*
        forms part of the 5th Anniversary Republic Festival.

        Pianist and Eoan répétiteur, Gordon Jephtas, leaves
        the country to seek job opportunities abroad.

District Six, a multi-cultural neighbourhood in Cape Town, is zoned as a 'whites only' area. During the following years the entire population of this suburb, including the Eoan Group headquarters in Hanover Street, is forcibly removed to residential areas 20 kilometres away from the city centre.

South Africa's prime minister, Dr Hendrik Verwoerd, regarded as the architect of apartheid, is assassinated on 6 September in parliament.

1967 Joseph Gabriels leaves the country to study singing in Italy.

The Seventh Opera Season is presented, including Giacomo Puccini's *Madama Butterfly*, Gaetano Donizetti's *L'Elisir d'Amore* and Giuseppe Verdi's *La Traviata*.

The New York producer Stanley Waren directs Eoan's (and South Africa's) première of the Rodgers and Hammerstein musical *Oklahoma!*.

In London Ismail and Carmen Sydow try in vain to persuade Gordon Jephtas to return to South Africa and become Manca's successor. They do, however, succeed in raising R34 000 from the Netherlands to help build the new Eoan Group Cultural Centre in Athlone.

1968 In March, Eoan produces the Rodgers and Hammerstein musical *South Pacific*, directed by David Bloomberg and performed in the Alhambra in Wynberg (for whites) and the Luxurama (for coloureds). Opening night is attended by the state president and members of cabinet.

Due to the illness of a number of principal singers, leading to insufficient preparation, the Eighth Opera Season is cancelled at the eleventh hour causing yet another financial crisis for the group. This seems to be the beginning of an ever-worsening relationship between the board of the Eoan Group and the Eoan Group Trust.

1969 An operatic concert, *Opera for All*, is given in March, showcasing the group's soloists.

The Eighth Opera Season takes place in October and November, during which Giuseppe Verdi's *La Traviata, Il Trovatore* and *Rigoletto* as well as a new addition to their repertoire, Gioachino Rossini's *Il Barbiere di Siviglia*, are performed.

In November the Eoan Group Cultural Centre in Athlone on the Cape Flats opens. The centre consists of the Joseph Stone Auditorium, studios, practice rooms and offices. Eoan has now been removed from the central position it enjoyed in the cultural life of Cape Town for more than three decades. The total cost for the building is R287 000, of which R167 000 was raised by the Eoan Executive Committee.

1970 Stanley Waren returns from New York to produce the musical *Carmen Jones* by Rodgers and Hammerstein in the Joseph Stone Auditorium.

1971 The Ninth Opera Season takes place in October with Pietro Mascagni's *Cavalleria Rusticana*, Ruggiero Leoncavallo's *I Pagliacci* and Giuseppe Verdi's *Rigoletto* and *La Traviata*. Eoan also performs Verdi's *Rigoletto* for the 10th Anniversary Republic Festival to coloured-only audiences.

Joseph Gabriels debuts at the Metropolitan Opera House in New York in the role of Canio in Ruggiero Leoncavallo's *I Pagliacci*. He later settles with his family in Milan, Italy.

250

1972 Helen Southern-Holt passes away in Canada.
The Alhambra Theatre in Riebeeck Street in Cape Town, where many of Eoan's opera and ballet productions took place, is demolished.

1973 Eoan performs many operatic concerts during this year bringing in much-needed revenue.

The Cape Town City Hall is renovated to its original state of 1905, making the venue unfit for operatic productions.

Manca reveals in a letter that community support for the group has declined drastically since 1960, when Eoan had almost 2 000 members, to a mere 370 in this year.

1974 The Tenth Opera Season takes place in March in the Green & Sea Point Civic Centre comprising Gioachino Rossini's *Il Barbiere di Siviglia*, three short ballets as well as a number of operatic concerts.
Manca is awarded a Gold Medal from the Suid-Afrikaanse Akademie vir Wetenskap en Kuns.

1975 The Eleventh Opera Season takes place in February and March, during which Giuseppe Verdi's *La Traviata* is performed. This is the last opera season the group presents to Cape Town audiences.

From July to August the group undertakes its first and only tour abroad, travelling to the United Kingdom to take part in the International Festival of Youth Orchestras and Performing Arts in London and Aberdeen, Scotland. The choir consists of 26 young singers accompanied by four senior soloists (Ronald Theys, Gerald Samaai, Vera Gow and May Abrahamse) and support staff. Six ballet dancers are also invited to take part in special training programmes.

1976 **The student uprising against the use of Afrikaans
in black schools starts in Soweto on 16 June. During
a protest march in Soweto on this day, police open
fire on the students, killing 23 (according to official
reports, but believed to be many more).**

**The Erika Theron Commission is tasked by govern-
ment to probe the social and political circumstances
of the coloured community. The commission's recom-
mendation that political rights be restored to coloured
people in parliament is, however, rejected.**

1977 Joseph Manca (aged 69) resigns on grounds of ill-
health after being with the group for 34 years.
Members claim they have not been forewarned and no
formal farewell celebration is held.

**In September, Steve Biko, leading founder of the Black
Consciousness Movement in South Africa, is killed in
detention.**

1978 Ismail Sydow resigns, also due to ill-health, and
Veronica Allan is elected the new chairperson. At the
same meeting, however, four more executive members
resign, Mr M Modak, Mrs S Gierdien, Olga Magnoni
and Carmen Sydow. Dick Jaffer becomes the new
wardrobe master.

1979 Gordon Jephtas is appointed artistic director of the
Eoan Group. In March he and May Abrahamse present
a recital in the Nico Malan Opera House. Jephtas
resigns before the end of the year due to conflict with
the Eoan executive.

In the years to come Eoan's ballet and drama sections
continue to be active, but formal opera activities are
minimised after this date.

1980 Royston Stoffels, head of Eoan's drama section, compiles the report *Reasons Why the Eoan Group is No Longer a Viable Arts Project* that is discussed during the annual general meeting in June. The minutes of the meeting mention that the group now often performs to empty houses.

Eoan's voice trainer and stalwart producer Alessandro Rota retires.

The tenors Ronald Theys and Keith Timms join the Cape Performing Arts Board (CAPAB) as the first coloured singers to be part of their opera department.

The South African Council on Sport (SACOS), an organisation against apartheid in sport, calls on the coloured community in Cape Town to boycott Eoan's performance because the group accepts funding from the apartheid government.

1981 The Group decides not to take part in 20th Anniversary Republic Festival.

1983 **In August, the United Democratic Front is launched in the coloured suburb of Mitchells Plain. Political activist Reverend Allan Boesak serves as keynote speaker at the launch, which is attended by 10 000 people.**

1985 Joseph Manca passes away on 10 October.

1987 **Due to political violence across the country, a State of Emergency is declared in South Africa.**

In July, the Cape Flats activist Ashley Kriel is killed in detention.

1989   The Eoan Group Trust under the chairmanship of Michael van Schalkwyk decides to discontinue its annual application for government funds.

1990   The ANC, SACP, PAC, COSATU and other political organisations are unbanned and Nelson Mandela is released from prison.

1992   Gordon Jephtas passes away in New York.

1994   The first democratic elections are held in South Africa, and the ANC comes into power.

2000   The record company GSE Claremont releases the first and only commercial CD recording of Eoan's 1960 performance of Giuseppe Verdi's *Rigoletto*.

2004   Vera Gow receives the Order of Ikhamanga in Silver 'for her excellent contribution to the development of arts and culture in South Africa and sterling performance in the field of operatic music'.

2005   May Abrahamse and Johaar Mosaval receive Molteno medals from the Tercentenary Foundation in Cape Town for their lifelong contribution to arts and culture.

2007   May Abrahamse (aged 76) is awarded a Kanna from the Klein Karoo National Arts Festival for her lifelong contribution to arts and culture.

2008   The Eoan Archive is transferred to the Documentation Centre for Music at the University of Stellenbosch.

List of
Interviewees

May Abrahamse was the longest serving principal soprano for the Eoan Group. In the years after opera ceased to be formally produced, she taught singing at the group, served as secretary on the executive committee and was a confidant to Gordon Jephtas. May was interviewed by Christine Lucia on 9 July 2009.

Dirk Alexander was a member of the Eoan Group Choir in the 1940s. He was interviewed by Santie de Jongh on 21 September 2009.

Sophia Andrews-van Rooyen was the principal mezzo-soprano for the group from 1956 until the early 1970s, known for her roles in *Il Trovatore* and *The Barber of Seville*. She was interviewed by Hilde Roos on 19 June 2009.

Benjamin Arendse was a principal baritone for many years. He was interviewed by Ruth Fourie on 14 May 2009. Bennie passed away in October 2011, aged eighty-four.

Gerald Arendse was a soloist for Eoan in the late 1960s and was one of the few singers who supplemented his income in the entertainment business. He was interviewed by Ruth Fourie in June 2008.

The mezzo-soprano **Judith Bailey** was one of the star soloists of the group during their tour to England in 1975. She attracted the attention of Claudio Abbado and had vocal training at La Scala in Milan, Italy for a year. Judith was interviewed by Hilde Roos on 14 September 2009.

As a child, **Sheila Beukes** lived next door to Ismail and Carmen Sydow. Carmen taught her to sew and she helped to make many costumes for Eoan's opera and ballet productions. Sheila was interviewed by Ruth Fourie on 10 July 2009.

Amanda Botha was a journalist for *Die Burger Ekstra* in the 1970s and '80s, and often reported Eoan's activities in those years. Amanda was interviewed by Hilde Roos on 8 December 2009.

Mimi Coertse, the South African soprano, sang with the Vienna State Opera from the 1950s to the 1970s. She showed a keen interest in upcoming local singers, offering prizes through the Mimi Coertse Singing Competition. She was interviewed by Stephanus Muller on 24 September 2009.

Virginia Davids, currently professor in singing at the University of Cape Town, was a young soloist during the last productions of the Eoan Group in the 1970s. She was one of the first coloured singers to sing for the arts councils during the 1980s. Virginia was interviewed by Wayne Muller on 7 July 2009.

Leon Dreyer was a member of the Eoan Group Choir in the 1940s and sang the role of Gastone in Verdi's *La Traviata* in 1956 and 1958. Leon was interviewed by Ruth Fourie on 4 June 2009.

Winifred du Plessis was a principal soprano for the Eoan Group in the 1960s. She was interviewed by Phillip Swales on 12 September 2009.

Elizabeth Engelbrecht-April was a soprano soloist in the early choral productions of Eoan in the 1940s. She was interviewed by Ruth Fourie on 14 July 2009.

Merle Falken danced for Eoan in the 1970s. She lost her job due to her involvement with Eoan. Merle was interviewed by Hilde Roos on 10 December 2009.

Ruth Fourie is the widow of Eoan's principal baritone, Lionel Fourie, who passed away in 1963. Over the years she has kept close contact with the Eoan members and was part of the committee that put this book together. She was interviewed by Christine Lucia on 22 June 2009.

Mabel Gabriels-Kester is the widow of Eoan's star tenor, Joseph Gabriels. After leaving the country in 1967, Joseph sang in a number of opera houses in Europe and the United States and settled in Milan, Italy. Mabel was interviewed via email by Santie de Jongh in February 2010.

Ruth Cookson-Goodwin was a principal soprano for the group from 1956 until the early 1960s when she withdrew from the group due to political reasons. She was interviewed by Ruth Fourie on 21 May 2009.

Ruth Grevler-Manca is the daughter of Joseph Manca, Eoan's director for thirty-four years. As a child she experienced the group at close range and at times also served as makeup artist for their productions. Ruth was interviewed by Hilde Roos on 31 May 2009.

Alethea Jansen was involved with the management of Eoan in the 1940s and worked closely with Helen Southern-Holt. She was interviewed by Ruth Fourie on 7 May 2009.

Cecil Jacobs was a dancer who taught ballet at the Eoan Group for many years. He currently runs his own dance school in Muizenberg. Cecil was interviewed by Stephanus Muller on 15 September 2009.

Lydia Armino-Johnson was trained as a ballet dancer at UCT and taught ballet at Eoan for many years. She was one of the dancers who received special training in Europe during the group's 1975 tour. She was interviewed by Hilde Roos on 26 September 2009.

Martin Johnson was a principal tenor for the group from the mid 1960s onwards, singing many lead roles with Patricia van Graan. He was interviewed by Phillip Swales on 19 August 2009.

Valerie Johnson was a chorus member and travelled with Eoan to the United Kingdom in 1975. She was interviewed by Ruth Fourie in September 2008.

Pieter Kooij has been a music critic for *Die Burger* for more than forty years and reviewed many Eoan opera productions and concerts. He was interviewed by Wayne Muller on 23 September 2009.

Anna-Maria Kuipers-Liliefeldt joined the Eoan Group as a small child doing ballet. In later years she also sang in the choir. She was interviewed via email by Santie de Jongh in June 2009.

Jocylyn Liedeman is the daughter of Josephine Liedeman, a principal soloist and executive committee member for Eoan in the 1970s and '80s. The group's activities were part of her life from childhood. Jocylyn was interviewed by Hilde Roos on 3 June 2009.

Abeedah Medell is the current head of the ballet section at the Eoan Group. She was interviewed by Ronnie Samaai on 28 August 2009.

As a child **Phil Pienaar** was the neighbour of Eoan soloist Vera Gow in Woodstock before the enforcement of the Group Areas Act. He later worked for the Department of Coloured Affairs. Phil was interviewed by Hilde Roos on 22 September 2009.

Trevor Pretorius joined the Eoan Group in the mid 1960s and sang leading roles in the musicals *South Pacific* and *Carmen Jones*. Trevor was interviewed by Phillip Swales on 26 August 2009.

Shafiek Rajap is the current head of the Eoan Group and facilitated the transfer of the Eoan Group Archive to the Documentation Centre for Music (DOMUS) at the Universitiy of Stellenbosch. He was interviewed by Stephanus Muller on 19 August 2009.

Emma Renzi was one of South Africa's leading sopranos and enjoyed a singing career in Europe from 1954 to 1979. She has always taken a keen interest in opera in South Africa and at times worked closely with Gordon Jephtas. She was interviewed by Christine Lucia in July 2009.

Gerald Samaai was one of Eoan's principal tenors who enjoyed a longstanding singing career with Eoan from 1964 onwards. Gerald was interviewed by Wayne Muller on 12 May 2009.

Ronnie Samaai is a violinist who experienced Eoan at close range through his brother Gerald, a soloist for Eoan. Ronnie was interviewed by Wayne Muller on 6 October 2009.

Fuad Sawyer, formerly Frank Sawyer, joined the Eoan Group Choir in 1968 at the age of eleven and travelled with the group to the United Kingdom in 1975. He was interviewed by Wayne Muller on 25 August 2009.

Phillip Swales was a principal baritone for the Eoan Group in the early 1970s and later served as chairman of the Eoan Group Trust. Phillip was part of the book committee. He was interviewed by Christine Lucia on 6 July 2009.

Ronald Theys was a principal tenor for Eoan and one of the first coloured singers to join the Cape Performing Arts Board in 1980. He has enjoyed a long singing career and still sings for Cape Town Opera. Ronald was interviewed by Wayne Muller on 8 July 2009.

Reverend **John Ulster** was a soloist with the Eoan Group Choir in the early days of the group. His brother Dan Ulster conducted the choir before Joseph Manca joined the group. Reverend Ulster was interviewed by Phillip Swales on 16 September 2009. He passed away in January 2012, aged eighty-nine.

Tillie Ulster joined the group as a small child in 1938 and later married Dan Ulster, the first conductor of the Eoan choir. Tillie was involved in administration as well as music productions. She was interviewed by Ruth Fourie in September 2009.

John van der Ross was a soloist during Eoan's tour to the United Kingdom in 1975. He was later employed as a baritone at the Natal provincial arts council. He was interviewed by Hilde Roos on 26 September 2009.

Professor **Richard van der Ross** was the first coloured person to serve on the Eoan Group Trust of which he later became chairman. He also served as Vice-Chancellor of the University of the Western Cape from 1975 to 1986. Van der Ross was interviewed by Stephanus Muller on 5 August 2009.

Patricia van Graan was a soprano soloist for Eoan in the late 1960s and left the group in 1972 to pursue vocal training in England. Patricia was interviewed by Hilde Roos on 19 November 2008. She passed away in February 2012 in London.

Michael van Schalkwyk was chairman of the Eoan Group Trust during the late 1980s and it was under his chairmanship that the group decided to terminate annual applications for government funding. He was interviewed by Hilde Roos on 11 September 2009.

Peter Voges was a ballet dancer with the group in the early 1960s and took part in the musicals that Eoan performed in 1968 and 1971. He joined the management team of Gordon Jephtas in 1979/80. Peter was interviewed by Stephanus Muller on 11 September 2009.

Joan Watson joined the Eoan Group Choir in 1973 and toured abroad with the group in 1975. She was interviewed by Santie de Jongh via email in August 2009.

Jennifer Wheatley joined the Eoan Group Choir in the 1970s and toured abroad with the group in 1975. She was interviewed by Santie de Jongh in August 2009.